Developments in the Japanese Documentary Mode

Developments in the Japanese Documentary Mode

Editors

Marcos Centeno
Michael Raine

MDPI • Basel • Beijing • Wuhan • Barcelona • Belgrade • Manchester • Tokyo • Cluj • Tianjin

Editors
Marcos Centeno
Department of Cultures and
Languages, Birkbeck,
University of London
UK

Michael Raine
Film Studies Program,
Western University
Canada

Editorial Office
MDPI
St. Alban-Anlage 66
4052 Basel, Switzerland

This is a reprint of articles from the Special Issue published online in the open access journal *Arts* (ISSN 2076-0752) (available at: https://www.mdpi.com/journal/arts/special_issues/developments_japanese_documentary_mode).

For citation purposes, cite each article independently as indicated on the article page online and as indicated below:

LastName, A.A.; LastName, B.B.; LastName, C.C. Article Title. *Journal Name* **Year**, *Volume Number*, Page Range.

ISBN 978-3-03943-913-3 (Hbk)
ISBN 978-3-03943-914-0 (PDF)

Cover image courtesy of Komura Shizuo.

© 2020 by the authors. Articles in this book are Open Access and distributed under the Creative Commons Attribution (CC BY) license, which allows users to download, copy and build upon published articles, as long as the author and publisher are properly credited, which ensures maximum dissemination and a wider impact of our publications.

The book as a whole is distributed by MDPI under the terms and conditions of the Creative Commons license CC BY-NC-ND.

Contents

About the Editors vii

Preface to "Developments in the Japanese Documentary Mode" ix

Marcos P. Centeno-Martín and Michael Raine
Tracing Tendencies in the Japanese Documentary Mode [†]
Reprinted from: Arts **2020**, *9*, 98, doi:10.3390/arts9030098 1

Jinshi Fujii
Yanagita Kunio and the Culture Film: Discovering Everydayness and Creating/Imagining a National Community, 1935–1945 [†]
Reprinted from: Arts **2020**, *9*, 54, doi:10.3390/arts9020054 17

Daisuke Miyao
What's the Use of Culture? Cinematographers and the Culture Film in Japan in the Early 1940s
Reprinted from: Arts **2019**, *8*, 42, doi:10.3390/arts8020042 33

Koji Toba
On the Relationship between Documentary Films and Magic Lanterns in 1950s Japan
Reprinted from: Arts **2019**, *8*, 64, doi:10.3390/arts8020064 43

Marcos P. Centeno Martín
Legacies of Hani Susumu's Documentary School
Reprinted from: Arts **2019**, *8*, 82, doi:10.3390/arts8030082 53

Justin Jesty
Image Pragmatics and Film as a Lived Practice in the Documentary Work of Hani Susumu and Tsuchimoto Noriaki
Reprinted from: Arts **2019**, *8*, 41, doi:10.3390/arts8020041 65

Miyo Inoue
The Ethics of Representation in Light of Minamata Disease: Tsuchimoto Noriaki and His Minamata Documentaries
Reprinted from: Arts **2019**, *8*, 37, doi:10.3390/arts8010037 83

Lauri Kitsnik
Record. Reenact. Recycle. Notes on Shindō Kaneto's Documentary Styles
Reprinted from: Arts **2019**, *8*, 39, doi:10.3390/arts8010039 95

Bill Mihalopoulos
Documenting a People yet to Be Named: History of a Bar Hostess
Reprinted from: Arts **2019**, *8*, 44, doi:10.3390/arts8020044 107

Jennifer Coates
Blurred Boundaries: Ethnofiction and Its Impact on Postwar Japanese Cinema
Reprinted from: Arts **2019**, *8*, 20, doi:10.3390/arts8010020 117

About the Editors

Marcos Centeno is a lecturer in Japanese Studies and coordinator of the Japanese programme at Birkbeck, University of London. Before that, he worked for the department of Japan and Korea at SOAS where he taught several courses on Japanese Cinema and convened the MA Global Cinemas and the Transcultural. Centeno Martín was also a Research Associate at Waseda University and a Research Fellow at the Universitat de València. His research interests revolve around Japanese documentary film, Hani Susumu, film theory, transnationality, postwar avant-garde, and representation of minorities.

Michael Raine is an Associate Professor of Film Studies in the Department of English and Writing Studies at Western University, Canada. He has written widely on Japanese cinema, with an emphasis on the transmedia transition to sound in prewar Japan, wartime image culture, and the postwar 'cinema of high economic growth'. He has published most recently on the Japanese musical, Imamura Shōhei's The Insect Woman, and wartime cinema in Occupied Shanghai. His anthology, *The Culture of the Sound Image in Prewar Japan* (co-edited with Johan Nordström), 2020 is published by Amsterdam University Press.

Preface to "Developments in the Japanese Documentary Mode"

Writing on Japanese cinema has prioritized aesthetic and cultural difference, and obscured Japan's contribution to the representation of real life in cinema and related forms. Donald Richie, who was instrumental in introducing Japanese cinema to the West, even claimed that Japan did not have a true documentary tradition due to the apparent preference of Japanese audiences for stylisation over realism, a preference that originated from its theatrical tradition. However, a closer look at the history of Japanese documentary and feature film production reveals an emphasis on actuality and everyday life as a major part of Japanese film culture.

That 'documentary mode'—crossing genre and medium like Peter Brooks' 'melodramatic mode' rather than limited to styles of documentary filmmaking alone—identifies rhetoric of authenticity in cinema and related media, even as that rhetoric was sometimes put in service to political and economic ends. The articles in this Special Issue, 'Developments in the Japanese Documentary Mode', trace important changes in documentary film schools and movements from the 1930s onwards, sometimes in relation to other media, and the efforts of some post-war filmmakers to adapt the styles and ethical commitments that underpin documentary's "impression of authenticity" to their representation of fictional worlds.

Marcos Centeno, Michael Raine
Editors

Editorial

Tracing Tendencies in the Japanese Documentary Mode †

Marcos P. Centeno-Martín [1],* and Michael Raine [2]

1. Department of Cultures and Languages, School of Arts, Birkbeck, University of London, London WC1E 7HX, UK
2. Department of English and Writing Studies, Western University, London, ON N6A 3K7, Canada; mraine3@uwo.ca
* Correspondence: m.centeno@bbk.ac.uk
† The Japanese names in this Special Issue follow the Japanese convention (family name first name).

Received: 29 July 2020; Accepted: 29 August 2020; Published: 21 September 2020

1. Introduction

The documentary mode has not had the recognition it deserves in the western historiography of Japanese cinema. The 'discovery' of that cinema at film festivals in Europe and the United States in the 1950s, and the growth of academic and popular writing that followed, prioritized aesthetic and cultural difference and obscured Japan's contribution to the documentary mode. Canonical authors such as Donald Richie, who was instrumental in introducing Japanese cinema to the West, even claimed that Japan did not have a true documentary tradition due to the apparent preference of the Japanese audience for stylisation over realism, a preference that originated from its theatrical tradition (Richie 1990, p. 60). And yet, over 130,000 documentary films were made between 1945 and 2010 (Murayama 2010, pp. 240–46), and postwar Japanese documentary films regularly won prizes at specialist film festivals.[1] Beyond documentary film production itself, a closer look at the history of Japanese feature film production also calls Richie's assertion into question. "Semi-documentary" and "documentary touch" were clichés of postwar feature film criticism, in response to a renewed emphasis on actuality and ordinary life in at least one strand of Japanese studio and independent production. This special issue, *Developments in Japanese Documentary Mode*, seeks to challenge the predominance of fiction film in the literature on Japanese cinema, and in particular the assumption of a stylised Japanese aesthetic. It reveals a broad sense in Japan of the film medium as connected to material and phenomenological authenticity, even as that rhetorical effect was sometimes put in service to political and economic ideologies.

As Bill Nichols has argued, film as "document" is an inherent power of this apparently automatic medium, visible in its early uses as a scientific recording apparatus, an exhibitionist purveyor of "attractions", and in the earliest actualities. But, Nichols continued, in order to become a genre, that documentary aspect of film had to be supplemented by the subjective intentionality of filmmakers (what John Grierson called the "creative treatment of actuality" (Grierson 1933, p. 8)). Those filmmakers crafted their material into stories, as part of a group of practitioners supported by institutions, making films that helped organize the ambitions of fellow filmmakers and the expectations of audiences. At the same time, that narrative aspect of documentary film opens the door to its apparent other: the fiction film. If documentary must employ storytelling in order to tell us about our world, the fiction film can draw on the documentary's "impression of authenticity" (Nichols 2017, p. xii) by foregrounding

---

1. See The Educational Film Producers Association of Japan Inc. (ed). *Short Films of Japan*, bulletin of the Association for the Diffusion of Japanese Films Abroad.

its material aspects of unglamourised people in real locations leading ordinary lives. Even Grierson recognized the "documentary value" of the fiction film (Grierson 1979, p. 25). Rediscovering, organising, and assessing Japanese contributions to the documentary mode from narrative, aesthetic, and theoretical points of view, the articles in this special issue embrace the ambiguity of documentary as what Bill Nichols called a "fiction (un)like any other" (Nichols 2017, p. 4).

The scope of this special issue goes beyond documentary film alone. Rather than a distinct genre, the articles in this issue trace a "documentary mode" characterised by a rhetoric of truthfulness that, like Peter Brooks' influential "melodramatic mode" (Brooks 1976, p. 12), spans multiple media and genres. This tendency may operate in different formats, from newsreels to fiction films, from magic lanterns to television and can be observed in disciplines from film theory to folklore studies. In this sense, the selected articles interrogate documentary movements, schools, and ways of approaching reality, challenging the limiting understanding of documentary as a self-contained category and proposing a renewed framework for the study of "nonfiction film" that is not necessarily limited to "nonfiction" or even "film". Each article in this issue focuses on an aspect of documentary in Japan, from the intertextual grounding of the prewar culture film (*bunka eiga*) through theoretical debates in postwar documentary and developments in ancillary media, such as magic lantern images and photography, to the incorporation of the tension between objectivity and subjectivity, characteristic of documentary, into feature film production. In this introduction we provide some historical and theoretical context for the developments and debates presented in the articles. That history is necessarily incomplete, but rather than establish a single narrative line we hope that through these diverse articles, readers will gain an enhanced understanding of the history and possibilities of the documentary mode in Japan.

2. Early Developments and Terminologies

Since its inception, Japanese nonfiction and adjacent formats have evolved and adopted different terminologies. In fact, the literal translation of "documentary" in Japanese (*dokyumentarī* or *kiroku eiga*) was neither the earliest nor the most common expression used in Japan until at least the end of World War II. The terminological confusion is compounded by shifts between media and ambiguities over the epistemological status of film images. Komatsu Hiroshi went so far as to argue that there was no conceptual distinction between fiction and nonfiction in the early period of Japanese filmmaking. The dominant form of early film drama, the so-called *kyūgeki*, had such strong intertextual connections to the existing theatre that they were in some ways documents of a dramatic performance. On the other hand, films that supposedly showed conditions on the ground during the Russo–Japanese war of 1904–1905 regularly featured models and scenes restaged in Japan. Audiences only objected when the models and the staging were poor (Komatsu 1992).

The first nonfiction film in Japan can be found in the earliest moving images ever shot in the country. They were thirty-three sequences, dating back to 1897 and 1898, shot by August Lumière's French camera operators François-Constant Girel and Gabriel Veyre, as well as the Japanese apprentice Shibata Tsunekichi, using a cinematograph, which had been acquired by the industrialist Inabata Katsutarō (Koga 1995, pp. 31–43; Anderson and Donald 1982, p. 146; Nornes 2003b, pp. 2–3). The films were so-called "actualities", short sequences that proliferated during the first decades of the twentieth century, as they were cheaper and easier to produce than narrative fiction films, which required a script, actors, settings, and so on (Musser 1994, p. 232). Japanese entrepreneurs saw in these actualities a profitable business and developed a new nonfiction format, a sort of proto-newsreel called *jiji eiga* ("real-life movies") during the Boxer Rebellion (1898–1901). As in other countries, many of these proto-newsreels were "fabricated news films" (*kōsei sareta nyūsu eiga*), based on real events but re-enacted in studios, while others were directly "fake news films" (*nise nyūsu eiga*), completely fabricated events (Komatsu 1992, p. 238). By the 1910s nonfiction practices were re-evaluated based on new expectations of truthfulness, which were largely motivated by the emergence of permanent film theatres (Komatsu 1992). These venues replaced travelling troupes, and audiences began to regard cinema as a valuable source of information, rather than merely as entertainment (Greenberg 2001, p. 7), though that information was still often presented in the form of scripted and/or re-enacted scenes.

The rhetoric of truthfulness mentioned above not only evolved into these *jiji eiga*, but also into a more elaborate format, the *travelogue* or travel documentary in the 1910s. The American entrepreneur William Selig pioneered this genre and sponsored the first two travelogues in Japan, *In Japan* (1911) and *The Ainus of Japan* (1913), shot by Frederick Starr. Of course, the concept of virtual tourism was not invented with the film actuality. For example, the way Japanese *Wajin* and Ainu are represented in these travelogues reproduced already existing patterns of representation that had been developed decades before in photography. Film in the early twentieth century was a "new medium" that adopted existing practices of "documentary" exhibition. In the nineteenth century books and illustrated journals showed readers engravings of places they could not visit, often based on daguerreotypes or other photographic processes (Lerebours 1842). John L. Stoddard and Burton Holmes, stars of the illustrated lecture circuit, travelled extensively and used photographs and then moving pictures for their sophisticated audiovisual performances (Lastra 2000, p. 100). Both had major presentations on Japan, and commissioned staged photographs of "typical" scenes, as well as made original images to convince their audiences that magic lantern presentations were "a better way to see the world than travel itself" (Barber 1993, p. 77).

In the 1920s, despite the ambiguous boundary between fiction and nonfiction, there was a growing belief in the ability of cinema to portray current events. The genre of newsreels was transformed into a new medium that would complement print journalism, although they were still released irregularly (Nornes 2003b, p. 15). As an example, the Japanese Ministry of Education commissioned *The Great Kantō Earthquake* (Kantō daishinsai, 1923), a documentary filmed by Shirai Sigueru, which marked the start of government involvement in film production. Commercial companies also produced earthquake documentaries to satisfy public fascination with the disaster, and the drama film studios made earthquake melodramas as soon as they were able. Although those films were dismissed as unserious in some quarters, they drew more attention to realism in the fiction film. The Nikkatsu studio in particular, though it could not reproduce the production values of Hollywood films about similar disasters, used location shooting and paratextual discourses on the traumatic experiences of the stars on the screen to create powerful forms of identification and rememoration in the audience (Lewis 2019, pp. 53–81). That potential for fictional narratives to engage the experience of real events and places is explored in several articles in this issue.

Even as the state became increasingly involved in documentary film production, the field remained widely populated by progressive or left-wing filmmakers who sympathised with Marxism, proletarian culture movements, and the class struggle that arose in the 1920s. As a response, the Japanese government sought to eliminate political dissidence and in 1925 enacted the "Peace Preservation Law" (also known as the Public Security Preservation Law), specifically designed to control the Left. In the following years, many artistic, intellectual, and culture leaders were arrested, interrogated, and imprisoned. However, activism continued in the documentary scene until at least the mid-1930s. Prokino (Nippon Puroretaria Eiga Dōmei or "Japan Proletarian Film League"), an organ of the Japanese Communist Party founded in 1929, produced documentary films and *Puroretaria nyūsu* (Proletarian News), as well as propaganda films, fiction films, and animated films, until its dissolution due to police persecution in 1934 (Nornes 2003b, p. 37). Even as activists performed ideological apostasy (*tenkō*) in order to continue working, ideas about film's special ability to register the materiality of things and everyday life still circulated through such groups as the Materialism Study Society (Yuibutsuron Kenkyu Kai) (Nornes 2003b, pp. 121–47). Those ideas also motivated a shift toward realism in the feature film that was formative for the postwar generation of realist filmmakers, such as Shindō Kaneto, then working as assistants in the studios.

Despite the rise of militarism in Japan and the subsequent attacks on freedom of the press, the 1930s can be defined as a "Golden Age" of documentary. The state promoted the production of educational films (*kyōiku eiga*), while the fifteen-year conflict in Asia (1931–1945) was characterized by an unprecedented prominence of nonfiction, fuelled by the new needs of representation and social mobilization (Salomon 2011, pp. 77–78, 116–18). Film theory and feature film production also saw an efflorescence of realist theories in this period (Yamamoto 2020). This rise of documentary modes in cinema resulted in a variety of terms that began to circulate in the discussions of the time: *jissha eiga* (cinema of real events), *kiroku eiga* (documentary cinema), *nyūsu eiga* (news cinema), and *dokyumentarī eiga*, borrowed from English. Also, the expression *bunka eiga* (culture film) was coined in 1933 as a translation of the German *kulturfilm*, the mainly scientific cinema produced by UFA. The term ended up designating all kinds of wartime documentary production, particularly once it was adopted in the 1939 Film Law (*Eigahō*).

The development of newsreels (*nyūsu eiga*) gave extraordinary prominence to nonfiction in the 1930s. Between 1934 and 1936, the Japanese press established the first five regular newsreels: *Asashi Sekai News*, *Daimai Tōnichi News* (by *Mainichi* newspaper), *Yomiuri News*, *Dōmei News* (by the eponymous news agency), and *Tōhō Hassei* (by the Tōhō film studio) (Imamura and Tadao 1986, p. 45). Simultaneously, "newsreel theatres", which also showed short cartoons and documentaries, emerged in the cities (Hori 2017, p. 125). The new genre experienced an extraordinary boom after the outbreak of the war with China in 1937 (Hamasaki 1999, pp. 34–35). As the number of households with relatives at the front grew, so did the number of citizens who attended cinemas to be informed about the war (Nornes 2003b, p. 50; Shimizu 1991, pp. 2–3). After the enactment of the Film Law, Japanese newsreel companies were unified under the company Nippon Eigasha (or Nichiei), following the model of Nazi Germany. The full monopolisation of Japanese newsreels was realised once Nichiei absorbed the Tōhō and Shōchiku "culture film" departments and created *Nippon News*.

Once Japan went to war against the Allies after the bombing of Pearl Harbour, the need for propaganda increased even further. Nichiei's budget was enlarged from two to seven million yen between 1941 and 1942. Additionally, as the Japanese Empire expanded over the Philippines, Malaysia, Thailand, French Indochina, Burma, and Chinese regions, Nichiei created branches with local versions of *Nippon News*, which worked as a key medium for nationalist propaganda and to promote the Pan-Asian ideal of "The Greater East Asian Co-prosperity Sphere" (Dai Tōa Kyōeiken).

3. Wartime Tensions and the Demand for Nonfiction

The Film Law also fuelled demand for nonfiction, since it required theatres to screen at least 250 m of "culture films" in each programme. As a result, documentary film production increased from 985 in 1939 to 4460 in 1940 (Nornes 2003b, p. 63). The films were deeply ideological, presenting a view of Japanese total mobilization that was pre-scripted by the state. Official narratives of famous events, such as the attack on Pearl Harbour, were presented in newspapers, contextualized by documentaries, and fictionalized in blockbuster propaganda films. In all cases, their adherence to the official narrative was supported by the documentary mode of film and photography, in which the presence of apparently realistic military hardware and uniforms reinforced the ideological claims of the figures on the screen.

However, not all nonfiction films of the 1930s followed militaristic policies. As noted above, the documentary film circles had been a stronghold for the Japanese left and ironically, much of the wartime propaganda film was made by filmmakers opposed to nationalism (Hori 2017, pp. 114–53). The most notorious example was the case of Kamei Fumio, a documentary maker linked to the Japanese Communist Party and a former member of Prokino, who proposed a kind of antimilitarist approach in his trilogy on the conflict in China: *Shanghai* (1937), *Nanking* (1937), and *Peking* (1938). Kamei was accused of promoting Marxism and antiwar consciousness in his films and was incarcerated in 1941 (Nornes 2003b, p. 177; Nornes 2006, p. 26). His supposed propaganda documentary *Fighting Soldiers* (Tatakau Heitai, 1939), which follows Japanese troops through the trenches in China, was banned.

Kamei was an isolated example, the only filmmaker to be arrested during the war. Other filmmakers resolved the tensions between national policy (*kokusaku*) and their political and aesthetic subjectivity in complex ways. What, from one perspective, seems like a humanist interest in the texture of everyday life or a modernist fascination with new forms of mobility or new modes of perception, could also be a deeply ideological discourse on national culture and the relation of individual to the collective. As Fujii Jinshi argues in this issue, the ethnographic turn toward ordinary people, first in feature films and then in *bunka eiga*, helped create/imagine a unified sense of the national character of the Japanese people through their representation of nonmetropolitan life. Other filmmakers emphasized the new modes of perception enabled by airplanes and optical weapons, or enlisted the perceptual apparatus of cinema to engage audiences more intensely in the war effort. Those "filmlike films" (*eiga teki eiga*) had more in common with ambitious feature films than what Mark Nornes called the orthodox "hard style" of more typical documentaries. Ironically, those formally ambitious films were often the most successful with audiences, and were made by liberal filmmakers who went on to support progressive post-war documentary movements, as well as movements to democratise post-war intellectual life, such as the *Shiso no kagaku* (Science of Thought) group (Tsurumi 1969, pp. 233–53).

It is also important to highlight women's roles in Japanese documentary film during this period. War circumstances and the increasing demand for propaganda films provided women with an opportunity to become directors, since women were replacing men in many sectors, including the film industry. Sakane Tazuko, who worked as an editor and assistant director for Kenji Mizoguchi, became the first female director in Japan with *New Clothing* (Hatsu Sugata, 1936). In 1940, Sakane started working for the Riken documentary company where she directed *Fellow Citizens in North* (Kita no doho, 1941). In 1942, Sakane moved to Manchuria to work for Man'ei (Manchurian Film Association), one of the largest film studios in Asia at the time (Yomota 2019, pp. 91–92), where she directed fourteen nonfiction films until 1945. Atsugi Taka also became a key figure for in documentary scene in wartime Japan. Atsugi had a stronger political commitment than Sakane: she had been a member of Prokino until its dissolution, and questioned the dominant ideology during and after the war. In 1934, she became the only woman employed at P.C.L. (Photo Chemical Laboratory, later part of Tōhō Studios), where she began her writing career. In 1939, her husband Mori Kōichi was arrested for his left-wing activism and Atsugi joined the documentary producer Geijutsu Eigasha (GES), where she worked as the scriptwriter for *Record of a Nursery* (Aru hobo no kiroku, 1942). Atsugi incorporated her opposition to nationalist education into the script, taking the approach of showing how mothers and teachers teach children a commitment to life rather than death (Ikegawa and Ward 2005, p. 266). From 1941, the mobilization of women became mandatory and the Japanese media multiplied their representations of female labour. As a consequence, Atsugi worked on various documentaries that positively portrayed the effort of women during the war, such as *This Is How Hard We Are Working* (Watashitachi wa konnani hataraiteiru Mizugi Sōya, 1945), in which she showed young female workers in a factory making military uniforms. Atsugi's contributions to the documentary field also include her translation in 1938 of Paul Rotha's book *Documentary Film*. She translated documentary film as "culture film" (*bunka eiga*), which sparked extensive discussion among Japanese directors.

4. Postwar New Approaches

4.1. Revival of Japanese Documentary Film

Although *gendaigeki* (modern day films), such as Gosho's *Where Chimneys are Seen* and Ozu's *Tokyo Story*, won prizes in Berlin and London, the postwar Japanese films that drew attention at international film festivals were mostly *jidaigeki* (period dramas). Filmmakers such as Kurosawa Akira, Mizoguchi Kenji, Kinugasa Teinosuke, Imai Tadashi, and Inagaki Hiroshi astonished western audiences with exotic images of a legendary Japan, receiving Academy Awards in the US as well as prizes at the Cannes, Venice, and Berlin film festivals during the 1950s. This imbalance was recognized by both contemporary and more recent writers (Giuglaris and Giuglaris 1957; Yamamoto 1983; Bordwell 1994; Centeno-Martín 2018a). However, while the Japanese production of fiction films reached its peak in this decade—1958 marked a record with 547 entertainment films (VV.AA 1963, p. 63)—the number of documentary films was even greater, reaching 1794 productions in the same year (Uni Japan 1961, p. 2). This figure clearly indicates that the production of nonfiction did not vanish with the propaganda films after the Japanese surrender. In fact, Japanese documentary films were not unknown in the West. In addition to tourist films (*This is Tokyo*), adventure films (*Karakoram*) and painstaking science films (*Mikuro no Sekai*) won prizes at western film festivals (Kusakabe 1980, back matter pp. 7–9).

In the aftermath of World War II, the documentary film industry underwent a profound restructuring. While the obligation to screen culture films disappeared with the abolition of the 1939 Film Law and theatres were reluctant to expand their programmes by including short documentaries (Yoshihara 2011, pp. 79–97), the industry experienced a revival thanks to two types of productions: "educational films" (*kyōiku eiga* or *kyōzai eiga*) and "PR films" (*PR eiga*). The initial impetus for the revival of the industry was the importation of American short documentaries by the Civil Information and Education (CIE) division of the Allied Occupation. The films needed to be localized by (light) reediting and the recording of a Japanese voice over. That work was carried out by existing documentary companies and branches of the feature film studios, and soon led to commissions for Japanese-made "CIE films" to be shown on donated Natco projectors at nontheatrical sites around Japan (Nakamura 2012). Although urban populations were well-supplied with commercial cinemas, the CIE films were the main form of entertainment (as well as propaganda) for rural and child audiences throughout Japan (Wada-Marciano 2019, p. 98). The interest in these films continued in the mid-1950s, as the Japanese ministries, mainly the Ministry of Education, were keen to show how the educational system had changed since the years of militarism.

In this context, Iwanami Eiga emerged as a pivotal company for the production of postwar documentary films, leaving a catalogue of around 4000 titles. Iwanami's documentary modes mainly developed around PR films, educational films, and science films, although the company also produced TV programmes and feature films. Iwanami also became a sort of documentary school where many leading figures of Japanese documentary started their careers—for example, Hani Susumu, Ogawa Shinsuke, Tsuchimoto Noriaki, and Kuroki Kazuo. Alongside these authors, two female filmmakers, Haneda Sumiko and Tokieda Toshie, made significant educational films in which they added a renewed gender perspective. Both were promoted as directors at Iwanami at the end of 1950s, during a period in which the Ministry of Education was sponsoring educational films about women.

The development of documentary film was closely linked to Japanese economic growth, and towards late-1950s this materialised in the proliferation of the PR films, which mostly were commissioned by the strategic industries of reconstruction: the steel, automobile, naval, or electrical sectors. A significant example was the *Sakuma Dam* series (Sakuma Damu, 1954–1957), funded by the company Dengen Kaihatsu on the construction of the first major hydroelectric dam in postwar Japan. In the process of adaptation to the postwar circumstances, these films provided the documentary producers with some financial stability (Tsuchimoto 1988, pp. 248–69; Hani 2012, pp. 30–31). However, these productions caused a great deal of frustration among documentary makers. Their promotion of capitalist power contradicted the Marxist idea of educating the masses, which was widely shared among postwar documentary circles (Irie 2006, p. 248; Hani 2012, p. 31). Where other artist groups could intervene in education or the regional avant-garde, using reportage and social realism as a means of social "engagement" (Jesty 2018), documentary filmmakers at companies such as Iwanami Productions, Nihon Eigasha, and Shin Riken Eiga Kaisha worked in the service of the high-growth capitalist economy. This contradiction prompted artistic and ethical debates among documentary makers from the early sixties, such as those published in *Kiroku eiga* (Yamane 1993). Authors such as (Mamiya 1962) rejected the notion that PR films could be a laudable task for documentary makers. Similarly, the veteran Yoshino Keiji showed a feeling of defeat toward the end of their career and questioned whether these films had been useful for society (cited by Hani 1985, p. 138). While sharing the same concern, others like Kuroki Kazuo claimed that the PR film might be used for artistic experiment with cinematic language (cited in Yamane 1993). Hani also noted that the technical and artistic quality of many PR films had been overlooked (Hani 1985). More recently, authors have highlighted the films' historical value as exceptional witnesses to an era (Hani 2012, pp. 83–165; Toba 2010).

While cinema had become the main medium to foster documentary modes of representation in the previous decades, this role started to be taken over by television from the 1950s. Since the first NHK broadcast in 1953, the number of television broadcasts increased rapidly, reaching 10 million by 1960 (Toda 2006, p. 155). The big studios tried to keep their hegemony in the entertainment sector and did not allow films to be broadcast on television, and as a consequence, much of the programming was filled by American films during the first years (De Castillon 1975, p. 17). However, television companies reached agreements with the film studios from 1955, and from that time the development of documentary modes in cinema and television became intertwined. News and reportage programmes were shot on film, and both documentary and feature filmmakers transferred from cinema to television. Thus, television stations became a meeting point for directors, as well as scriptwriters and professionals with different backgrounds (newsreels, journalism, art, and entertainment film). Also, many companies, including those outside the big studios such as Iwanami, engaged in the production of documentaries for television, for which Masaaki Segawa coined the term *terementarī*, a combination of the Japanese words for television and documentary.[2] Hani applied this concept to all information and social programmes made for television, and noted that *terementarī* was not merely an exhibition format but also entailed a new style that demanded a renewed personal approach to reality (Hani 1960, pp. 69–76).

As the number of nonfiction genres produced for television increased, so did the discussions on the possibilities of the television documentary proliferated from the end of the decade. Many of them were led by the first generation of filmmakers, who worked for television such as Hani Susumu, Ushiyama Yunichi, Okamoto Yoshihiko, and Yoshida Naoya (see Hani et al. 1959). Authors in general believed that television would allow a closer engagement with reality and had high expectations in the degree of truthfulness it might bring. Hani, for example, highlighted the realism found in fiction series such as *Watashi wa kai ni naritai* (Okamoto Yoshihiko, KRT 1958), in which characters acted with great naturalness and seemed to play themselves (Hani 1959, p. 199).

4.2. New Critical Approaches

Japan has a long history of image and film theory. Filmmakers, as well as theorists and critics, engaged in prolific debates about documentary practice and the nature of images from the 1930s to the 1970s. While these discussions have been neglected in English language scholarship for decades, recent work has discussed, for example, the conflict between Iwasaki Akira and Imamura Taihei about realism in documentary film and its ideological implications (Irie 2010, pp. 71–75). In Japan, Atsugi Taka's translation of Paul Rotha's *Documentary Film* also triggered intense debate, which involved a wide range of intellectuals such as Hasegawa Nyōzekan, Tosaka Jun, Kamei Katsuchirō, and Nakai Masakazu (Nornes 1999). Other debates, such as the ethical concerns about the filmmaker's social responsibility, developed by Iijima Tadashi, Tsumura Hideo, and Futaba Jūzaburō, still wait for scholarly scrutiny. Many of those critics, such as Imamura Taihei, recognized the documentary aspect of both fiction and nonfiction film. The self-reflexive criticism developed by postwar filmmakers has also been recognized in recent years (Furuhata 2007, 2013; Raine 2012; Centeno-Martín 2018b, 2020a). Articles in this special issue continue that exploration, both in wartime (Fujii, Miyao) and postwar periods (Kitsnik, Centeno-Martín, Jesty, Mihalopoulos, Inoue, Coates).

The enormous growth of documentary as a field after World War II produced an astonishing intellectual ferment around politics, aesthetics, and genre. The hidebound feature film studios were strongly hierarchical and run by anticommunist leaders, so many ex-student radicals ended up working in documentary alongside leftists who were pushed out of the Toho studio after a series of postwar strikes. That political engagement, opposed to previous wartime propaganda, initiated critical discussions of current affairs and engaged in topics that had been taboo during the war. *The Japanese*

---

[2] The text by Segawa Masaki. 1959. Dokyumentari no hōkō (Documenatry Direction). *Kinema Junpō* 8 is cited in (Hani 1960, p. 69).

Tragedy (Nihon no Higeki, 1946) is an early example, in which Kamei Fumio accused Japanese leaders, including the emperor, of war crimes. Kamei went on to make antinuclear films and a series of documentaries that mobilised support against the expansion of the US air base at Tachikawa in the 1950s (Raine 2019). Later, in the context of the protests against the US–Japan Security Treaty, a younger generation of documentary makers, such as Ogawa Shinsuke, Tsuchimoto Noriaki, and Adachi Masao, epitomised the Japanese militant cinema from the 1960s. Those filmmakers were often at odds with the established cultural policies of the Japanese Communist Party (JCP), creating a split that was symptomatic of the rise of the "New Left" in Japan.

That political division was in part driven by aesthetic differences. Where the established left had a strong concept of the "party line", new filmmakers wished to liberate directors from social, political, and authoritarian constraints and explore individual freedom in capturing reality. They shared that interest in authorship and subjectivity with the proliferating culture circles, formed in the aftermath of World War II, in which writers, journalists, painters, critics, filmmakers, and other artists proposed alternative modes of authenticity to the reportage and social realism established on the Left (Matsumoto 2012). These alliances between avant-garde circles and documentary films have recently become an object of inquiry (Matsumoto and Kenji 2008; Toba 2010; Raine 2012; Furuhata 2013; Key 2011; Centeno-Martín 2019), which is expanded further in this special issue by Toba. Filmmakers such as Matsumoto Toshio, Teshigahara Hiroshi, Kuroki Kazuo, and Hani Susumu engaged in a quest for new methods to explore reality. Some decades later, that New Left social orientation was challenged in turn by radical notions of subjectivity that underpinned intimate documentaries about filmmakers' private lives, including close depiction of partners and other family members. Documentary filmmakers such as Kazuo Hara in the 1970s, Kawase Naomi in the 1990s, and Yang Yong-hi in the 2000s have dismantled the traditional distinction between filmed subject (*shutai*) and filmed object (*taishō*), making it necessary to update previous debates about the filmmaker's role in the profilmic world.

Strikingly, much of the hardest thinking about the documentary aspect of cinema took place in out-of-the-way areas of the Japanese film industry, such as the producers of educational and PR films. Matsumoto Toshio, who would become an important avant-garde filmmaker and theorist, had attended the study group for the Documentary and Educational Film Producers Conference (Kiroku Kyōiku Eiga Seisaku Kyōgikai, known as Seikyō), led by prewar leftist filmmakers Noda Shinkichi and Atsugi Taka. The group went on to publish *Kiroku eiga*, a journal that, after Matsumoto and his allies took over editorial control in 1960, attracted contributions from theorists of art, literature, and fiction as well as nonfiction filmmaking (Raine 2012). In this "age of the document" (kiroku no jidai, Toba 2010), critical explorations of the documentary mode also questioned the boundary between fiction and nonfiction formats. Filmmakers, both inside and outside the major film studios, strove for a "cinema of actuality" (Furuhata 2013) that broke through the artificial wall of conventional "storyism" (Yoshida 1960). Many other groups, such as the Documentary Art Group (Kiroku Geijutsu no Kai), produced journals such as *Gendai geijutsu* that continued those debates. Matsumoto was also a marginal member of the Blue Group, a study group centred on young filmmakers at Iwanami to discuss both their current work and the projects they could not realize at the company (Nornes 2007, pp. 16–19). That group formed the nucleus of a series of documentary filmmakers, especially directors and cinematographers such as Hani Susumu and Tamura Masaki, who went on to work in both fiction and nonfiction genres during the 1960s and 1970s.

5. Goals and Structure of This Special Issue

The documentary mode is an essential part of Japanese film culture, whose role in film history has been recognized only recently. Some authors have provided a general historical overview of the documentary film (Satō 2010; Kurosawa et al. 2010), while others have focused on certain aspects: short documentaries (Yoshihara 2011; Harada 2012; Fujii 2002), Iwanami Eiga productions (Kusakabe 1980; Hani 2012; Tsunoda 2015), the variety of nonfiction genres (Takeda 2017), prewar and wartime non-fiction (Okudaira 1986; Kurasawa 1987; Fujii 2001; Hori 2002; Nornes 2003b; Centeno-Martín 2017;

Morita 2018) and postwar movements (Nornes 2003a; Centeno-Martín 2020b). In recent years, there has been a growing interest in treating certain documentary makers as *auteurs*, such as Sakane Tazuko (Ikegawa 2011; McDonald 2007), Tsuchimoto Noriaki (Jesty 2011; Bingham 2009; Gerow and Noriaki 2014; Inoue 2018), Ogawa Shinsuke (Nornes 2007); Hani Susumu (Briciu 2013; Centeno-Martín 2015), Matsumoto Toshio (Matsumoto and Kenji 2008; Raine 2012), and Hara Kazuo (Ruoff and Ruoff 1993).

Although there are older histories of documentary film that survey early actualities, *bunka eiga*, educational films, PR films, socially committed documentaries, television documentaries, and so on (Satō 1977), and more focused volumes on single production companies (Kusakabe 1980), few works have recognized Nichols' stipulation that documentary is a "fiction (un)like any other". Documentary is not just a genre but a mode (or modes); filmmakers in Japan have long explored the special power of cinema to compel a sense of authenticity, even when put in service of fictional worlds. From 1920s earthquake documentaries to the 1930s films influenced by contemporary debates over materialism, and from the ideological hypostatisation of a unitary Japanese nation in wartime culture films to 1960s radical documentaries that unashamedly "stood on the side of the subject" (Nornes 2007, p. 30), the putative boundary between documentary and dramatic films was frequently crossed in Japanese cinema. If terms such as "documentary touch" and "semi-documentary" were mere journalistic shorthand in post-war film criticism, Coates, Kitsnik, and Mihalopoulos make clear in this volume that some filmmakers made more stringent efforts to develop fictional worlds using at least some of the rhetorical forms and ethical commitments that underpin documentary's "impression of authenticity". In that context, it is vital that current studies develop more comprehensive approaches by interrogating the alliances and dialogues between documentary and other media and artistic practices, to avoid compartmentalising documentary films away from the rest of film history. *Developments in Japanese Documentary Mode* proposes new approaches to the history and theory of nonfiction genres and adjacent formats that contribute to identifying, analysing, and categorising distinctive uses of the documentary mode in Japan.

In his article, Fujii Jinshi identified an "inversion", through which, despite their shared goal of representing the ignored margins of Japan, the historical coincidence and methodological compatibility of the wartime documentary (*bunka eiga*) and Japanese ethnography (*minzokugaku*) supported the Japanese State in its ideological construction of a unitary and homogenous "Japanese Nation". Motivated by a "discourse of the vanishing", which described traditional Japanese culture as retreating in the face of forced modernization, both *bunka eiga* and *minzokugaku* drew on a contemporary intertextual field of ethnographic photography and reportage to attempt to document the disappearing lifeways of Japan. However, reviewing the "cameraman–viewfinder debate" between Miki Shigeru and Kamei Fumio, Fujii showed that cameraman–director Miki's collaboration with famous ethnographer Yanagita Kunio, recapitulated the tension in all documentary practices between a respect for the real and a desire to control it. Miki and Yanagita's documentary and spinoff photographic album covered over the heterogeneity of Japan, with representative images that came to stand for what could not be seen. Rather than a true representation of reality, their work served as an escape from it.

Miyao Daisuke also drew on the "cameraman–viewfinder debate" to highlight the tension between two longstanding discourses on documentary filmmaking: the film image as a mechanical reproduction of reality and documentary cinema as the creative treatment of actuality. He argued that wartime commentators played down the creative aspects of documentary in favour of the immediacy of the newsreel, a kind of zero degree recording that was even praised in feature films as an example of "documentary spirit" (*jissha seishin*). Through a discourse analysis of articles mostly in the influential trade journal *Eiga gijutsu*, he showed how that tension was resolved for makers of *bunka eiga* (culture films) by a strategic use of the world "culture". Culture was used not in Raymond Williams' modern sense of ordinary life (Williams 1958), but in the sense of education and refinement: cultured documentary filmmakers were both *au fait* with the modern science and technology of optics and imported cameras that produced their apparently automatic images and at the same time knowledgeable about the Japanese culture that they were newly commissioned to support. Concluding in a similar vein to Fujii, Miyao showed how that cultural knowledge was implicitly in opposition to Americanised popular culture, and complicit with the cultural nationalism of wartime Japan.

Toba Koji cast light on the documentary scene in Japan since the 1950s. This article provides keys to understand certain aspects of the media production of the time by exploring the interactions between magic lantern and documentary films. Toba proposed an innovative analysis of the relationship between Japanese documentary film and the cultural context of the time, including changes in postwar education, political activism, and the postwar "democracy" spirit in cultural productions and collaborative works. Toba demonstrated how the documentaries expanded beyond cinema and should be studied in relation to what is not in the film, becoming a sort of macrotext, which is comprised of a various media and artistic works that complement each other (mainly magic lantern productions, but also poetry, illustrated books, and so on). This approach also entails paying attention to the filmmaker's alliances with social actors, without which the films cannot be completely understood, ranging from artists, such as sculptors and painters, as well as local communities (students, teachers) and local historians.

The following three articles (Centeno-Martín, Jesty, and Inoue) explored the documentary scene from 1950s Japan and analysed tendencies that were articulated through shared innovative approaches to filmmaking. Centeno-Martín took Hani's film theory and practice as a starting point to demonstrate how this author pioneered a filmmaking method based on an extraordinary engagement with the filmed environment and created a sort of "documentary school". Centeno-Martín explained how Hani's theoretical framework was aimed at exploring inner worlds existing in the external world by following his principle of filming "protagonists who do not act". The article illustrates how Hani applied his methodology to a film without living characters, which focused instead on the architecture of Hōryūji temple. This example became one of the boldest attempts of the time to explore subjectivities and inner universes in the filmed objects and shows how the avant-garde documentary movement evolved in a variety of unexpected directions in late 1950s. The analysis is contextualised within the intellectual and artistic scene, including (trans)national influences as well as the ideological and aesthetic rupture among Japanese New Left artists. Centeno-Martín traced how Hani's method was expanded to Teshighara and Adachi's avant-garde documentaries, interrogating subjective dimensions in rural, urban, and architectural landscapes.

The relationship among these directors, largely unexplored to date, is essential to a comprehensive view of the documentary scene in post-war Japan. Assessing these artistic links and common practices, rather than studying films as isolated works, is instrumental to identifying collective tendencies of the time. Jesty explored this issue further by analysing how Hani's theories and films from the 1950s were expanded by Tsuchimoto in the early 1970s. The article provides a sharp and in-depth understanding of Hani's methodological framework, the nature of his collective works founded on the rejection of scripts, actors, and staged shooting, as well as its reliance on long-running involvement with the subjects in the film. Jesty engaged in important epistemological keys, such as Hani's singular notion of performance (*engi*), which is only true to life when shots capture changes in individuals as a consequence of being exposed to unfamiliar environments. Jesty explained how, to a certain extent, Tsuchimoto expanded Hani's approach in his lifelong engagement with Minamata victims. The article also demonstrates that despite apparent similarities with *cinéma vérité* in the US and France, Japanese authors developed an original pragmatic method seeking to reveal the dynamics of the subject's "life-world", which was not conceived to exist apart from the filmmakers. Films require partial mediation that should be carried out through receptivity and long observation. Thus, Jesty defined this film practice shared by Hani and Tsuchimoto as an "intersubjective" process, since the moving image's ability to project the subject's life-world emerges from the interdependence of the people involved in the film, both filmmakers and filmed subjects.

Inoue expanded Jesty's analysis by engaging in a discussion of the ethical dimension of Tsuchimoto's documentary practice. The article shows how Tsuchimoto's close gaze on the human being, which is based on interactions between individuals, becomes problematic when representing filmed subjects (*shutai*) who remain unconscious or unable to express themselves, like victims of Minamata disease. How can filmmakers deal with subjects who can't interact? Is it ethically right to film them in the first place? Inoue engaged in this ethical debate that has relevant implications for contemporary media practices. By comparing Tsuchimoto's films with Eugene Smith's photography, Inoue showed how the threshold between an abusive usage of a subject's life and an ethical representation is extremely subtle but equally meaningful. Tsuchimoto's concerns about the potential danger that the camera may trigger on filmed subjects is precisely what makes his approach valuable.

Kitsnik analysed Shindō Kaneto's interest in working with real events and using a variety of documentary film resources, tropes, and patterns of representation as part of the filmmaker's engagement with postwar cinematic experiments on the boundaries between reality and fiction. The article raises crucial questions through the close observation of Shindō's oeuvre: questions of ethics and the impossibility of making "nonfiction" films given the unavoidable existence of an author and the subsequent cinematic artifice that makes any attempt to capture reality objectively unattainable. Thus, Kitsnik illustrated how Shindō's work is a mixture of documentary and fiction formats, articulated in a hybrid and stylised manner. This study is also useful to understand the context in which other avant-garde filmmakers of the time, such as Oshima and Matsumoto, engaged in this film experienced challenging the boundaries between fiction and nonfiction by combining historic events, media footage, and interviews with re-enactments or fictional stories.

Turning to Imamura Shohei, a filmmaker whose career spans both feature films and documentaries, Bill Mihalopoulos argued that many of Imamura's films are characterized by a promiscuous fusion of the "immediacy and authenticity associated with documentary film-making" and the "character development and dramatic arc" typical of the fiction film. When Imamura turned to documentary filmmaking in the 1960s, the films were similarly experimental and reflexive. Focusing on Imamura's 1970 documentary *History of Post-war Japan as Told by a Bar Hostess*, Mihalopoulos argued that the juxtaposition of interview and newsreel documentary modes, layered in the same shot, disrupted the dominant narrative of post-war Japan. The interval between the two modes allows us to perceive, simultaneously and ambivalently, the interview subject's shameless vitality as well as her self-commodification and indifference to her complicity in the public events shown behind her. Unlike the wartime films discussed by Fujii and Miyao, the dialectic of public and private in the film foregrounds the heterogeneity of life as it is in Japan. Mihalopoulos concluded that in place of the orthodox story of democratization and economic growth, Imamura's film suggests a "radical change in personality", in which Japanese respond to intensified postwar capitalism with "greed, violence, and cold indifference".

Jennifer Coates also cast a wide net over the history of documenting practices in the cinema. Starting with the earliest actualities, Coates questioned national and genre divisions in film analysis. Drawing on the concept of ethnofiction from visual anthropology, Coates extended its definition from subjects improvising their own lives on camera to argue that scripted prewar documentaries were a form of ethnofiction, as were wartime films that, like ethnofiction, dramatized real events. This historical revisionism enabled a critique of origins: ethnofiction is usually traced to French *cinema verité*, but Coates argued that it was a common-sense approach in Japan from the 1950s to the present day, from Japanese filmmakers such as Imamura Shohei to filmmakers working in Japan, such as Hou Hsiao Hsien. Ethnofictional practices in those films included research into real people's lives and a provocative or reflexive relation between filmmaker and subject/character. Coates went on to argue that recognizing Japanese feature films as ethnofictions allows us to recognize that blend of fictional and documentary techniques as a polycentric global innovation with geographic and temporal specificities.

We would like to thank these authors for responding to our initial call for papers, and for their careful revisions of their essays. We are pleased to present their work in public and hope the various arguments and histories documented here will spark further research and discussion among our readers.

Conflicts of Interest: The authors declare no conflict of interest.

References

Anderson, Joseph, and Richie Donald. 1982. *The Japanese Film: Art and Industry*. Princeton: Princeton University Press, (originally published in Tokyo, Rutland VT.: C.E. Tuttle Co, 1959).

Barber, X. Theodore. 1993. The Roots of Travel Cinema: John L. Stoddard, E. Burton Holmes, and the Nineteenth-Century Illustrated Travel Lecture. *Film History* 5: 68–84.

Bingham, Adam. 2009. Filmmaking as a way of life: Tsuchimoto, Ogawa, and revolutions in documentary cinema. *Asian Cinema* 20: 166–75. [CrossRef]

Bordwell, David. 1994. *Film History: An Introduction*. New York: McGraw Hill.

Briciu, Bianca. 2013. Love and power: The objectification of the adolescent body in Hani Susumu's *Hatsukoi jigokuhen/Nanami, inferno of first love* (1968). *Journal of Japanese and Korean Cinema* 5: 59–76. [CrossRef]

Brooks, Peter. 1976. *The Melodramatic Imagination: Balzac, Henry James, Melodrama and the Mode of Excess*. New Haven: Yale University Press.

Centeno-Martín, Marcos P. 2015. Susumu Hani (1950–1960): The Theoretical and Practical Contribution to the Japanese Documentary and Youth Cinema. An Approach to Hani's Case as a Precursor of the New Wave. Ph.D. dissertation, University of Valencia, Valencia, Spain.

Centeno-Martín, Marcos P. 2017. Transnational Circulation of Images of the Pacific War (1941–1945): The Japanese Empire Seen through Spanish Newsreels. *Irish Journal of Asian Studies (IJAS)* 3: 1–13.

Centeno-Martín, Marcos P. 2018a. Introduction. The Misleading Discovery of Japanese National Cinema. *Arts* 7: 87. [CrossRef]

Centeno-Martín, Marcos P. 2018b. The Limits of Fiction: Politics and Absent Scenes in Susumu Hani's Bad Boys (Furyō Shōnen, 1960). A Film Re-reading through its Script. *Journal of Japanese and Korean Cinema* 10: 1–15. [CrossRef]

Centeno-Martín, Marcos P. 2019. Postwar Narratives through Avant-garde Documentary: Tokyo 1958 and Furyō Shōnen. In *Persistently Postwar. Media and the Politics of Memory in Japan*. Edited by Artur Lozano, Dolores Martínez and Blai Guarné. New York and Oxford: Berghahn Books, pp. 41–62.

Centeno-Martín, Marcos P. 2020a. From Japan to Africa: Transnationality in Hani Susumu's Theory and Cinematic Experience from Japan to Africa". In *Japan beyond Its Borders: Transnational Approaches to Film and Media*. Edited by Marcos P. Centeno-Martín and Morita Nori. Tokyo: Seibunsha, pp. 113–26.

Centeno-Martín, Marcos P. 2020b. Crónicas de Paisaje. Nuevas formas de subjetividad en la vanguardia documental japonesa. In *Memoria y paisaje en el cine japonés de posguerra*. Edited by Pedro Iacobelli and Claudia Lira. Santiago de Chile: Ediciones Universedad Católica de Chile, pp. 287–335.

De Castillon, Pierre. 1975. Notes et Etudes Documentareis. *Le Cinéma Japonais* 8: 16.

Fujii, Jinshi. 2001. Torarenakatta shotto to sono unmei: Jihen to eiga 1937–1941 (Shots that could not be taken and their fate: The China Incident and cinema, 1937–1941). *Eizōgaku (Visual Studies)* 67: 23–40.

Fujii, Jinshi. 2002. Films That Do Culture: A Discursive Analysis of Bunka Eiga, 1935–1945. *Iconics* 6: 51–68.

Furuhata, Yuriko. 2007. Returning to Actuality: Fūkeoron and the Landscape Film. *Screen* 48: 345–62. [CrossRef]

Furuhata, Yuriko. 2013. *Cinema of Actuality: Japanese Avant-Garde Filmmaking in the Season of Image Politics*. Durham: Duke University Press.

Gerow, Aaron, and Tsuchimoto Noriaki. 2014. Tsuchimoto Noriaki. Documentarists of Japan No. 7. Documentary Box. Available online: http://www.yidff.jp/docbox/8/box8-2.html (accessed on 21 May 2020).

Giuglaris, Shinobu, and Marcel Giuglaris. 1957. *Le cinema Japonais*. Paris: du Cerf.

Greenberg, Larry. 2001. The Arrival of Cinema in Japan. In *The Benshi. Japanese Silent Films Narrators*. Edited by Matsuda Eigasha. Tokyo: Urban Connections, pp. 6–12.

Grierson, John. 1933. The Documentary Producer. *Cinema Quarterly* 2: 7–9.

Grierson, John. 1979. Flaherty's Poetic Moana. In *The Documentary Tradition*, 2nd ed. Edited by Lewis Jacobs. New York: W. W. Norton, pp. 25–27, Originally published under the byeline The Moviegoer in *New York Sun*, 8 February 1926.

Hamasaki, Koji. 1999. Nyūsu eiga kōkogaku: Katsudō shashin 1 Shadan hōjin Nihon Nyūsu-eiga-sha setsuritsu made: 1896–1940 (Newsreel Archaeology. 1 From action photos to the creation of Nihon Nyūsu eiga-sha: 1896–1940). *Kawasaki-shi Shimin Myūjiamu kiyō* 11: 34–35.

Hani, Susumu. 1959. Terebi prodyūsā e no chōzenjō. Kagami ni natteshimatta mado (Letter to Challenge Television Producers. The Window which became a Mirror). *Chūo Kōron* 74: 199.

Hani, Susumu. 1960. *Terementarī ron (Terementari Theory) in Gendai terebi kōza*. Edited by Kakutarō Kanazawa. Tokyo: Daviddosha, pp. 69–76.

Hani, Susumu. 1985. Aru tokuina rīdā ni tsuite no kaisō. Iwanami Eiga ni okeru jinzai ikusei o sasaeta mono (Reflection on some singular leaders. Training talents at Iwanami Eiga). *Rekishi to shakai* 6.

Hani, Susumu. 2012. Boku to Iwanami Eiga (Iwanami Eiga and I). In *Iwanami Eiga no 1-oku furēmu (Images of Postwar Japan. The Documentary Films of Iwanami Productions)*. Edited by Niwa Yoshiyuki and Yoshimi Sun'ya. Tokyo: Tokyo Daigaku Shuppankai, pp. 21–38.

Hani, Susumu, Ushiyama Yunichi, Okamoto Yoshihiko, and Yoshida Naoya. 1959. Warera wa terebi prodyūsā (We, Television Producers). *Chūō Kōron* 74: 225.

Harada, Ken'ichi. 2012. CIE Eiga/Suraido no Nihonteki Juyō: "Niigata" to iu Jirei Kara (Japanese Reception of CIE Films/Slides: From the case of "Nigata"). In *Senryō suru Me, Senryō suru Koe: CIE/USIS Eiga to VOA Rajio*. Edited by Yuka Tsuchiya and Yoshimi Shun'ya. Tokyo: Tokyo Daigaku Shuppankai.

Hori, Hikari. 2002. Senchū, senryōki kōteki media ni okeru joseizō no hensen (Images of Women in Newsreels of Wartime and Occupation Japan). *Journal of Gender Studies Japan* 4: 29–46.

Hori, Hikari. 2017. *Promiscuous Media. Film and Visual Culture in Imperial Japan, 1926–1945*. Ithaca: Cornell University Press.

Ikegawa, Reiko. 2011. *Teikoku no eiga kantoku Sakane Tazuko*. (Sakane Tazuko, Empire's Film Director). Tokyo: Yoshikawa.

Ikegawa, Reiko, and Julian Ward. 2005. Japanese Women Filmmakers in World War II: A Study of Sakane Tazuko, Suzuki Noriko and Atsugi Taka. In *Japanese Women Emerging from Subservience, 1868–1945*. Edited by Gordon Daniels and Hiroko Tomida. Folkestone: Global Oriental, pp. 258–77.

Imamura, Shōhei, and Satō Tadao, eds. 1986. *Sensō to Nihon eiga (War and Japanese Film)*. Tokyo: Iwanami Shoten.

Inoue, Miyo. 2018. Exhibition, Document, Bodies: The (Re)presentation of Minamata Disease. Ph.D. dissertation, University of California, Berkeley, CA, USA.

Irie, Takanori. 2006. Iwanami Eiga no ni nenkan (Two Years in Iwanami Eiga). *Seiron* 417: 244–53.

Irie, Yoshirō. 2010. Approaching Imamura Taihei and the Originality of His Film Theory. *Review of Japanese Culture and Society* 22: 60–79.

Jesty, Justin. 2011. Making mercury visible: The Minamata documentaries of Tsuchimoto Noriaki. In *Mercury Pollution: A Transdisciplinary Treatment*. Edited by Michael C. Newman and Sharon Zuber. Abingdon: Taylor and Francis, pp. 139–60.

Jesty, Justin. 2018. *Art and Engagement in Early Postwar Japan*. Ithaca: Cornell University Press.

Key, Margaret S. 2011. *Truth from a Lie: Documentary, Detection, and Reflexivity in Abe Kobo's Realist Project*. New York: Lexington Books.

Koga, Futoshi. 1995. 'Meiji no Nihon' kara 'Rumieru eiga Nihon-hen'e (From Meiji Japan to Lumière Films Japan Edition). In *Eiga Denrai*. Edited by Yoshishige Yoshida, Masao Yamaguchi and Naoyuki Kinoshita. Tokyo: Iwanami Shoten.

Komatsu, Hiroshi. 1992. Some characteristics of Japanese Cinema before World War I. In *Reframing Japanese Cinema. Authorship, Genre, History*. Edited by Arthur Nolleti and David Desser. Bloomington: Indiana University Press, pp. 238–44.

Kurasawa, Aiko. 1987. Japanese Film Propaganda in Java 1942–1945. *Indonesia* 44: 59–116. [CrossRef]

Kurosawa, Kiyoshi, Yomota Inuhiko, and Yoshimi Shunya. 2010. *Nihon eiga wa ikiteiru dai 7 kan: Fumikoeru dokyumentari (Japanese Cinema is Alive Volume 7: Documentary that Overcomes)*. Tokyo: Iwanami Shoten, pp. 111–30.

Kusakabe, Kyūshirō. 1980. *Eizō o tsukuru hito to kigyō: Iwanami Eiga no sanjūnen (Filmmakers and Companies: Thirty Years of Iwanami)*. Tokyo: Mizuumi Shobō.

Lastra, James. 2000. *Sound Technology and the American Cinema*. New York: Columbia University Press.

Lerebours, N. P. 1842. *Excursions Daguérriennes: Vues et Monuments les plus Remarquables du Globe (Daguerrian Excursions: The Most Remarkable Views and Monuments in the World)*. Paris: Rittner et Goupil.

Lewis, Diane Wei. 2019. *Powers of the Real: Cinema, Gender, and Emotion in Interwar Japan*. Cambridge: Harvard University Asia Center.

Mamiya, Norio. 1962. 1962-nen no 'watashi' (The 'Me' of 1962—How To Shoot PR Films). *Kiroku Eiga* 11.

Matsumoto, Toshio. 2012. A Theory of Avant-Garde Documentary. *Cinema Journal* 51: 148–54.

Matsumoto, Toshio, and Ishizaka Kenji. 2008. *Dokyumentarii no Umi e: Kiroku Eiga Sakka Matsumoto Toshio to no Taiwa (Toward a Documentary Sea: A Conversation with Documentary Filmmaker Matsumoto Toshio)*. Tokyo: Gendai Shokan.

McDonald, Keiko I. 2007. Daring To Be First: The Japanese Woman Director Tazuko Sakane (1904–1971). *Asian Cinema* 18: 138–46. [CrossRef]

Morita, Noriko. 2018. Geijutsu eiga-sha ni yoru seisaku genba no hen'yō: Senji-ki Nihon ni okeru "dokyumentarī" no hōhō-ron no jissen. (The Transformation of the Production Site by Geijutsu Eigasha: The implementation of the "Documentary" Method in Wartime Japan). *Eizogaku* 100: 10–31.

Murayama, Hideo. 2010. Kiroku eiga no hozon to genjō (Contemporary Situation of Documentary Film Preservation). In *Shirīzu Nihon no dokyumentarī 4. Sangyō, kagaku hen*. Edited by Satō Tadao. Tokyo: Iwanami Shoten.

Musser, Charles. 1994. *The Emergence of Cinema: The American Screen to 1907*. Berkeley: University of California Press.

Nakamura, Hideyuki. 2012. Akatsuki ni au made: 'Iwanami Eiga' to 'me' no shakaiteki sōzō (Meeting at Sunrise: Iwanami Eiga and the Creation of a Social Gaze). In *Iwanami Eiga no 1-oku furēmu (Images of Postwar Japan. The Documentary Films of Iwanami Productions)*. Edited by Niwa Yoshiyuki and Yoshimi Sun'ya. Tokyo: Tokyo Daigaku Shuppankai, pp. 39–58.

Nichols, Bill. 2017. *Introduction to Documentary*, 3rd ed. Bloomington: Indiana University Press.

Nornes, Abe Mark. 1999. Pôru Rûta/Paul Rotha and the Politics of Translation Part 1. *Cinema Journal* 38: 91–108.

Nornes, Markus. 2003a. The Postwar Documentary Trace: Groping in the Dark. *Positions: East Asia Cultures Critique* 10: 39–78. [CrossRef]

Nornes, Abé Mark. 2003b. *Japanese Documentary Film: The Meiji Era through Hiroshima*. Minneapolis: University of Minnesota Press.

Nornes, Abe Mark. 2006. El magisterio de Fumio Kamei. In *El Cine de los Mil Años: Una Aproximación Histórica y Estética al Cine Documental Japonés (1945–2005)*. Edited by Carlos Muguiro. Pamplona: Colección Punto de Vista, p. 22, (The Typical Genius of Kamei Fumio, Yamagata International Documentary Film Festival, originally published in 2001.).

Nornes, Abé Mark. 2007. *Forest of Pressure: Ogawa Shinsuke and the Postwar Japanese Documentary*. Minneapolis: University of Minnesota Press.

Okudaira, Yasuhiro. 1986. Eiga no Kokka Tōsei. In *Kōza Nihon eiga 4: Sensō to Nihon eiga*. Tokyo: Iwanami Shoten.

Raine, Michael. 2012. Introduction to Matsumoto Toshio: A Theory of Avant-Garde Documentary. *Cinema Journal* 51: 144–47. [CrossRef]

Raine, Michael. 2019. The Cold War as Media Environment in 1960s Japanese Cinema. In *The Cold War and Asian Cinemas*. Edited by Poshek Fu and Man Fung Yip. London: Routledge.

Richie, Donald. 1990. *Japanese Cinema. An Introduction*. Hong Kong, New York and Oxford: Oxford University Press.

Ruoff, Kenneth J., and Jeffrey K. Ruoff. 1993. Filming at the Margins: The Documentaries of Hara Kazuo. *Image Theory, Image Culture, and Contemporary Japan. Iris* 16: 115–26.

Salomon, Harald. 2011. *Views of the Dark Valley—Japanese Cinema and the Culture of Nationalism, 1937–1945*. Wiesbaden: Harrassowitz Verlag.

Satō, Tadao. 1977. *Nihon kiroku eizōshi (History of the Japanese Documentary Image)*. Tokyo: Hyōronsha.

Satō, Tadao. 2010. *Shirīzu Nihon no dokyumentarī (Japanese Documentary Series)*. Tokyo: Iwanami Shoten.

Shimizu, Akira. 1991. *Nichi-Bei eigasen (Japanese-American War Films)*. Tokyo: Seikyūsha.

Takeda, Tōru. 2017. *Nihon nonfikushon shi: Ruporutāju kara akademikku jānarizumu made (A History of Japanese Non-Fiction: From Reportage to Academic Journalism)*. Tokyo: Chūō Kōron Shinsha.

Toba, Kōji. 2010. *1950 nendai: 'Kiroku' no jidai (1950s: The Documentary Age)*. Tokyo: Kawade Shobō Shinsha.

Toda, Keita. 2006. Iwanami Eiga Seisakujo to 60 nendai dokyumentarī eiga no shuppatsu: Tsuchimoto Noriaki sakuhin ni miru shoki terebi to no kakawari wo chūshin ni (Iwanami Eiga Productions and the beginning of 1960s Documentaries: Focusing on Noriaki Tsuchimoto and his Early Television Work). *The Sociologist. Journal of the Musashi Sociological Society* 8: 145–271.

Tsuchimoto, Noriaki. 1988. Shiron, Dokyumentarī eiga no 30 nen (My Theory, 30 Years of Documentary Film). In *Kōza Nihon eiga 7: Nihon eiga no genzai*. Tokyo: Iwanami Shoten, pp. 248–69.

Tsunoda, Takuya. 2015. The Dawn of Cinematic Modernism: Iwanami Productions and Postwar Japanese Cinema. Ph.D. dissertation, Yale University, New Haven, CT, USA.

Tsurumi, Shunsuke, ed. 1969. *Kataritsugu Sengoshi I (Passed-Down Postwar History, Part 1)*. Tokyo: Shisō no Kagakusha.

Uni Japan. 1961. *Japanese Films 1961. Non-Dramatic Subjects*. Tokyo: Uni Japan, Association for the Diffusion of Japanese Films Abroad.

VV.AA. 1963. *Eiganenkan*. Tokyo: Jijitsūshinsha.

Wada-Marciano, Mitsuyo. 2019. Educational Films in Postwar Japan: Traces of American Cultural Policies in the Cold War Period. In *The Cold War and Asian Cinemas*. Edited by Poshek Fu and Man-Fung Yip. New York and London: Routledge.

Williams, Raymond. 1958. Culture is Ordinary. In *Conviction*. Edited by Norman MacKenzie. London: MacGibbon and Key.

Yamamoto, Kikuo. 1983. *Nihon eiga ni okeru gaikoku eiga no eikyō (The Influence of Foreign Cinema on Japanese Cinema)*. Tokyo: Waseda Daigaku Shuppanbu.

Yamamoto, Naoki. 2020. *Dialectics without Synthesis: Japanese Film Theory and Realism in a Global Frame*. Berkeley: University of California Press.

Yamane, Sadao. 1993. Changes in 1960s Documentary Cinema from PR films to Image Guerilla. In *Japanese Documentaries of the 1960s*. Tokyo: Yamagata Film Festival, pp. 14–20.

Yomota, Inuhiko. 2019. *What is Japanese Cinema? A History*. New York: Columbia University Press.

Yoshida, Kijū. 1960. Eiga no kabe: Stōrī-shugi hihan (The Wall of Cinema: A Critique of Storyism). *Shinario* 16: 84–87.

Yoshihara, Junpei. 2011. *Nihon tanpen eizōshi: Bunka eiga, kyōiku eiga, sangyō eiga (History of Japanese Short Films: Culture Films, Educational Films, Industry Films)*. Tokyo: Iwanami Shoten.

© 2020 by the authors. Licensee MDPI, Basel, Switzerland. This article is an open access article distributed under the terms and conditions of the Creative Commons Attribution (CC BY) license (http://creativecommons.org/licenses/by/4.0/).

Article

Yanagita Kunio and the Culture Film: Discovering Everydayness and Creating/Imagining a National Community, 1935–1945 [†]

Jinshi Fujii

Faculty of Letters, Arts and Sciences, Waseda University, Tokyo 162-8644, Japan; jinfujii@waseda.jp

† Translated by Michael Raine, Marcos P. Centeno-Martín, and Maiko Kodaka. This article was originally published as Fujii Jinshi. 2003. Yanagita Kunio to bunka eiga: Shōwa jyūnendai niokeru nichijōseikatsu no hakken to kokumin no sōzō. In *The Politics of Cinema* (Eiga no seijigaku). Edited by Hase Masato and Nakamura Hideyuki. Tokyo: Seikyūsha, pp. 265–301. This translation is printed by permission of the original publisher. The author discusses the conflicted definition of "culture film" (*bunka eiga*) in relation to Japanese folklore studies (*minzokugaku*). Those fields are referred to by their English translations throughout this article. All names in the text are given in Japanese order (family name first) with the exception of the author attribution above.

Received: 11 February 2020; Accepted: 2 April 2020; Published: 26 April 2020

Abstract: In wartime Japan, folklore studies (*minzokugaku*) as an academic discipline emerged at the same time as the rise of the culture film (*bunka eiga*). Both helped mobilize peripheral areas and firmly created the image of a unitary nation. This paper focuses on *Living by the Earth* (*Tsuchi ni ikiru*, 1941), directed by Miki Shigeru, and its spinoff photo album titled *People of the Snow Country* (*Yukiguni no minzoku*, 1944). Miki filmed rural life and ordinary people in the Tohoku region under the strong influence of Yanagita Kunio, a founder of Japanese folklore studies, and published the photo album in collaboration with Yanagita. In this project, vanishing customs were paradoxically regarded as objects impossible to photograph. However, that paradox enhanced the value of the project and made it easier to construct an imagined national community through the discourse of folklore studies.

Keywords: documentary film; the culture film; folklore studies; documentary photography

---

No one dies so poor that he does not leave something behind.

Blaise Pascal[1]

1. The Culture Film and Folklore Studies

1.1. The "Discovery" of Rural Japan

Japanese folklore studies, as an academic discipline, emerged at the same time as the rise of the culture film. I do not think this was a coincidence. The discourses on folklore studies and the culture film had formal similarities, and moreover, they formed archetypal expressions of an *inversion* that they shared with the hegemonic discourse following the "China Incident" that led to the outbreak of the Second Sino-Japanese War in 1937.

First, let us focus on folklore studies. As an academic discipline, it was established during the 1930s, with Yanagita Kunio at its center. Yanagita was already in his sixties when he published two books of methodology, *Folklore Theory* (*Minkan denshō ron*) in 1934 and *Methodology for the Study of*

---

[1] Quoted in (Benjamin 1996, p. 313).

Regional Ways of Life (Kyōdo seikatsu no kenkyū-hō) in 1935.[2] In addition to those books, in 1935, Yanagita created a study circle, the Association of Folklore (Minkan denshō no kai), at his home and published the journal known as *Folklore (Minkan denshō)*, through which his students started their systematic studies. This sequence of events, driven by the force of Yanagita's personality, established folklore studies as an academic discipline and gained it wide recognition in Japanese society.[3] However, it is important to note that Yanagita resisted the label of folklore studies, because his comprehensive oeuvre expanded beyond existing disciplinary boundaries.[4] Despite Yanagita's concerns, it cannot be ignored that his work circulated as the "Yanagita School" of folklore studies, and he became an authority in the field. The aim of this article is neither to clarify Yanagita Kunio's true purpose nor to explore the contemporary validity of his texts. Even if the image of his work is superficial, it has had enormous social influence, so there is still value in carefully analyzing its functions and effects. That is the sense in which this paper treats "Yanagita Kunio" and folklore studies.

So, what about the culture film? What was the culture film after all? I have already discussed this question elsewhere (Fujii 2001a)[5] and can summarize my argument as follows. The term "culture film" is usually considered to be a synonym for a "documentary film" (*kiroku eiga*) made during wartime, but this common understanding was only possible in retrospect. Culture film was an empty sign that could be discussed endlessly precisely because it had no fixed definition. In fact, references to the culture film circulated widely in the discursive space of the second decade of the Shōwa period (1926–1989), appearing in various print media. The background to that was the "discovery" of the commercial value of non-fiction films with the popularity of newsreels after the China Incident in 1937 and the start of the compulsory exhibition of culture films in film programs one year after the enactment of the Film Law in 1939. Additionally, it cannot be overlooked that the discourse on culture films made it possible to ignore the twisted "reality" in Japan that was a consequence of the China Incident.[6]

While folklore studies and the culture film developed in their own way between 1935 and 1945, they became decisively intertwined after the China Incident. The film critic Tsumura Hideo, who participated in the "Overcoming Modernity" symposium, stated in an article published in 1941:

> The impact of the China Incident on the politics and culture of Japan was profound in many respects. But the most significant is the nation's interest in the "rural" (*chihō*) and "rural people". In the context of total war and the creation of the military state, the problem is how to understand the particularity of rural Japan and develop it appropriately, with a view to the destiny of the nation as a whole, in an organic relation to the urban.
>
> Tsumura (1941, pp. 21–22)

According to Tsumura, the total war system following the China Incident caused the nation to turn its gaze toward rural areas, and indeed, the number of films featuring villages suddenly increased in this period. As the editor of the bulletin of Fumin Kyōkai (Association for Enriching Japanese Nationals), Kimura Taijirō, stated:

> Recently, a particular cinematic genre of "peasant film" has appeared. As a critique of films that until now were too focused on the city, and for social reasons to do with the increased interest in rural villagers and farmers in the current circumstances, it is a clear step forward

---

[2] The former reprinted in (Yanagita 1998), the latter in (Yanagita 1998). The advertisement when the first book was published by Kyōritsusha read: "The first systematic study of folklore" in *Tabi to densetsu* (Travel and Folklore), October, 1934.

[3] It is also significant that many introductory texts on "folklore" were translated in the 1920s. See (Makita 1972, pp. 131–32).

[4] *Folklore Theory* begins: "It seems a little early to use the word Folklore Studies as a common noun in Japan". See also (Karatani 1993, pp. 258–80).

[5] This was translated by Jeffrey Isaacs as "Films That Do Culture—A Discursive Analysis of Bunka Eiga, 1935–1945" in *Iconics* 6 (2002).

[6] In a narrow definition, culture films were only films that had been authorized by the Ministry of Education according to the Film Law criteria. However, it was clear from the discourse on culture films at the time that the definition was more inclusive than that.

for Japanese cinema, which has finally developed into a cinema based on a comprehensive sense of the masses that includes rural villages and people.

Kimura (1939)[7]

Kimura mentioned films such as *Earth* (Tsuchi, 1939), *Airplane Roar* (Bakuon, 1939), *Nightingale* (Uguisu, 1939), and later *Horse* (Uma, 1941) as good examples. Those are all feature films, but culture films were also subject to the same phenomenon. According to Aihara Shūji's research, between January and June 1941, 58 of the 135 authorized culture films (43% of the total) were "related to domestic production and culture". Within this category, films about "agriculture and farming" numbered 38, comprising 28% of the total (Aihara 1942).[8] As Aihara argues, many of the 18 "natural science related" films could also be categorized as "agriculture and farming", which indicates the rapidly growing interest in rural villages in culture films of the time (although this chaotic categorization also illustrates the confusion about this concept). Therefore, the culture film and folklore studies shared an overlapping interest in rural areas.[9] Filmmakers were aware of this intimate relationship between culture films and folklore studies.[10] As the cameraman Midorikawa Michio stated, addressing young filmmakers in the manual of the state-controlled Film Association of Imperial Japan:

> The Japanese study of traditions and ethnology is limited to an extremely specific group of researchers, a state of affairs that we feel sure is closely linked to the current state of our lives. We put too much value on individualism due to our excessively open connection with the world.
>
> However, in the current situation I am happy to see an important new movement that emphasizes Japanese cultural awareness. In fact, the leaders of this movement have never been asleep *and good results will come from their example* (...) We have come to the time when we should look back on tradition. We are becoming aware of the chaos which emerges if our lives do not take root in tradition.

Midorikawa (1940, pp. 69–71)

As the emphasis in the quotation shows, what had been "discovered" was not something that had appeared recently. It had been there all along, but it did not attract any attention since it was too quotidian.

A sense of loss was necessary to "discover" rural life, which had become so familiar that no one noticed its importance. After the First World War, the migration to cities to serve in heavy industry triggered a sudden population crisis in rural areas, and the military enlistment of the younger generations after the China Incident added to the pressures on farming and fishing villages. Those accelerated changes threatened traditional life with extinction. As a direct result, the everyday life of rural Japan came to be retrospectively held dear. Borrowing Midorikawa's expression, this was discovered by those who "looked back" and became aware of the chaotic situation. As Tsumura Hideo wrote: "I have been

---

[7] The ideal peasant film mentioned in this article was the American film *Our Daily Bread* (1934), which shows that the concern was not limited to Japan. For instance, the first International Agrarian Film Competition was held at the 15th general meeting of the International Institute of Agriculture in Rome in 1940. See (Donini 1941).

[8] The background to this phenomenon was a letter from the Home Office that stated, "films about production, especially agriculture, should be encouraged", printed in *Kinema Junpō*, January in 1941, and quoted in (Kinema Junpō Sha 1976, p. 83); the promotion of rural lives was encouraged in (Cultural Department of the Imperial Rule Assistance Association 1985).

[9] The interest in rural Japan was thematized in literature earlier than film. For instance, *Before the Dawn* (Yoakemae) by Shimazaki Tōson was completed in 1935, followed immediately by the serialization of Kawabata Yasunari's *Snow Country* (Yukiguni). Uchida Tomu's *Earth* was also based on the original novel by Nagatsuka Takashi published in 1910, though it was influenced by the success of an adaptation by the Shin Tsukiji troupe in the Tsukiji little theatre. Shikiba Ryūsaburō, who joined Yanagi Sōtetsu's Mingei movement, stated that it was literature that first found value in rural Japan, and this "literature of the soil" (distinguished from proletarian literature) was inherited by the culture film (Shikiba 1941).

[10] Reflecting on the culture films of 1940, Tsumura Hideo pointed out an impasse in their production. Since "relying only on culture film producers might limit the range of expression (...) a way forward for exploring rural lives would be to get advice from Yanagita's Association of Folklore. Understanding folklore studies is also necessary" (Tsumura 1941, p. 145).

thinking of various things since the emergence of the culture film in Japan. Most importantly, that these films allowed us to see the 'faces' of rural areas and rural people" (Tsumura 1941, p. 21). This statement does not mean Tsumura never saw faces of people from the countryside. It simply highlights the fact that without this discovery, Tsumura would not have noticed the value of those "faces", which sparked "a certain emotional impression" when they were seen. This "discovery" was made at the historical crossroads/crisis situation (conjuncture) in which everyday rural life was vanishing by virtue of being ignored, retroactively bestowing value on that life precisely because of the urgency of the crisis that threatened it.

1.2. Created/Imagined Japan

The southern and northern parts of Japan provide extreme examples of the situation described above. The former is Okinawa and the latter is the Tohoku region, which has very snowy winters. Although it has been widely argued that Okinawa played a key role for Yanagita Kunio and the establishment of folklore studies,[11] the relationship between the culture film and Okinawa shall be discussed in a separate paper, since films featuring the snow country were the core of this film genre. The following section will focus on some culture films which were clearly produced from an ethnographic interest in the snow country, but before that, it is worth taking a glance at a film on the subject that was not created from such an ethnographic approach. This will help us understand the image of the snow country in the context of contemporary culture films.

Culture films were considered boring until the release of Ishimoto Tōkichi's *Snow Country* (*Yukiguni*, 1939), which was the first masterpiece of the genre.[12] It was not only commercially successful but also had a warm reception among critics and won a prize from the Ministry of Education.[13] The film was produced by Omura Einosuke´s Geijutsu eigasha, a studio that also published the journal *Folklore Research* (*Minzokugaku Kenkyū*). Geijutsu eigasha was as important as the Tōhō studio in the production of culture films. The entire shoot took three years and was edited from footage taken in various areas such as Yamagata and other places in Tohoku, Hokkaido, and Hokuriku.

The film begins with a scene of a running steam train. First, we see black soil farms, white mountains appearing gradually from the distance, and a man removing snow alongside the tracks when the train enters the snow country. This introduction, getting gradually closer to the destination, functions as a stereotypical "story of arrival" that often conceals estrangement in the encounter with the other.[14] It could be argued that the film is quite literally passing through Kawabata Yasunari's "tunnel" in his novel *Snow Country* (Karatani 1997, pp. 42–44). Here, the chain of short shots emphasizes the feeling of movement and the beauty of the remaining machinery from the 1920s, while, at the same time, the locomotive breaking explosively through the heavy snow suggests the ultimate victory of human beings over nature.

After the opening sequence, "the fight of man against snow" in the snow country can be read in different ways, but it shows the influence of a tendency toward social reformism found in Paul Rotha's theory of documentary (Rotha 1938). The portrayal of postmen on snowshoes, the scenes of removing snow and the renovated housing with roofs of a fifty-degree incline on which the snow cannot stick are like a "triumph" over the snow. The voiceover explaining that it is only Japan among the countries of the developed world that suffers from such heavy snow conveys a foreign (Euro-American) perspective

---

[11] See (Murai 1995; Koyasu 1996, pp. 1–54).
[12] See (Fujii 2001a).
[13] *Yukiguni*, first screened at the Hibiya Theatre, which specialized in Western films, was unexpectedly successful (it was rare to screen Japanese films in cinemas for Western films). The award from the Ministry of Education was accompanied by the citation: "depicting snow in Japan's coastal area, it succeeded not only as documentation but also as an indication of the proper way to make culture films" (Advertisement for *Yukiguni* in *Nihon Eiga* 5.6, 1940, p. 117). There must also have been pressure from the letter from the Home Office, mentioned in note 8 (*Earth* was also given an award at the same time).
[14] See (Kitakouji 2003).

on the snow country that was internalized among Japanese people.[15] In fact, *Snow Country* was not sent to the Venice Film Festival despite its popularity. According to Hasegawa Nyōzekan's report, although *Snow Country* was widely recognized as a good culture film, "it was not chosen because of a potentially misleading interpretation of the 'uncivilised' Orient by Western people" (Hasegawa 1939, p. 5). However, Kamei Fumio, a prominent filmmaker in the culture film section of the Tōhō studio, praised the film:

> Among the films I have seen this year, although it is strange to say it in front of Mr. Ishimoto, *Snow Country* is one of the best. There is room for discussion in terms of technical aspects; however, I think it is a groundbreaking film because it raises the problem of rural Japan, though many people believe that the value of documentary films lies in showing exotic places, such as *Umi no seimeisen* [*Lifeline on the Sea*, 1933] produced by Yoko-cine and *Dotō wo kette* [*Through the Angry Waves*, 1937], *Shanghai* [1937], *Nanjing* [1938], and *Beijing* [1938] produced by Tōhō.
>
> Kamei et al. (1940, p. 21)

According to Kamei, the value of the film was the "discovery" of everyday life, and *Snow Country* played a decisive role in the process through which the culture film discovered everyday life. *Snow Country* contains scenery from various locations. Through this structure, the individual uniqueness of each place is removed. It neglects the diversity of the nation and creates/imagines a general image of "Japan". For example, the film never focuses on poverty in the countryside or intense agrarian disputes. These views of rural Japan produced under the wartime totalitarian order concealed the harsh "reality" as well as contradictions between people in the nation.[16] Following the remark on the turn to rural subjects quoted earlier, Tsumura Hideo went on to mention this deception hidden in the "discovery" of rural Japan:

> The concept of the national people (*kokumin*) should acquire a new interpretation in modern Japanese society. When considering the systematic idea of *nation*, it is essential to look differently at rural areas and their people than we have in the past. Rural areas and rural people will gain new value and meaning, which will give birth to a new idea of a *Japanese nation*.
>
> Tsumura (1941, p. 25)

2. Miki Shigeru and Yanagita Kunio

2.1. Living by the Earth (Tsuchi ni ikiru, 1941)

In the autumn of 1939, a cameraman and a producer visited Yanagita Kunio's home in Seijō, Tokyo. Their goal was to ask Yanagita for advice on shooting and directing a film about a village in Tohoku. According to the producer from the Tōhō Culture Film Department, while Yanagita seemed confused by the sudden visit at first, he was eventually swept up in the enthusiasm of this cameraman, who had a reputation for his unique persuasiveness. This cameraman was Miki Shigeru. He had originally started his career in fiction film and gained a strong reputation with films such as Mizoguchi Kenji's *The Water Magician* (Taki no shiraito, 1933). However, this was not enough to satisfy Miki, and he sought to explore his subjectivity by jumping into the newly flourishing field of the culture film.

---

[15] Regarding this point, the architect Bruno Taut, who stayed in Japan during the 1930s and taught the idea of Japanese beauty, is significant here. His widely read *Nihon no bi no saihakken* (*The Rediscovery of Japanese Beauty*) was published by Iwanami Shoten in 1939 and included a reference to snow country (Akita in winter) (Taut 1939).

[16] It is interesting to note that the perspective on rural Japan at that time seemed to avoid Hokkaido. The difference of its indigenous people was violently erased as a result of the assimilation policies of the Japanese empire. Under the nationalist regime, Hokkaido was probably too problematic a subject. In fact, this land had dairy farms with vast fields that did not fit within the generalized image of the "Japanese countryside" of the time.

His work *The Black Sun* (Kuroi taiyō, 1936) received international accolades for his successful shooting of a total solar eclipse. In addition, his work on Kamei Fumio's films, which depicted battlefields on the continent such as *Shanghai* (1938) and *Fighting Soldiers* (Tatakau heitai, 1939) was highly regarded.[17] Miki, who was eager to take control of the films he worked on, attempted to persuade studio managers to let him take responsibility for directing and shooting; however, he surprisingly chose Yanagita Kunio as general supervisor even though they had never met before.

The proposal that Miki put to Yanagita was to bring a camera to a village in the Tohoku region and to document the lives of its people, capturing the spirit of the farmers who lived and died on that land. Since Miki had been impressed by two books by Yoshida Saburō, *Notes of an Oga Kanpū Farmer* (*Oga Kanpū sanroku nōmin shuki*) (Yoshida Saburō 1935) and *Journal of an Oga Kanpū Farmer* (*Oga Kanpū sanroku nōmin nichiroku*) (Yoshida Saburō 1938), he wanted to film the location where they were written, Wakimoto village in Akita prefecture. Yanagita was moved by Miki's enthusiasm and introduced him to Nara Kannosuke, a renowned ethnologist from southern Akita. As a result, Miki wandered around Akita alongside Nara shooting footage with a Rolleicord twin lens camera and eventually constructed a narrative around that material (Mura 1963).

The film was entitled *Living by the Earth* (*Tsuchi ni ikiru*, 1941). As the producer Mura Haruo recalls, spending a long time shooting a culture film on location was a reckless idea, because its commercial success was unlikely. "The customs in the village were about to vanish due to the worsening of the wartime situation. In those conditions, Miki attempted to portray customs that were rapidly disappearing like snow in early spring" (ibid., p. 179). It was precisely because they were on the point of vanishing that they gained aesthetic value when recorded on film.[18] Of course, Miki put a strong emphasis on the "ordinariness" of the locations (Miki 1941b) because his point of view was one that gave retrospective value to absolutely ordinary things.

Given the exceptional nature of this work, film magazines paid great attention to the filming of *Living by the Earth* and anticipated its completion. In January 1941, *Bunka Eiga* published three pages of snapshots of the film locations and an essay by Miki. The first page features a huge portrait of Miki holding a small-format handheld camera (Figure 1). It presented the film as a work of art and Miki Shigeru as an "author". Miki also appears in four out of the total eight snapshots. In one featuring the director on location, the caption states "Miki working hard, wearing a beret".

As has already been noted, there was no cameraman at the time whose face was as familiar in the media as Miki (Fujii 2001b). He took on the role of representing all the cameramen of culture films after the "cameraman-viewfinder debate" with Kamei Fumio, published in *Bunka Eiga Kenkyū* in 1940.[19] So, when Miki shot *Living by the Earth* with the authority of an "author", the film gained great prestige within the world of the culture film. On the one hand, Miki represented himself as a cameraman looking through the viewfinder and, on the other hand, as a director standing next to the camera. Kamei had started the "cameraman-viewfinder debate" by stating that "a cameraman only looking through the viewfinder is like a blinkered horse" (Kamei et al. 1940, p. 24). In contrast to Kamei's claim, Miki acted as a director of culture films who also looked through the viewfinder.[20]

The shoot for *Living by the Earth* lasted for a whole year, starting in the summer of 1940, and the film was released on 28 October 1941 at feature length with a voiceover by Tokugawa Musei. The last locations were filmed around Honjō village, Yuri-gun area in Akita prefecture, including Wakimoto

---

[17] See (Fujii 2001b).
[18] Miki stated his motive for making *Living by the Earth* in the following way: "peasant customs have changed dramatically in recent years. From straw sandals to rubber shoes, straw rain coats to rubber rain coats, sedge hats to service caps. Women are influenced by the cities and in the summer wear lightweight clothes. They eat curry and rice, ice lollies, Chinese ramen and dumplings. Villages are changing and it is difficult to find peasants like those of the old days" (Miki 1941a, p. 54).
[19] Editors' note: see Disuke Miyao. "What's the Use of Culture? Cinematographers and the Culture Film in Japan in the Early 1940s" in this issue for a discussion of the debate.
[20] The journal *Bunka eiga* features photogravures entitled "Tsuchi ni ikiru hitobito" (People Who Live by the Earth). Additionally, a Special Issue on *Living by the Earth* was published before the completion of the film.

and Oiwake villages in the south, as well as Katanishi and Yonaizawa villages in the north. The film depicts the process of rice farming, the Namahage festival, the reclaimed land of Hachirōgata Lake, emigration to Manchuria, and the reclamation of land for vacation spots (Miki 1941a). However, *Living by the Earth* was not commercially successful and did not have a warm reception among critics either. Ishimoto Tōkichi criticized the film, arguing that it ended up with a simplistic portrayal of superficial beauty (Ishimoto 1942). Considering that Shigeno Tatsuhiko had a similar opinion, this was probably a common impression of the film (Shigeno 1941).

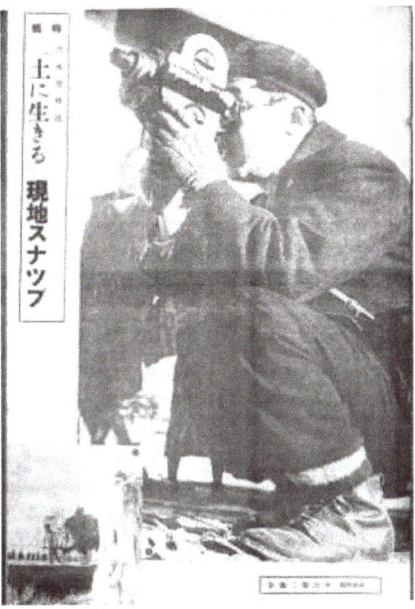

Figure 1. "Miki working hard, wearing a beret", *Bunka Eiga*, 1941, vol. 1, issue 1, p. 7. In public domain.

Although the film cannot be said to have met expectations, I would like to discuss the two works by Yoshida Saburō that inspired Miki Shigeru, *Notes of an Oga Kanpū Farmer* and *Journal of an Oga Kanpu Farmer*, which had been published as a bulletin of the Attic Museum (later restructured as the Institute for the Study of Japanese Folk Culture) established by Shibusawa Keizo.[21] Yoshida was a peasant who had lived in the foothills of Mt. Kanpū, Oga peninsula in Akita. As the name suggests, *Notes of an Oga Kanpū Farmer* was a collection of Yoshida´s jottings made during his farm work. Ōnishi Goichi who worked at the Nippon Seinen kai (Association of Japanese Youth) recommended Yoshida's writings to Shibusawa. As soon as Shibusawa read them, he decided to publish them. Then, he visited Yoshida´s village with other ethnologists in order to take pictures.[22] Publishing *Notes of an Oga Kanpū Farmer* was also encouraged by Yanagita; however, the question is what motivated a peasant such as Yoshida to write these notes. It was the urgent sense of a crisis brought about by sudden changes in village life taking place in front of his eyes. "The village today is affected by modern culture and has almost lost the traces of the past (...) villagers favor theatres and motion pictures rather than monotonous traditional dance" (Yoshida Saburō 1935, p. 73).

---

[21] For more information on Keizo Shibusawa, see (Satō 1987).
[22] *Notes of an Oga Kanpū Farmer* included many pictures taken with a 16-mm film camera that Shibusawa had bought in London. It is said that Shibusawa used to bring this camera on his travels to produce ethnographic visual materials (Kawasaki and Harada 2002, p. 22). As I will discuss later, this use of images was unusual in contemporary Folklore Studies.

Journal of an Oga Kanpu Farmer, published three years later, was more interesting. It was a photo diary of farming during the entire year, starting on 13 March 1935, with 370 pages of text. A map of farming fields, graphs of incomes and expenses, and records of daily meals were included in the appendix. However, these notes on the daily life of a peasant family, unusual only for its scrupulousness, were regarded as a highly valuable ethnographic record. It is astonishing that it was published in such an expansive format.

Why was Miki prompted by these books to take a camera and document everyday life in the provinces? Yoshida Saburō's work contained rich visual resources. The images became very popular in the media of the time and were later regarded as blazing a trail for "ethnographic photography" (*minzoku shashin*). The reason behind this popularity can be traced to the growth of "new photography" (*shinkō shashin*) since the 1920s; the rise of mass production; the reduction in prices of equipment; the spread of small-format, lighter cameras; and the development of transportation, which facilitated an increase in tourism.[23] To sum up, Miki's interest in the Tohoku region was born from his contact with Yoshida Saburō's books, but as we can see from the fact that Yoshida's writing was given value by the already-existing system of folklore studies and that "ethnographic photography" was established by the contemporary conditions of media circulation, the gaze turned toward rural Japan in this period was mediated in multiple ways, made possible by the fact that the desiring relation toward rural Japan at the time was profoundly socially constructed. To understand the prominence of a single peasant's life portrayed in Yoshida's voluminous *Journal of an Oga Kanpu Farmer*, we must take into account that it was the result of a collaboration between culture film and folklore studies, complemented by the discovery of the value of rural life in the "ethnographic photography" published by the mass media of the time. Kumagai Motoichi also documented the countryside by combining graphs with drawings and text in *Photographic Document of Kaichi Rural Village* (*Kaichi mura: Nōson no shashin kiroku*) published in 1938 with the support of Itagaki Takao, an art historian and advocate for "machine aesthetics" who had a big impact on Kumagai. The publication caused a sensation and marked a period in which the daily lives of the common people could be widely transmitted and commoditized through the media.[24]

This is the context in which *Living by the Earth* was produced. Unfortunately, only 15 minutes of footage are left now, so it is impossible to assess the entire film. However, the legacy of the encounter between Miki Shigeru and Yanagita Kunio fortunately remains in another form.

2.2. The People of the Snow Country (Yukiguni no minzoku, 1944)

While he was shooting *Living by the Earth*, Miki took more than two thousand photographs. Some of them were of fast-vanishing customs so they became precious documents from an ethnographic perspective.[25] The pictures were to be published as a single photo album. However, the publication was unexpectedly delayed because Miki moved to Southeast Asia as a member of a Military Information Corps, and Mura Haruo took over all the responsibilities of composition and editing. It is said that Mura sought advice from Yanagita Kunio about the selection of photographs and the content of the captions. The completed photo album was titled *Yukiguni no minzoku* (*People of the Snow Country*) and published as a joint work of Miki and Yanagita in 1944. Despite its high price during wartime of 13.10 JPY, five thousand copies of the first edition sold out immediately (Mura 1963).[26]

---

[23] See (Kikuchi 2001, pp. 149–51).
[24] Later regarded as a pioneering work of folklore studies, Suzuki Bokushi's *Hokuetsu Seppū* (1936–1942) was revised by the meteorologist Okada Takematsu, Yanagita's childhood friend, and published in 1936 by Iwanami Bunko. The development of the Life Composition Movement (*seikatsu tsuzurikata undō*) and "amateur writing" (*shirōto bungaku*) should be considered in the same context. For an account of amateur writing, see (Fujii 2002).
[25] Miki pointed out that the popularization of the solar calendar in Japanese society after the China Incident changed annual customs in rural areas dramatically (Yanagita and Shigeru 1944, p. 31). The solar calendar in Japan was adopted in 1873; however, there were some areas that still used the old lunar calendar in the 1930s.
[26] According to Murai Osamu, the publication of *Folklore Studies* was excepted from the suppression of speech under the militaristic government (Murai 1999, p. 263). In that respect, folklore studies accommodated itself to the wartime system.

The photo album consists of 367 photographs taken by Miki with captions depicting daily life in snow country villages, and the essays "Stories of the Snow Country" (*Yukiguni no hanashi*, pp. 1–23), written by Yanagita and "The Annual Events and Customs of Southern Akita" (*Shu to shite Akita-ken Minami Akita chihō ni okeru nenjū gyōji to shūzoku*, pp. 25–58) by Miki. Apart from the focus on images, the album was similar to Yoshida Saburō's books, and so could clearly be categorized as ethnographic material with photographs. In the afterword, Miki states, "the photographs in this book are nothing like so-called "reportage photography" or "art photography"; therefore, if someone expects beautiful things they will be disappointed" (Yanagita and Shigeru 1944, p. 60). The way Miki emphasized "ordinariness" in his pictures marks his discovery of the value of the quotidian, supporting the value of photographing the world "as it is" (*ari no mama*) (Yanagita and Shigeru 1944, p. 60). While this is a common idea, photographs that present an object "as it is" do not exist. The impression of representing reality "as it is" is created under specific conditions. Keeping this in mind, how can the photos of *People of the Snow Country* be viewed?

The album begins with a series of pictures of peasants titled "People Living by the Earth" (*Tsuchi ni ikiru hitobito*) (Figure 2). The series of photographs begins with standing figures of the farmers, moves on to close-ups of faces, and then ends with a mix of group photographs and close-ups of hands. This structure guides the reader naturally through their everyday lives. The first photo stands as an emblem of the entire book. Its caption includes a quotation from Miyazawa Kenji, "Ame ni mo makezu" (undefeated by the rain) and continues as follows:

> Stone-like taciturnity, not sociable, but eyes overflowing with warmth, mouths hinting at quiet pleasure, a cow-like tenaciousness inscribed in wrinkles; the skin of their faces shines with a sturdy vitality inherited from their ancestors. These people still strongly and deeply possess what city people have long since lost. This is the true face of the Japanese people. (no page number).

This caption strips the idiosyncratic and individualistic characteristics of the countryside and its people and clearly intends to provide a general image of "Japan" and the "Japanese". The method of navigating towards a certain interpretation through a combination of photographs was originally developed by Natori Yōnosuke's *hōdō shashin* (his translation of "reportage photography") exhibited throughout the 1930s.[27] The shock function of the best reportage photography is of course removed here, and the photographs are to a great extent shaped in accordance with the wartime system. However, because camera perception is fundamentally different from human perception, the intention of those who apply the caption is always shadowed by the possibility of being betrayed by the photograph itself. Therefore, when a photograph is used for a specific purpose, captions become obligatory (Benjamin 1995, pp. 559–600).

As discussed when analyzing Ishimoto Tōkichi's *Snow Country*, attention towards the snow country in this period was not aimed at discovering differences within a standardized nation, but at imagining and creating a generalized image of "Japan". The album *People of the Snow Country* surely shared this perspective on the snow country, inviting the audience to adopt a similar perspective. Of course, we cannot equate the claims for modernization to "improve" rural life in the film *Snow Country* and the attempt to document a vanishing everyday life in the album *People of the Snow Country*. Nonetheless, we cannot ignore the fact that Social Reformism and folklore studies, which seem to be opposed, shared a deep connection and a common purpose of creating a national people (*kokuminka suru*).[28]

---

[27] On reportage photography, see Chapter 11 in (Kawasaki and Harada 2002). Also (Kaneko 2000).
[28] Iwasaki Masaya makes the important argument that agrarianism, originally a purely modernist movement, had a fantasy of modern materiality and was not accepted by peasants engaged in a traditional way of life. Eventually, in order to gain support from the peasants, agrarianism performed an about-face (*tenkō*) and was assimilated into fascism and imperialism (Iwasaki 1997).

Figure 2. Page from "People Living by the Earth", *People of the Snow Country* (*Yukiguni no minzoku*, Yanagita and Shigeru 1944). In public domain.

Yanagita Kunio appears at the end of this series of images in *People of the Snow Country*. As Kikuchi Akira also points out (Kikuchi 2001, p. 56), it is very strange that Yanagita's text, titled "Stories of the Snow Country", does not connect to the images in any way. There are references to ethnographic images in general but no references to any specific photograph, which seems to show Yanagita's strong desire to avoid making a direct connection between text and image. Yanagita begins by mentioning the "discovery" of the countryside: "by entering the era when train tracks criss-cross the country, we came to understand a new meaning of the snow country" (p. 4). In the following passage he mentions "photographs":

> In any case, many delicate customs remain in the Tohoku area, rescued from oblivion because they are connected to the memory of previous generations. To put it another way, I think that compared to other regions there is a strong sense of taking customary activities seriously, and feeling unsatisfied when those customs are abandoned. But the time is coming when we can no longer say that is true. Now, at last, it is time to say goodbye. It is a great shame that so many of those scenes take place inside gloomy households that cannot even be recorded on photographs. Moreover, it cannot be said that the people of the snow country are satisfied with the feeling of somehow looking down on the lifestyle of their previous world.

The "delicate customs" of the remote region of Tohoku vanish, and those "customs" unfortunately cannot be captured in photographs. Of course, in this quotation, Yanagita may simply be referring to the problem of low light levels. There may not be sufficient light in the peasants' houses, hidden under the deep snow in Tohoku, to capture those customs with a camera. However, this was not the first time that Yanagita made this kind of claim. In "Ethnic Art and the Culture Film" (Yanagita 2003),[29] Yanagita asserts: "the difficulty of documenting the uniqueness of ethnic art is a common problem among those engaged in folklore studies. The idea of films as a solution is something everyone comes up with". By "ethnic art", here Yanagita meant folk arts that fall into the category of song and dance practices (*kabu shōyō*), which cannot be preserved in the way that sculptures and drawings are. Moreover, they often embrace religious purposes and have a certain value when performed at night in a dark setting. Thus, even if one attempts to film it "as it is" with a camera, inevitably one has to move it to a bright place due to lighting issues. As a consequence, the putative essence of that "ethnic art" is lost:

> Especially nuances, colors or something special in ethnic art cannot be represented well enough with the current Japanese film technology. For instance, solemn acts such as a small vow to the mask before putting it and the purification of one's body by pouring cold water upon oneself before dancing are missed. Foreign films are better at depicting the atmosphere of churches because the centrality of musical instruments and hymns in Christianity creates a certain atmosphere.
>
> From this point of view, pessimistically, I think Japanese ethnic art will go extinct.
>
> Yanagita and Shigeru (1944, p. 24)

What is clear here is that Yanagita sees the peculiarity of Japanese ethnic art as the impossibility of capturing it in a photographic image[30] and that the inability to be recorded as a photographic image would lead to the "vanishing" (*shōmetsu*) of "ethnic art". Japanese "ethnic art" manifests itself as a tragic evanescence that announces its own death.[31] In that case, perhaps Yanagita's words gain a special privilege, as he attends to Japan's dying ethnic art. Images cannot fully represent that dying form; only Yanagita's words can record them. Perhaps in this way, Yanagita's text became unshakeable canon for Japanese folklore studies.[32]

According to Kikuchi Akira, the discourse of folklore studies originally structured the visual components on an abstract surface (Kikuchi 2001, pp. 191–92). Even though photography started to be used in folklore studies from the postwar period, the visual image was only used to strengthen a pre-existing written frame of reference. Each student of folklore studies could easily imagine Yanagita's version of "Japan" through the "rich visuality of his prose" (and not through visual images themselves).

As mentioned above, photographic images are always shadowed by the possibility of betraying the cameraman's intentions, because the camera brings a non-human perspective. If folklore studies rendered visual images abstract, perhaps this is the reason why. Perhaps for the same reason, Yanagita and traditional folklore studies did not actively engage with the ethnographic photography mentioned earlier. Just as strict monotheism bans idolatry, folklore studies rejected visual images in order to guarantee its authority.[33] In *Stories of the Snow Country*, Yanagita asserts the following, which is nothing

---

[29] In *Nihon Eiga* 4.13. At that time, Yanagita often published in film and photographic magazines and attended meetings associated with visual arts. Those publications were not included in *Teihon Yanagita Kunio shū geppō* (Monthly Report on the Revised Collected Works of Yanagita Kunio) so this material is not easily available for reference.

[30] This impossibility of recording corresponds to Yanagita's category of spiritual phenomena, as opposed to tangible culture and linguistic arts, in his classification of the materials of folklore studies (Yanagita 1998).

[31] Mishima Yukio states, "Even in the beginning, folklore studies smelled like death", in (Mishima 1976). For the idea of extinction (*metsubō*) in Yanagita, see (Murai 1999) and also (Ivy 1995).

[32] The distrust that Yanagita had for photography was based on the assumption that people tended to perform in front of cameras (Yanagita et al. 1943, pp. 40–41; Kikuchi 2001, pp. 151–64). In fact, Yanagita felt dissatisfied by the images of the peasants in *Living by the Earth*, which he thought betrayed an awkwardness caused by a consciousness of the camera (Mura 1963). Although Yanagita's distrust was understandable, such an attitude is connected to the process by which his written texts were canonized, and visual materials that could contradict them were suppressed.

[33] H.D. Harootunian (1988) sees a connection between Yanagita the ethnologist and his youthful rejection of photographic realism when he was active as a romantic poet and denied the value of the genre of literary sketch (*shaseibun*).

other than a declaration of victory for folklore studies: "A great task remains to be undertaken. Japan is a country truly worth the undertaking" (p. 21).[34]

3. "Tunnel" into Snow Country

Let us return to the discussion on the film *Living by the Earth* in relation to Miki Shigeru. Miki fought against director Kamei Fumio in the shooting of *Fighting Soldiers* (Tatakau Heitai, 1939) made during the war in China. The direct cause was that he did not film a Chinese boy whom Kamei had come across and wanted to film. The boy could not understand the situation and so got scared and ran away. Kamei caught him, holding him with a rope, and asked Miki to film him. However, Miki, looking at the boy's fearful face, could not do it.

As I have discussed elsewhere (Fujii 2001b), this rivalry between Miki and Kamei was historically significant because it was the first time a director had accompanied the shoot for this kind of war documentary. Before, the "director's job" was in the studio, editing footage that a cameraman had shot on location according to certain production plans. However, now, the director would join the shooting, and filmmaking was no longer the visualization of a preexisting plan—filming what the director wanted. The filmmaker was now exposed to a "reality" that developed in ways that could not be anticipated. In the case of the aforementioned fearful Chinese boy, the intention of a director became powerless in front of a "reality" that was constantly rewritten. Kamei, who experienced this as a documentary filmmaker for the first time, decided to impose by force his intentions over "reality", while Miki recoiled at that "reality". In other words, Kamei was assured that he could handle the "reality" as if it was in an editing room, while Miki lost his words in front of a "reality" that was beyond human intention.

What made Miki incline toward ethnographic studies was perhaps this sense of fear or reverence toward "reality". As a consequence, external elements appear not as objects of manipulation but rather as objects of emotional attachment. This was Miki's motivation to document a constantly renewed reality "as it is".[35] Nonetheless, I have argued here that the discourse of folklore studies was a system for avoiding "reality". Images themselves are just representations; however, the discourse on photography in the 1930s, as we see in "reportage photography", praised the image's role in both documenting and, at the same time, intervening in the world. This was supported by the series of pictures that were regarded as pioneering "ethnographic photography" and in some ways by the culture film. However, the function of photography in both documenting and intervening in "reality" was threatening for the discourse of folklore studies, which attempted to systematize itself in this period by canonizing Yanagita's texts. On the other hand, even though the discourse on the culture film tended to mimic reportage photography in praising the essential recording function of the camera, it indulged in a "speech without speaking", a deceptive attention to technique that avoided the reality that could threaten it (Fujii 2001a). Both folklore studies and the culture film pretended to engage with reality, but they were nothing more than forms to escape from it. Perhaps Miki Shigeru hoped to find in folklore studies a new field in which to engage his artistic subjectivity, but, in fact, he simply oscillated between two similar systems.[36]

---

[34] The meaning of this declaration of victory was made clear in (Yanagita 2003). Yanagita, who avoided any systematic theorization, fell into certain contradictions. For instance, at the end of his "Stories of the Snow Country" article, Yanagita hoped that visual materials would record the expansion of the Great East Asia Co-Prosperity Sphere, but even that was due to a specificity of Japan that had no parallel: "We Japanese have a capacity to sense things with the eyes more than in words, which is very rare among the rest of the world" (p. 20). Yanagita in another discussion also mentions the possibility of visual materials for recording intangible culture; however, he seems not to be satisfied with the technology of the time (Yanagita et al. 1943, p. 40).

[35] The following statement by Miki should be understood in this context: "culture films should not be 'directed'. Preparing scripts and directing according to the scenario ... this method is not appropriate for documentary films" (Tanaka et al. 1941, p. 41).

[36] Culture films and folklore studies were also similar in that they functioned refuges for Marxists during the war (Fujii 2001a; Tsurumi 1998).

Koyasu Nobukuni argues that the regional folk songs and diet of common people that folklore studies took as its object of study were absorbed as the material of a "One National Ethnography" (*Ichikoku minzokugaku*) with the "nation" as its subject (Koyasu 1996). Surely, this reminds us of Kamei Fumio's montage: the newly discovered details of everyday life are freely cut together, without ever leaving the editing room, in a "montage" that gives them a particular significance.[37] In fact, the first time Yanagita saw the scenery of the snow country that he had written of so many times was when he watched Ishimoto Tōkichi's *Snow Country*:

> I feel empathetic toward the snow country. It was my first time to actually see it in a film, although I had heard a lot of stories. It was profoundly moving to see adults with snowshoes creating a path over the deep snow and leading a group of children to school.[38]
>
> I have to confess is that I was never able to travel during winter due to my work. After getting old, it was even more difficult to enter the life of the snow country due to my physical condition. Therefore, until now I have only been to hot and tropical places.
>
> Yanagita and Shigeru (1944, p. 22)

So, the film was a "tunnel" into the snow country. Yanagita was already charmed by this tunnel: all he had to do was go through it to see a landscape that had already been prepared. A "tunnel" that makes it possible for us to avoid reality—the discourses on the culture film and folklore studies from 1935 to 1945 constituted such a tunnel.

Funding: This translation was supported by the Birkbeck Research Committee Strategic Fund.

Conflicts of Interest: The author declares no conflict of interest.

References

Aihara, Shūji. 1942. Seisaku kikaku no shōsatsu, Shōwa 16 nen kaiko (Reflections on the Production Plan: A review of 1941). *Bunka Eiga* 2.1: 22–26.

Benjamin, Walter. 1995. The Work of Art in the Age of Mechanical Reproduction. Translated by Kubo Tetsuj. In *Benjamin Korekushon 1: Kindai No Imi (Benjamin Collection 1: The Meaning of Modernity)*. Edited by Asai Kenjirō. Tokyo: Chikuma shobō, pp. 583–640. First published in 1936.

Benjamin, Walter. 1996. The Storyteller: Reflections on the Works of Nikolai Leskov. Translated by Akiko Miyake. In *Benjamin Collection 2 Essay no Shisō (Benjamin Collection 2: Philosophy in Essays)*. Edited by Asai Kenjirō. Tokyo: Chikuma shobō, pp. 283–334. First published in 1936.

Cultural Department of the Imperial Rule Assistance Association. 1985. Chihō bunka shinkensetsu no konpon rinen oyobi tōmen no hōsaku (Fundamental Concepts and Policies for the New Construction of Rural Culture). In *Shiryo Nihon Gendaishi 13: Taiheiyousensō ka no Kokumin Seikatsu (Archival Materials on Modern Japanese History vol. 13: National Life in WWII)*. Edited by Shirō Akazawa, Kenzō Kitagawa and Masaomi Yui. Tokyo: Ōtsuki shoten, pp. 248–50. First published in 1941.

Donini, A. 1941. The Result of the First International Agrarian Film Competition. Translated by Kitazawa Tōhei. *Bunka Eiga* 1.6: 42–43.

Fujii, Jinshi. 2001a. Bunka suru eiga: Shōwa Jūnendai ni okeru bunka eiga no gensetsu bunseki. *Eizōgaku* 66: 5–22. Translated by Jeffrey Isaacs. 2002. Films That *Do* Culture—A Discursive Analysis of *Bunka Eiga*, 1935–1945. *Iconics* 6: 51–68.

Fujii, Jinshi. 2001b. Torarenakatta shotto to sono unmei: Jihen to eiga 1937–1941 (Shots that could not be taken and their fate: The China Incident and cinema, 1937–1941). *Eizōgaku* 67: 23–40.

---

[37] It is also significant that Yanagita compared a central principle of folklore studies, the method of "substantiation by multiple occurrence" (*jūshutsu risshōhō*) to composite photography (*kasane dori shashin*) (Yanagita 1998, p. 62).

[38] Advertisement for *Yukiguni* in *Bunka Eiga*, 1939, vol. 2, issue 4, no page number.

Fujii, Jinshi. 2002. Kashi to fukashi no poritikkusu: Eiga *Kojima no Haru* to sōryokutaisei ka ni okeru 'rai' no hyōshō. (2) Kyōkai no hikinaoshi (Politics of the Visible and the Invisible: The Representation of Hansen's Disease in the Film *Spring on a Small Island* under the Total War System. (2) Redrawing the boundary). *UP* 31.12: 13–17.
Harootunian, H.D. 1988. Figuring the Folk: History, Poetics, and Representation. In *Mirror of Modernity: Invented Tradition of Modern Japan*. Edited by Stephen Vlastos. Berkeley and Los Angeles: University of California Press, pp. 144–59.
Hasegawa, Nyozekan. 1939. Kokusai eiga konkūru to Nihon (International Film Competitions and Japan). *Nihon Eiga* 4.8: 2–9.
Ishimoto, Tōkichi. 1942. Bunka eiga geppyō (Monthly Review of Culture Films). *Nihon Eiga* 7.1: 30–33.
Ivy, Marilyn. 1995. *Discourses of the Vanishing: Modernity, Phantasm, Japan*. Chicago: The University of Chicago Press.
Iwasaki, Masaya. 1997. *Nōhon-shisō no shakai-shi: Seikatsu to kokutai no kōsaku (The Social History of Agrarianism: Intersection of Lifestyle and National Polity)*. Kyoto: Kyoto Daigaku Gakujutsu Shuppankai.
Kamei, Fumio, Ken Akimoto, Yoshitsugu Tanaka, Kōzō Ueno, and Tōkichi Ishimoto. 1940. Nihon bunka eiga no shoki kara kyō wo kataru zadankai (Round-table on Bunka Eiga, from the beginnings to the Present Day). *Bunka Eiga Kenkyū* 3.2: 16–27.
Kaneko, Ryūichi. 2000. Hōdō shashin no ichi: Journalism to propaganda no kōsaten (The Position of Reportage Photography: Crossroads of Journalism and Propaganda). *Kokusai Kōryū* 88: 50–55.
Karatani, Kōjin. 1993. *Hyūmoa toshite no yuibutsuron (Materialism as Humor)*. Tokyo: Chikuma shobō.
Karatani, Kōjin. 1997. Kindai Nihon no hihyō: Shōwa zenki 1 (Critics of Modern Japan: The early Showa 1. In *Kindai Nihon no hihyō I: Shōwahen jō (Modern Japanese Criticism I: Showa, Part 1)*. Edited by Karatani Kōjin. Tokyo: Kōdansha, pp. 13–44.
Kawasaki, Kenko, and Ken'ichi Harada. 2002. *Okada Sōzō, Eizō no seiki: Gurafizumu, puropaganda, kagaku eiga (Sozo Okada: Century of Film. Graphism, Propaganda, Scientific Films)*. Tokyo: Heibonsha.
Kikuchi, Akira. 2001. *Yanagita Kunio to minzokugaku no kindai: Okunoto no Aenokoto No 20 seiki (Yanagita Kunio and the Modernity of Folklore Studies: The 20th Century of Aenokoto in Okunoto)*. Tokyo: Yoshikawa Kōbunkan.
Kimura, Taijirō. 1939. Korekara no nōmin eiga (The Future of Peasant Films). *Eiga to rebyū* 5.9: 50.
Kinema Junpō Sha. 1976. *Sekai no ega sakka 31 Nihon eigashi (The World of Film Makers 31: The History of Japanese Film)*. Tokyo: Kinema Junpō Sha.
Kitakouji, Takashi. 2003. Han-tōchaku no monogatari (Story of anti-arrival). In *Eiga no seijigaku (The Politics of Cinema)*. Edited by Hase Masato and Nakamura Hideyuki. Tokyo: Seikyūsha, pp. 303–51.
Koyasu, Nobukuni. 1996. *Kindaichi no arukeorogii: Kokka to sensō to chishikijin (The Archeology of Modern Thought: Nation, War, and Intellectuals)*. Tokyo: Iwanami Shoten.
Makita, Shigeru. 1972. *Yanagita Kunio*. Tokyo: Chūō kōron sha.
Midorikawa, Michio. 1940. Kameraman no seikatsu to kyōyō (Lifestyle and Education of the Cameraman). In *Eiga satsueigaku dokuhon (Textbook for Filmmaking)*, vol. 1. Tokyo: Dai Nihon Eiga Kyōkai, pp. 46–84.
Miki, Shigeru. 1941a. Tokushū kaisetsu *Tsuchi ni ikiru* (Special Comment on Living by the Earth). *Bunka Eiga* 1.10: 52–54.
Miki, Shigeru. 1941b. Kome to nōmin seikatsu ni kan suru eiga (Films about Rice and Peasant Life"). *Bunka Eiga* 1.1: 7–9.
Mishima, Yukio. 1976. Yanagita Kunio *Tōno Monogatari*: Meichō saihakken (Yanagita Kunio's The Legend of Tono: Rediscovery of a Masterpiece). In *Mishima Yukio zenshū (The Collected Works of Mishima Yukio)*, vol. 34. Tokyo: Shinchōsha, pp. 399–402.
Mura, Haruo. 1963. Yanagita sensei to kiroku eiga (Mr. Yanagita and Documentary Films). In *Teihon Yanagita Kunio shū geppō (Monthly Report of the Revised Collected Works of Yanagita Kunio)*, vol. 23. Tokyo: Chikuma Shobō, pp. 179–80.
Murai, Osamu. 1995. *Nantō ideorogii no hassei, Yanagita Kunio to Shokuminchi-Shugi (The Origins of the Southern Islands Ideology: Yanagita Kunio and Colonialism)*, Revised Edition. Tokyo: Ōta Shobō.
Murai, Osamu. 1999. Metsubō no gensetsu kūkan: Minzoku, kokka, kōshōsei (The Discursive Space of Ruin: The People, The State, and Oral Traditionality). In *Sōzō Sareta Koten: Kanon Keisei, Kokumin Kokka, Nihon Bungaku (Imagined Tradition: The Formation of the Canon, the Nation State, and Japanese Literature)*. Edited by Shirane Haruo and Suzuki Tomi. Tokyo: Shinyōsha, pp. 258–301.

Rotha, Paul. 1938. *Bunka Eigaron*. Translated by Atsugi Taka. Kyoto: Daiichi Geibunsha.
Satō, Kenji. 1987. Shibusawa Keizo to Attic Museum (Keizo Shibusawa and the Attic Museum). In *Nihon no kigyōka to shakai bunka jigyō: Taishō-ki no fuiransoropii (Japanese Entrepreneurs and Socio-Cultural Projects: Philanthropy during the Taisho Era)*. Edited by Kawazoe Noburo and Yamaoka Yoshinori. Tokyo: Tōyō Keizai Shinpōsha, pp. 124–43.
Shigeno, Tatsuhiko. 1941. Tsuchi ni ikiru. *Eiga hyōron* 1: 11.
Shikiba, Ryūzaburō. 1941. Eiga to chihō bunka (Films and Rural Culture). *Eiga Hyōron (Film Review)* 1.2: 79.
Tanaka, Toshio, Hideo Tsumura, and Shigeru Miki. 1941. Satsueisha no seishin ni tsuite; Tsuchi ni ikiru wo megutte (The Spirit of the Cameraman: On Living by the Earth"). *Eiga Gijutsu* 2.5: 32–43.
Taut, Bruno. 1939. *Nihonbi no saihakken (Rediscovering the Beauty of Japan)*. Tokyo: Iwanami shoten.
Tsumura, Hideo. 1941. *Eiga to kanshō (Films and Appreciation)*. Tokyo: Sōgensha.
Tsurumi, Tarou. 1998. *Yanagita Kunio to sono deshitachi: Minzokugaku o manabu Marukusu shugisha (Yanagita Kunio and His Students: Marxists Studying Japanese Ethnography)*. Kyoto: Jinbun Shoin.
Yanagita, Kunio. 1998. Minkan denshō ron (Folklore Theory). In *Yanagita Kunio zenshū dai 8 kan (Collected Works of Yanagita Kunio vol. 8)*. Tokyo: Chikuma shobō, pp. 3–194. First published in 1934.
Yanagita, Kunio. 1998. Kyōdo seikatsu no kenkyū-hō (Methodology for the Study of Regional Ways of Life). In *Yanagita Kunio zenshū dai 8 kan (Collected Works of Yanagita Kunio vol. 8)*. Tokyo: Chikuma shobō, pp. 195–368. First published in 1935.
Yanagita, Kunio. 2003. Bunka eiga to minkan denshō (The Culture Film and Folk Stories). In *Yanagita Kunio zenshū dai 30 kan (Collected Works of Yanagita Kunio vol. 30)*. Tokyo: Chikuma shobō, pp. 177–79. First published in 1939.
Yanagita, Kunio. 2003. Minzoku geijutsu to bunka eiga (Ethnic Art and the Culture Film). In *Yanagita Kunio zenshū dai 30 kan (Collected Works of Yanagita Kunio vol. 30)*. Tokyo: Chikuma shobō, pp. 232–34. First published in 1939.
Yanagita, Kunio, and Miki Shigeru. 1944. *Yukiguni no minzoku (People of the Snow Country)*. Tokyo: Yōtokusha.
Yanagita, Kunio, Ken Domon, Hiroshi Hamaya, Toshio Tanaka, and Manshichi Sakamoto. 1943. Yanagita Kunio shi wo kakonde; minzoku to shashin zadankai (Around Yanagita Kunio: The National People and Photography Round-Table). *Shashin Bunka* 27.3: 39–45.
Yoshida Saburō. 1935. *Oga Kanpū sanroku nōmin shuki (Notes of an Oga Kanpū Farmer)*. Tokyo: Achikkumyūzeamu.
Yoshida Saburō. 1938. *Oga Kanpū sanroku nōmin nichiroku (Journal of an Oga Kanpu Farmer)*. Tokyo: Achikkumyuūzeamu.

 © 2020 by the author. Licensee MDPI, Basel, Switzerland. This article is an open access article distributed under the terms and conditions of the Creative Commons Attribution (CC BY) license (http://creativecommons.org/licenses/by/4.0/).

Article

What's the Use of Culture? Cinematographers and the Culture Film in Japan in the Early 1940s

Daisuke Miyao

Department of Literature, University of California, San Diego, San Diego, CA 92093, USA; dmiyao@ucsd.edu

Received: 6 January 2019; Accepted: 22 March 2019; Published: 27 March 2019

Abstract: In the early 1940s Japan, cinematographers and critics feverishly discussed the notions of immediacy and authorship in relation to documentary practices. The status of cinematographers as the authors of the images that they shot was particularly questioned in those conversations due to the mechanical nature of the motion picture camera. This article mainly focuses on the discussions in the journal *Eiga Gijutsu* (Film Technology) in 1941–1942 over the notion of culture, and examines how cinematographers imagined their new roles in documentary practices in the cinema.

Keywords: documentary; cinematography; authorship; the culture film

1. Introduction

It is true that today's new media, personal portable devices—mobile phones and digital cameras in particular—and Web 2.0 platforms of video-sharing websites have been reshaping documentary practices. Not only the notion of immediacy, but also that of authorship have been widely discussed in relation to such practices.

However, before the "fourth screen" of the mobile devices appeared, or even before the second (television) and the third (computer), there were times when cinematographers and critics feverishly discussed the notions of immediacy and authorship in relation to documentary practices. The late 1930s to early 1940s in Japan was one such moment. The status of cinematographers as authors of the images they shot was particularly questioned in those debates due to the mechanical nature of the motion picture camera. This article mainly focuses on the discussions in the journal *Eiga Gijutsu* (Film Technology) in 1941–1942 over the notion of culture, and examines how cinematographers imagined their new roles in documentary practices in the cinema. *Eiga Gijutsu* was published in 1941–1943 by Eiga Shuppansha (Motion Picture Publication Company) for the purpose of contributing to "the establishment of motion picture science in Japan" (Kinyō naru eiga kagaku no kakuritsu 1941, p. 11). The journal is an appropriate data source for such filmmaking, as many cinematographers contributed to this journal and attempted to redefine their roles in filmmaking.

2. The Cameraman-Viewfinder Debate

During the late 1930s to early 1940s, when Japan entered wars with China and then with the United States and their allies, the documentary film became prominent. Wars were (and still are) suitable subjects for the newsreel. According to the film theorist Imamura Taihei, the number of spectators who thronged to the newsreel increased dramatically after 1937, when the Second Sino-Japanese War began (Imamura 1941, pp. 15–21). In 1940, the Nippon Newsreel Company (Nihon nyūsu eiga sha) was established as a merger of the newsreel operations of Japan's major newspapers: the *Aashi Shinbun*, the *Mainichi Shinbun*, and the *Yomiuri Shinbun*. The newsreel cinematographer Makishima Teiichi of the Nippon Newsreel Company claimed in 1940, "About one-half of newsreels deal with wars as their subjects, and nobody can become a newsreel cinematographer if he cannot photograph wars appropriately" (Makishima 1940, p. 325). Accordingly, a new subgenre of documentary, *senki eiga* (battle record films), which included films such as *Malayan War Front* (*Marē senki*, 1942) and *Oriental Song of Victory* (*Tōyō no gaika*, 1942), emerged and showcased fierce battles, marching soldiers, operation procedures, or conditions of native people and prisoners of war (POWs) (Kawamura 2010, p. 111). Even fiction films started to incorporate the documentary style, especially in the genre of war films. The term *jissha seisin*, or the documentary spirit, became widely used to (favorably in most cases) describe films in the documentary style. For instance, the war film *Five Scouts* (*Gonin no sekkōhei*, Tasaka Tomotaka 1938) was highly valued particularly because of its documentary-style cinematography accomplished by Isayama Saburō. According to the critic Murakami Tadahisa, it was film's "reportage-style" realistic expressions that could make "truly good war and military films" that would go beyond "simple publicity and propaganda" (Murakami 1938, p. 10).

As the popularity of the newsreel increased, large-scale documentaries, including the above-mentioned battle record films, became produced on a regular basis. As a result, according to the film historian Mark Nornes, the notion of the documentary film "director" emerged (Nornes 2003, p. 156). Before this period, the typical production style of documentary filmmaking involved a relatively autonomous cinematographer simply going out and shooting what he thought was appropriate, and an editor giving the footage structure and forming it into a finished film (Nornes 2003, p. 156).

The status of cinematographers was put at stake when the documentary film director emerged. In 1940, Kamei Fumio, one of the newly emerged documentary filmmakers, said in a roundtable discussion that was published in a journal *Bunka Eiga Kenkyu* (Study of Culture Film), "Cameramen see things only through the viewfinder. They are like horses with blinders on. Being in charge of the camera, this is inevitable. This is why the director is necessary in order to see the world behind and to the sides" (Fumio et al. 1940, p. 24; Nornes 2003, p. 157). In response, in the next issue of the same journal, the cinematographer Miki Shigeru wrote an open letter titled "A Letter to Culture Film Directors", in which he insisted that many directors knew nothing about the viewfinder and the technology of cinematography, and that they relied on the senses and techniques of their cameramen (Miki 1940a, p. 65; Nornes 2003, p. 157). In the following issue, Kamei responded:

> In a pure sense, cinematography is the creative recording of the "phenomena" of reality. Direction means grasping the essential meaning of "phenomena" and structurally deciding the cuts (and scenes) required for communicating that. "Cameramen see things only through the viewfinder. They're like horses with blinders on"—this comment is a metaphorical explanation for the character of the cinematographer who is in charge of recording "phenomena" in the work of filmmaking .... Film production supposedly integrates the various divisions of labor in one job, and now this antagonism—we must be disciplined! Here's toward a collaborative spirit where individual skills achieve their greatest strength, their total meaning. (Kamei 1940, pp. 116–18; Nornes 2003, pp. 157–58)

In the following issue, Miki claimed that Kamei's simplistic call for cooperation ignored some complicated relationships between directors and cameramen (Miki 1940b, pp. 182–85; Nornes 2003, p. 158).

The so-called cameraman–viewfinder debate (*kameraman rūpe ronsōu*) occurred in this manner. Nornes argues:

> The cameraman–viewfinder debate is important because it signals structural shifts in the industry that brought documentary to a new level. With its roots in the newsreel, the documentary started as a form deeply tied to a relatively simple rendering of history. Producers had yet to achieve a nuanced conception of nonfiction that recognized the constructed nature of the form, allowing them to shape their representations of the world in creative ways. With the documentary seen as a relatively unproblematic narration of events, the burden of creation rested on the cinematographers, with their visual records of events, and the editors who collated the images into coherence. (Nornes 2003, p. 158)

As Nornes indicated, the contest in the cameraman–viewfinder debate was between the idea of the mechanical reproduction of reality by the motion picture camera and that of cinema as the creative treatment of actuality. In short, Kamei regarded cinematographers as the operators of the motion picture cameras that mechanically reproduced images of reality while considering film directors, including himself, to be the creators of meanings out of those images. In contrast, while Miki recognized the mechanical nature of the camera and the cinematographers' technical skills with the camera, he opposed the idea that cinematographers lacked creativity in their treatment of actuality.

Film critics in Japan had already pointed out this dialectic. Hazumi Tsuneo, who was also working as the head of the publicity department of the film distribution company Tōwa Shōji, argued in 1935 that the mechanics of the camera that would only "imitate reality" should be distinguished from the cinematic realism that would "construct reality" (Hazumi 1935, p. 581). Similarly, Imamura Taihei emphasized in 1940 that what he called "cinematic records" were the "records of people's thoughts, the expression of what their minds understood", even though cinema tended to be regarded as "the record of the things in the world" because of its photographic nature (Imamura 1940, p. 89). The poet and film theorist Nagae Michitaro also claimed that documentary cinema was important not because of its "actuality", or the actual condition or facts of something, that is recorded as it is, but because of its expression that presents "reality" in the world in the way that the viewer can perceive (Nagae 1942, pp. 263–64). In the same year, the film critic Iijima Tadashi, who was also an expert in French literature, expressed the contest by saying, "The film technology made the objectivity of photography into subjective. It created a new objectivity" (Iijima 1942, p. 39).

The rapidly increasing popularity of the war newsreel fueled this debate. Especially in the war newsreel, actuality tended to overwhelm cinematographers' creativity. The cinematographer Kawaguchi Kazuo claimed, "[T]he value of cinematography could not help being secondary" in the newsreel, because "newsreel cameramen are required to precisely capture ever-changing phenomena in front of the camera under uncontrollable conditions" (Kawaguchi 1941, p. 38). The newsreel cinematographer Makishima Teiichi agreed, saying "When it comes to photographing the war, it is difficult to obtain the compositions that cinematographers have planned in advance. Even when cinematographers put their lives on the line to capture shots, the footage that they photographed may not impress viewers. There are many more failures than successes" (Makishima 1940, p. 327). The critic Ebisawa Koichi criticized a newsreel *Advance to French Indochina* (*Futsuin shinchu*, Ebisawa 1941) for its lack of visual images of the climactic battle between Japanese and French battalions. While the sound of the scene "[e]xtremely energized viewers' imagination", wrote Ebisawa, "I doubt if we correctly perceived what actually happened there" (Ebisawa 1941, p. 407). He knew very well that the cinematographer of the newsreel was not able to use his Eyemo camera very well in that particular circumstance. The Eyemo 35-mm camera, which has been produced by Bell and Howell since 1925, was so portable and durable that it was easier for newsreel cinematographers to photograph scenes in battlefields. It was the only available camera at that time that allowed hand-held photographing without a tripod. On the one hand, the newsreel played a significant role of publicizing Japanese national policy to its colonies, and Ebisawa valued newsreel cinematographers for their "reporting spirit serving of the nation" (Ebisawa 1941, p. 409). Yet, for Ebisawa, *Advance to French Indochina* revealed the limits of the newsreel. According to Ebisawa, the newsreel cinematographers were not "protectors" (*shin'eitai*) of cinema, but rather of "national politics" (Ebisawa 1941, p. 409). They were not so much cinematographers as reporters. As the newsreel cinematographer, Makishima admitted, "A newsreel cameraman does not need to be a cameraman, but he needs to have the skills of a newspaper journalist" (Makishima 1940, p. 316). The cinematographer Fukuda Torajirō of Riken Science Film Company shared the concerns of Ebisawa and Makishima and addressed them, saying "Photographing the newsreel needs to be completed in a limited time. Lighting cannot be easily manipulated", so that "the eyes of newsreel cinematographers become closer to those of their cameras, that mechanically capture the facts in front of them as they are" (Fukuda 1941, p. 346).

Indeed, the dispute between the idea of mechanical reproduction of reality by the motion picture camera and that of cinema as the creative treatment of actuality had existed globally since the era of the Lumière brothers. Film historians tended to call Lumière cinema *actualités*, or actuality films that captured moments of life around the turn of the 20th century. In his 1945 essay, which was later re-titled "The Ontology of the Photographic Image", the film critic André Bazin argued:

> Originality in photography as distinct from originality in painting lies in the essentially objective character of photography. For the first time, between the originating object and its reproduction, there intervenes only the instrumentality of a nonliving agent. For the first time, an image of the world is formed automatically, without the creative intervention of man ... All the arts are based on the presence of man; only photography derives an advantage from his absence. (Bazin 1960, p. 7)

For Bazin, cinema records the space of objects and between objects automatically, and without human intervention. Bazin claimed that the introduction of the "personality of the photographers" into the production by "automatic means" was limited only to the "selection of the object to be photographed and by way of the purpose he has in mind" (Bazin 1960, p. 7). However, this is of course false, since the cinematographer chooses the daylight, angle, distance, etc. According to the philosopher Jacques Rancière, the dialectics can be termed the "aesthetic" logic of romanticism, which emphasizes the passivity of the camera and the "representative" idea of art inherited from Aristotle, which makes fiction the arrangement of actions into a unified whole (Rancière 1998, p. 49). Indeed, the film historian André Gaudreault, among others, suggested that it would be more productive to discuss Lumière films by comparing them "synchronically with other work from the cultural practice" from which they were derived, because what the Lumière brothers did was to "amalgamate themselves with these products" (Gaudreault 2011, p. 43).

Arguably for the first time in the Japanese context, the cameraman–viewfinder debate made the dialectic between the camera's optical unconsciousness and the cameramen's creative involvement visible. The debate indicated a discursive shift on the role and the status of cinematographers in the Japanese film industry. Even after the direct exchanges of open letters between Kamei and Miki ended, cinematographers and critics who were conscious about the technology of cinematography continued the discussion, especially in the new journal *Eiga Gijutsu* (Film Technology).

3. The Culture Film for Cinematographers

During the debates, many cinematographers started to consider *bunka eiga*, or the culture film, to be an ideal entity that would mediate—or successfully achieve a balancing act between—the ideas of cinematic authenticity and the cinematic treatment of actuality. The culture film is a translation of the title of an education film series *kulturfilm* produced by the UFA (Universum Film-Aktein Gesellschaft) in Germany. The term "culture film" was also taken from the 1938 translation of Paul Rotha's *Documentary Film* into Japanese as *Bunka eiga ron* (Theory of the culture film). According to the film historian Fujii Jinshi, a film distribution company Tōwa Shōji Ltd. established a culture film section in 1935 as a distribution organization for the education film series separate from feature films (Fujii 2002, p. 52). Then, the new production company Toho established a culture film department in 1937 and produced two feature-length documentary films directed by Kamei: *Shanghai* (1938) and *Nanjing* (1938). The culture film became prominent after the Film Law was promulgated on 5 April and enforced on 1 October 1939. Under the Film Law, the Ministry of Education certified certain films as culture films to guarantee screenings. Or, to be more exact, the Ministry of Education made screening the culture film compulsory in 1940. The Film Law, although ambiguously, discussed the culture film as follows: "films that are specifically useful to the education of the people (*kokumin*)" (Article 15) and "films (other than feature films) recognized by the Ministry of Education as contributing to the nurturing of the people's knowledge or the cultivation of (their) national spirit" (Detailed Rules of Enforcement, Article 35) (Fujii 2002, p. 53). Fuwa Suketoshi of the Ministry of Education defined the culture film under the Film Law as "films about education, arts and sciences, national defense, health, and so on. They are not dramatic films, but rather the ones dealing with documentary and realistic methods. They need to be acknowledged by the Minister of Education as the ones that serve for enhancing the national spirit, directly inspiring knowledge of the Japanese people, and improving their skills" (Fuwa 1939, p. 15).

It is important to note that the definition of the culture film was very ambiguous. Fujii even called the culture film "an empty signifier that could be endlessly narrated ... [T]here was not one person at the time who could explain its difference from education film, record film (*kiroku eiga*), and science film" (Fujii 2002, pp. 52–53). In the discussions that followed the cameraman–viewfinder debate over the ideas of the motion picture camera's mechanical reproduction of reality and of cinema as the creative treatment of actuality, cinematographers tried to clarify the ambiguity of the culture film and fill the emptiness of signification of the genre for their own purposes. In other words, they worked to legitimize their status in filmmaking by strategically using the culture film—or, to be more exact, interpreting the term "culture" in their own ways—to make the case.

The big question in the cameraman–viewfinder debate was whether a cinematographer should be a technician or an artist to claim autonomy. The critic Kaeriyama Norimasa, who initiated the film modernization movement in Japan in the 1910s–1920s, asked the question during a roundtable among critics, cinematographers, sound technicians, and projectionists discussing "motion picture technologies" organized by *Eiga Gijutsu* following the cameraman–viewfinder debate (Konnichi no eiga gijutsu o kataru 1941, p. 107).

The answers from the cinematographers were unanimous. Isayama Saburo, the cinematographer of *Five Scouts*, juxtaposed art and technology in cinematography by saying, "[T]he notion of art is essential to the technology of photography" (Konnichi no eiga gijutsu o kataru 1941, p. 108). Miyajima Yoshio affirmed that "cameramen are technicians", but he did not forget to add that the levels of their cultural knowledge (*kyōyō*) would affect their techniques so that "cameramen's techniques would include the notion of art" (Konnichi no eiga gijutsu o kataru 1941, p. 108). In sum, they openly criticized the prevailing idea of cinematographers being a "tool" for the directors and the studios, and insisted on the significance of a "co-operation" between directors and cinematographers in order to agree on appropriate camera positions (Konnichi no eiga gijutsu o kataru 1941, p. 107).

In the culture film, the cinematographer Nagatomi Eijirō argued that cinematographers and directors would need to work closely together "to flexibly respond to constantly changing reality" during the production process (Nagatomi 1941, p. 35). For the culture film, continued Nagatomi, cinematographers were not only responsible for the photography, but also for the editing. He explained:

> In the culture film, connections between a shot and another are not as important as those in the fiction film. Camera angles in the culture film are often very explanatory, and most clearly show things in front of the camera. The culture film also needs a great number of shots of things that are totally unrelated. Such a smooth editing technique in the fiction film as match-on-action is rarely seen. So, there is always a chance in the culture film of being regarded as a compilation of shots whose meaning is incomprehensible. (Nagatomi 1941, p. 35)

Nagatomi seemingly presupposed two things in his conception of the culture film. The first was what Fujii called "the essentialism of documentary film" (Fujii 2002, p. 55). Nagatomi considered that the essence of the culture film lay in the mechanical recordings of reality. The Marxist film critic Iwasaki Akira wrote in 1939, "It is already an accepted notion that a primary cause for the rise of *bunka eiga* is its reconfirmation of film's capacity to record (*kirokusei*), its ability to reflect reality (*jisshasei*)" (Iwasaki 1939, p. 29; Fujii 2002, p. 55).

At the same time, by referring to editing, Nagatomi went beyond the broadly circulated assertion of the essence of the culture film as the recording of reality and acknowledged the creative treatment of actuality in the culture film. Nagatomi's twofold view on the cultural film was shared by other critics. For instance, Takagiba Tsutomu (the pseudonym of a Marxist linguist Miura Tsutomu) wrote in the June 1941 issue of the journal *Bunka Eiga* that the cinematographers of the culture film did not simply document "actuality" by the camera but simultaneously "expressed" the content by the cinematographer (Takagiba 1941, p. 52).

The roll of recording reality was not a problem for cinematographers because of their expertise in photoscience. However, in order to achieve the creative treatment of actuality, many cinematographers obsessively insisted on the necessity of acquiring "cultural knowledge". To them, the word "culture" in the culture film also meant "cultural knowledge" that the producers of those films should incorporate during their production. The cinematographer Kawasaki Kikuzō wrote, "We the cinematographers need to regard ourselves as painters who use cameras as pens, as well as poets who view human lives through viewfinders in order to become the directors' best partners, their eyes, and their pens." He then emphasized "developing artistic and cultural knowledge, including painting, sculpture, architecture, and literature, in addition to the science of photochemistry" as a basic requirement for cinematographers (Kawasaki 1941, p. 25). Similarly, another cinematographer Kawaguchi Kazuo argued, "The cinematography of the culture film targets objective and solemn reality . . . that follows its autonomous will and the law of nature." Kawaguchi insisted that, "In order to capture such reality and express it in cinema", the culture film cinematographers also had to have their own "worldview, cultural knowledge, and humanistic sensibility" to confront that reality (Kawaguchi 1941, p. 39).

The cinematographer Miki Shigeru put these debates over the culture film into practice in *Living on Earth* (*Tsuchi ni ikiru*, 1940–1941). Miki based his film on two published volumes. One was a social–scientific analysis, and the other was a cultural–anthropological analysis of a farmer's life in Akita prefecture: *Oga Samukazesanroku Nomin Mokuroku* and *Oga Samukazesanroku Nomin Shuki*. Following those two books as his inspiration of "cultural knowledge", Miki recorded the actual life of a farmer from 1940 to 1941. Miki lived with the farmer, "looked at agriculture and farmers lives" with his own eyes, and "learned with awe that everything of their lives—food, clothing and shelter—is connected to the earth and rice farming". His "awe" became the "theme" and the basis of his cinematographic plan of the film (Tanaka et al. 1941, p. 32).

Miki compared the tones (*gachō*) of *Living on Earth* with *Shanghai*, which is a documentary film that he photographed with the director Kamei Fumio, and said "[T]he techniques of cinematography were better in *Shanghai*" in the sense that they "looked more beautiful". However, argued Miki, "they were so beautiful that they did not express the smell of the earth" (Tanaka et al. 1941, p. 34). Miki admitted that in *Shanghai*, the brightness of the sun was too consistent to give the same "beautiful" tone throughout the film. There, the director's creative treatment of actuality subverts the essence of documentary film: a record of reality. The balancing act that was necessary in the culture film was failing.

Miki insisted that he "found his way in this culture film [*Living on Earth*] to live not just as a cameraman, but as an author" so it was a "shame" if he was still being considered to be simply a "cameraman" (Tanaka et al. 1941, p. 34). "To become a really good cinematographer", Miki was no longer satisfied with "being fully committed to the camera technology"; instead, he was willing to explore "the author spirit" (*sakka seishin*) (Tanaka et al. 1941, pp. 35–36). "The creativity of the culture film author" for Miki was not to write a fictional screenplay that had the theme and structure in advance, not to photograph things beautifully on location, not to direct or edit, but to have "the skill of selecting materials from reality" to express the film's theme. "The toil of farmers" was "the reality" in the case of *Living on Earth* that even bewildered Miki (Tanaka et al. 1941, pp. 39–40). His goal was to emulate the documentary filmmaker Robert Flaherty, "who had both techniques and subjectivity as an author", even though Miki criticized Flaherty's *Man of Aran* (1934) for "its surface beauty of waves and seaweeds and its lack of profound depiction of human lives" (Tanaka et al. 1941, p. 37). In other words, for Miki, Flaherty's work achieves a perfect balancing act between the idea of the mechanical reproduction of reality by the motion picture camera and that of cinema as the creative treatment of actuality based on the cultural knowledge on the region. Miki declared that in making a culture film, he aimed to become "the author of a film that only a cinematographer can make" (Tanaka et al. 1941, p. 41). To do so, in addition to obtaining scientific and technical knowledge in such areas as mechanics, photochemistry, optics, and electricity, Miki concluded that cinematographers "need to have profound cultural knowledge as artists" (Tanaka et al. 1941, p. 36). *Living on Earth* was an ideal culture film for Miki, because he thought he was able to achieve the combination of the two as a cinematographer—technical and cultural knowledge—and become an author.

4. Coda

As we have seen, following the cameraman–viewfinder debate mainly between Kamei and Miki, who made documentary films such as *Shanghai* together as a director and a cinematographer, cinematographers and critics discursively and practically attempted a balancing act between the ideas of the motion picture camera's mechanical reproduction of reality and cinema as the creative treatment of actuality. The culture film became the major site of such discussions and practices. Cinematographers were particularly keen on achieving such a balancing act, because they wanted to legitimize their status in filmmaking not only as the technician but also as the artistic author.

In the discussions that tried to define the culture film, some filmmakers and cinematographers started to articulate "culture" as the notion that would embrace the dichotomy between science and art, documentary record and artistic expression, mechanical reproduction and creative representation of actuality. For instance, Ueno Kozo argued in his 1940 monograph *Eiga no ninshiki* (The recognition of cinema) that the culture film should question the widely believed dichotomy between "artistic" fiction films and "scientific" documentary films (Ueno 1940, p. 223).

In an essay titled "Cameramen's Lives and Cultural Knowledge" published in *Cinematography Reader* (*Eiga satsuei gaku dokuhon*), which was an official textbook for cinematographers preparing for the exam to become certified cinematographers under the 1939 Film Law, Nipponese Society for Cinematographers head Midorikawa Michio tried to rearticulate the term "culture" in the culture film. Midorikawa insisted, "Apparently, our lives are in chaotic conditions because we have depended too much upon a trend that is not based upon [our culture]. The righteous camera eyes must enlighten the Japanese people for the good of tomorrow's society, with pedagogical consciousness and in the name of the culture film" (Midorikawa 1940, pp. 70–71). What Midorikawa meant by the "trend", which he distinguished from "culture", was most likely Hollywood films. Mark Nornes claimed, "As Japan became increasingly isolated in the world with its expansion across Asia, the values attached to 'culture' came under interrogation, and the associations connected to the word transformed. The *bunka* of *bunka eiga* signaled a return of the demand for disciplined, self-sacrificing dedication to non-personal goals serving the development of the nation, even while retaining traces of the previous era's concept of culture as an elitist bulkhead against the vagaries of popular culture" typified by Hollywood films (italics original. Nornes 2003, p. 56).

Midorikawa's use of the term "culture" was strategic. While criticizing it as a "trend", he did not intend to ignore the cinematographic technology of Hollywood cinema at all. Midorikawa maintained the necessity of learning "photoscience" to become "camera technicians", and introduced his profound knowledge of technology and techniques of cinematography, which was in accordance with the discourse of the American Society for Cinematographers (Midorikawa 1940, pp. 78–81). For instance, Midorikawa wrote, "In cinema, architecture is the object to be photographed and the viability of its existence completely depends on light: the most important element in cinematic expression" (Midorikawa 1940, p. 65).

Moreover, when Midorikawa insisted that Japanese cinematographers should "develop their cultural knowledge", he particularly recommended *A Study of Japanese Landscape* (*Nihōn fukei ron*), which was an 1894 nonfiction book by Shiga Shigetaka (1863–1927), a journalist and geographer (Midorikawa 1940, p. 57). While Shiga was known as the advocate of *kokusui shugi* (maintenance of Japan's cultural identity), which had the goal of arousing national awareness and cultural pride that would go against European imperialism, he fully employed scientific and technical knowledge that he had learned from academia in the West, in order to praise Japan's landscape in terms of its sublimity. For Shiga, "cultural knowledge" was based on familiarity in science and technology. As did Shiga, Midorikawa connected cultural knowledge to science and technology.

As the head of the Nipponese Society for Cinematographers, Midorikawa justified the "cultural knowledge" of cinematographers with their expertise in photoscience. Midorikawa went further. Once it came to the issue of actually photographing Japanese architecture in the culture film, Midorikawa emphasized that it would be important to consult Tanizaki Jun'ichirō's *In Praise of Shadows* ("Inei raisan," 1933–1934), which was a study of the use of lights and shadows in the traditional spaces of Japanese culture written by the acclaimed novelist. Midorikawa quoted nearly four pages from *In Praise of Shadows*, in which Tanizaki discussed Japanese architecture and connected it to his conception of traditional aesthetics of shadow in Japan (Miyao 2013, p. 209). The historian Harry Harootunian claimed, "In Japan and elsewhere, modernity was seen as a spectacle of ceaseless change (the narrative of historical progress and the law of capitalist expansion) and the specter of unrelieved uncertainty introduced by a dominant historical culture no longer anchored in fixed values but in fantasy and desire" (Harootunian 2000, p. xix). As a result, Harootunian argued, "Provoked by a growing sense of homelessness and the search for 'shelter'", the concern for "laying hold of an experience capable of resisting the erosions of change and supplying a stable identity—difference—in a world dominated by increasing homogeneity and sameness" became "the way discourse recoded the historical problem of the interwar period" (Harootunian 2000, p. xix). What emerged was "an immense effort to recall older cultural practices (religious, aesthetic, literary, linguistic) that derived from a remote past before the establishment of modern, capitalist society, and that were believed to be still capable of communicating an authentic experience of the people[,] . . . race[,] or folk that historical change could not disturb" (italics by the author. Harootunian 2000, p. xxvi). Along this line, according to Harootunian, people such as Tanizaki "looked longingly to some moment in the past, or simply the past itself as an indefinite moment, as the place of community or culture, that would serve as the primordial and original condition of the Japanese folk". Harootunian continued, "This image of culture and community was as timeless and frozen as the commodity form itself." He claimed that a "social discourse devoted to fixing the ground of cultural authenticity and the source of originality and creativity" defended the cultural spirit (*bunka seishin*) (Harootunian 2000, p. xxvi). Referring to Tanizaki, Midorikawa demonstrated how cinematographers should connect their scientific knowledge of film technology to the traditional culture of Japan. Thus, he used the notion of culture strategically to defend the status of cinematographers in filmmaking over the debates over the documentary nature of images by the motion picture camera, and the creative treatment of actuality in the rising popularity of documentary practices. Yet, because of his strategic adoption of culture as the basis of their autonomy, Midorikawa among other cinematographers started to cooperate with the wartime cultural policy that formulated and defended the national spirit.

Funding: This research received no external funding.

Conflicts of Interest: The author declares no conflict of interest.

References

Bazin, André. 1960. The Ontology of the Photographic Image. Translated by Huge Gray. *Film Quarterly* 13. 4: 4–9. [CrossRef]

Ebisawa, Koichi. 1941. "Kiroku eiga ni okeru eizo no genjitsusei sonota ni tsuite" (About the reality of images and other things in documentary film). *Eiga Gijutsu* 1.6: 407–9.

Fujii, Jinshi. 2002. Films That Do Culture: A Discursive Analysis of Bunka Eiga, 1935–1945. *Iconics* 6: 51–68.

Fukuda, Torajiro. 1941. "Kagaku suru kokoro satsuei hokoku" (Report of photographing Heart of Science). *Eiga Gijutsu* 1.5: 345–46.

Fuwa, Suketoshi. 1939. "Bunka eiga no mokuhyo" (The goals of cultural film). *Bunka Eiga* 2.6: 14–17.

Gaudreault, André. 2011. *Film and Attraction: From Kinematography to Cinema*. Translated by Timothy Barnard. Urbana: University of Illinois Press.

Harootunian, Harry D. 2000. *Overcome by Modernity: History, Culture, and Community in Interwar Japan*. Princeton: Princeton University Press.

Hazumi, Tsuneo. 1935. "Eiga riarizumu no teisho" (Suggestions on the cinematic realism). *Kinema Junpo*, December 1. Reprinted in Hazumi, Tsuneo. 2018. In *Nihon senzen eiga ronshu: Eiga riron no saihakken (Rediscovering Classical Japanese Film Theory: An Anthology)*. Edited by Aaron Gerow, Iwamoto Kenji and Mark Nornes. Tokyo: Yumani Shoten, pp. 577–81.

Iijima, Tadashi. 1942. "Eiga to gijutsu" (Cinema and technology). *Shin Eiga* 2.1: 38–41.

Imamura, Taihei. 1941. "Bunka eiga ni okeru kagaku to geijutsu no mondai" (The problem of science and art in the culture film). *Bunka Eiga* 1: 15–21.

Imamura, Taihei. 1940. *Kiroku eiga ron (Theory on Documentary Cinema)*. Tokyo: Daiichi Geibun Sha.

Iwasaki, Akira. 1939. *Eiga to Genjitsu (Cinema and Reality)*. Tokyo: Shunyodo Shoten.

Kamei, Fumio. 1940. "Miki-san no 'Bunka eiga enshutsusha e no tegami' no igi" (The meaning of Miki's "A letter to culture film directors"). *Bunka Eiga Kenkyu* 3.4: 116–18.

Fumio, Kamei, Akimoto Takeshi, Ueno Kozo, Ishimoto Tokichi, and Tanaka Yoshiji. 1940. "Nihon bunka eiga no shokai kara kyo o kataru zadankai" (Roundtable on the Japanese culture film from early days to today). *Bunka Eiga Kenkyu* 3.2: 24.

Kawaguchi, Kazuo. 1941. "Bunka eiga no fotogurafi ni tsuite" (About the photography in culture film). *Eiga Gijutsu* 2.4: 38–39.

Kawamura, Kenichiro. 2010. "Senki eiga ni tsuite: Kameraman ga 'sakka' ni naru toki" (About battle record films: When cameramen become 'authors'). In *Nihon eiga wa ikiteiru dai 7 kan: Fumikoeru dokyumentari (Japanese Cinema is Alive Volume 7: Documentary that Overcomes)*. Edited by Kurosawa Kiyoshi, Yomota Inuhiko, Yoshimi Shunya and Ri Bonu. Tokyo: Iwanami Shoten, pp. 111–30.

Kawasaki, Kikuzo. 1941. "Enshutsu to satsuei no kankei ni tsuite" (About the relationship between direction and cinematography). *Eiga Gijutsu* 2.4: 24–25.

1941. "Kinyō naru eiga kagaku no kakuritsu" (Urgent necessity to establish film science). *Eiga Gijutsu* 1.1: 11.

1941. "Konnichi no eiga gijutsu o kataru" (Talking about today's film technology). *Eiga Gijutsu* 1.2: 107–11.

Makishima, Teiichi. 1940. "Nyusu eiga no satsuei" (Cinematography of news film). In *Eiga satsueigaku dokuhon: Jo kan (Cinematography Reader: Volume 1)*. Edited by Tane Shigeru. Tokyo: Dainihon Eiga Kyokai, pp. 309–31.

Midorikawa, Michio. 1940. "Kameraman no seikatsu to kyoyo" (Cameramen's lives and cultural knowledge). In *Eiga satsueigaku dokuhon: Jo kan (Cinematography Reader: Volume 1)*. Edited by Tane Shigeru. Tokyo: Dainihon Eiga Kyokai, pp. 46–83.

Miki, Shigeru. 1940a. "Bunka eiga enshutsusha e no tegami" (A letter to culture film directors). *Bunka Eiga Kenkyu* 3.3: 65.

Miki, Shigeru. 1940b. "Futatabi bunka eiga enshutsusha e no tegami" (Another letter to culture film directors). *Bunka Eiga Kenkyu* 3.5: 182–85.

Miyao, Daisuke. 2013. *The Aesthetics of Shadow: Lighting and Japanese Cinema*. Durham: Duke University Press.

Murakami, Tadahisa. 1938. "Hoga katagata" (Segments of Japanese cinema). *Kinema Junpo* 10.

Nagae, Michitaro. 1942. *Eiga, hyogen, keisei (Cinema, Expression, Formation)*. Tokyo: Kyoiku Tosho.

Nagatomi, Eijiro. 1941. "Bunka eiga kameraman zakkan" (Various thoughts on culture film cameramen). *Eiga Gijutsu* 2.3: 34–35.

Nornes, Abé Mark. 2003. *Japanese Documentary Film: The Meiji Era through Hiroshima*. Minneapolis: University of Minnesota Press.

Rancière, Jacques. 1998. L'historicité du cinéma. In *De l'histoire au Cinema*. Edited by Antoine de Baecque and Christian Delage. Bruxelles: Éditions Complexe, pp. 45–60.

Takagiba, Tsutomu. 1941. "Bunka eiga ron hihan" (Criticizing the theory of the culture film). *Bunka Eiga* 1.6: 52–53.

Tanaka, Toshio, Tsumura Hideo, and Miki Shigeru. 1941. "Satsueisha no seishin ni tsuite: *Tsuchi ni ikiru* o megutte" (About cinematographers' spirit: On *Living on Earth*). *Eiga Gijutsu* 2.6: 32–43.

Ueno, Kozo. 1940. *Eiga no Ninshiki (The Recognition of Cinema)*. Tokyo: Daiichi Geibun Sha.

 © 2019 by the author. Licensee MDPI, Basel, Switzerland. This article is an open access article distributed under the terms and conditions of the Creative Commons Attribution (CC BY) license (http://creativecommons.org/licenses/by/4.0/).

Article
On the Relationship between Documentary Films and Magic Lanterns in 1950s Japan

Koji Toba

Faculty of Letters, Arts and Sciences, Waseda University, Tokyo 162-8644, Japan; toba@y.waseda.jp

Received: 22 March 2019; Accepted: 10 May 2019; Published: 17 May 2019

Abstract: In this paper, I explore three cases from postwar Japanese media history where a single topic inspired the production of both documentary films and magic lanterns. The first example documents the creation of Maruki and Akamatsu's famed painting *Pictures of the Atomic Bomb*. A documentary and two magic lantern productions explore this topic through different stylistic and aesthetic approaches. The second example is *School of Echoes*, a film and magic lantern about children's education in rural Japan. The documentary film blurs distinctions between the narrative film and documentary film genres by utilizing paid actors and a prewritten script. By contrast, the original subjects of the documentary film appear as themselves in the magic lantern film. Finally, the documentary film *Tsukinowa Tomb* depicts an archeological excavation at the site named in the title. Unlike the monochrome documentary film, the magic lantern version was made on color film. Aesthetic and material histories of other magic lanterns include carefully hand-painted monochrome films. Monochrome documentary films in 1950s Japan tended to emphasize narrative and political ideology, while magic lantern films projected color images in the vein of realism. Through these examples of media history, we can begin to understand the entangled histories of documentary film and magic lanterns in 1950s Japan.

Keywords: magic lantern; documentary film; popular history movement

1. Introduction

Documentary films and magic lanterns share intertwined production and viewing histories in wartime and postwar Japan. In 1930s and early 1940s Japan, documentary film and magic lanterns both faced strict government regulation regarding production and distribution. This complex and intertwined relationship continued under the Allied Occupation's regulation of cultural production. During the postwar period specifically, documentary film and magic lantern productions often shared narrow historical or social topics, as well as similar production and release timelines. These media simultaneously addressed similar social realities, albeit from varying creative and ideological positions. In this paper, I will introduce three cases from 1950s Japan in which magic lanterns and films or other media had direct, yet unique relationships. Unlike their wartime media counterparts, the magic lanterns and documentary films produced in the 1950s could be considered the fruits of Japan's so-called "Postwar Democracy". As we will find in the examples below, ordinary people gathered to participate in the production of both media forms. Thus, this study extends beyond the facts within the frame, arguing that the fundamental historical basis for postwar magic lanterns or documentary films necessarily includes the often-entangled processes by which these media were produced. In this sense, they should be considered additional forms of what Justin Jesty has described as "engagement", "a promise, a commitment, but one that is not coerced" (Jesty 2018, p. 36).

2. Material and Cultural History of Magic Lanterns in Japan from Wartime to Postwar

Magic lanterns, also known by the Latin name laterna magica, project images to a screen by illuminating transparent glass or film. Today, magic lanterns are known as an early form of projected media that flourished in the 19th century for the purposes of education and entertainment. In education, the magic lantern's direct successor was the slide projector, which itself has been replaced by PowerPoint today. The rise of cinema in the early 20th century gradually displaced magic lanterns for entertainment in the West. Magic lanterns as a media of entertainment follow a similar historical trajectory in Japan as well. In the Japanese case, however, the magic lantern (gentō in Japanese) survived even after cinema's emergence as the dominant media of entertainment. This is especially true for magic lanterns as the media of education. Beginning in the early 1930s, the Japanese Ministry of Education introduced magic lantern media to schools as an inexpensive way to show visual materials to children. In 1941, the Ministry redefined and regulated a new form of magic lantern, one which projected still images of 35 mm movie films, rather than glass plates. The Ministry promoted this new system of magic lantern media and scripts nationally alongside wartime propaganda films (Washitani 2013, pp. 81–91). From the earliest stages, film and magic lanterns in Japan possess an entangled media history, rather than a relationship of replacement or obsolescence.

After the war, the Allied Occupation's Civil Information and Education (CIE) section introduced "audio–visual education" to Japan. They lent 1300 Natco 16 mm talkie projectors and 650 Beseler magic lanterns to Japan's Ministry of Education. CIE and the Ministry of Education distributed educational films across Japan. Half of the films were imported from the US and half were produced in Japan (Yoshihara 2011, pp. 92–96). In 1946, only 5.8% of Japanese cities, towns, and villages had movie theaters (Harada 2012, p. 265). People in Japan who had never seen a movie before welcomed these Occupation and Ministry-distributed films. On average, Japanese people had watched more than ten CIE movies by July 1951 (Tsuchiya 2009, p. 131). CIE also provided 35 mm magic lantern films to the public, though the physical media differed from Japanese magic lanterns. CIE distributed vertically oriented magic lantern film, like the 35 mm film used in movies. The Japanese projector was oriented horizontally, similar to 35 mm still cameras. Japanese magic lantern films were therefore easily produced using ordinary film cameras. Although the CIE magic lantern as a physical media format failed to take hold, the tradition of magic lanterns as projected media continued from Japan's wartime period.

One reason magic lanterns survived in Postwar Japan was their utility in disseminating trailers of independently produced films. Low-budget film productions could affordably and rapidly produce magic lantern film trailers that could be screened in rural villages, even those without movie theaters. Independent film-makers produced and distributed magic lanterns for use as mobile film trailers. More than forty examples of magic lantern trailers produced by independent film-makers are extant today.[1] In addition to entertainment media producers, activists frequently made use of magic lanterns to promote social or political movements. One such example concerns the 63-day strike for wage increases undertaken by the Japan Coalminers' Union from October to December of 1953. The Coalminers' Union produced the magic lantern film *How We Fight: The 63-Day Struggle*. More than one-thousand copies of this film were then reproduced by the magic lantern film distributor Nihon Gentō Bunkasha. When subsequently shown throughout Japan, the film played a significant role in promoting the strike. With *How We Fight*'s success, many labor unions began producing magic lantern films as a propaganda tool (Kamiya and Washitani 2012, pp. 72–74).

Like their magic lantern counterparts, documentary films share similarly complex histories of wartime and postwar government control. Documentaries, called "culture films" (bunka eiga) from the

---

[1] For example, Kōbe Eiga Shiryōkan holds physical copies of more than forty trailers. These include Yamamoto Satsuo's *Zone of Emptiness* (Shinkū Chitai, 1952), Kamei Fumio's *Woman Walking Alone on the Earth* (Onna Hitori Daichi o Yuku, 1953), and Imai Tadashi's *Here is a Fountain* (Kokoni Izumi Ari, 1955).

German film genre "Kulturfilm", were also used for media propaganda in wartime Japan. The Japanese government promulgated a movie law (eiga hō) modeled on Italian and German policies, which came into effect in 1939. The law made it the duty of every movie theater in Japan to show at least one culture film and one news film for each narrative film screened (Okudaira 1986, pp. 49–253). This law brought on a golden age of Japanese documentary films as budgets available to documentary filmmakers ballooned in order to meet demand. Production companies producing documentary films during wartime continued on during the postwar period, supported by the Ministry of Education for educational purposes and by private companies for public relations purposes.

Fruitful comparisons between documentary films and magic lanterns exist beyond their relationship with government control. They also demonstrate the complexities of historicizing aesthetic trends in postwar media, particularly the history of color projected media and conceptions of realism in relation to technological advancement. Whereas the majority of documentary films were produced using monochrome film, magic lanterns were generally projected using color slides or frames. Paradoxically, viewers of magic lantern productions found reality expressed by the color and details of the film, despite their lack of movement. Documentary films, on the other hand, tended to embrace stylistic elements found in narrative films while conveying leftwing ideology. As was the case with production history, adding color embellishments to monochrome film or slides for magic lanterns—or using expensive color film from the start—began during wartime. The Asahi Shimbun reported on the military's use of "natural color (ten'nen-shoku)" magic lantern films from 1943 to 1944.[2] As it was too expensive to use color film in the production of documentaries during the war, magic lantern films played a supplementary role to the aesthetic tendencies of monochrome documentary films.

3. Efforts to Record the Tragedy of the Atomic Bomb: *Pika-Don* (1952) and *Pictures of the Atomic Bomb* (1953)

The first examples I would like to discuss are the documentary film and two magic lantern films produced about *Pictures of the Atomic Bomb* (*Genbaku no Zu*), popularly known as "The Hiroshima Panels". The panels themselves were produced between 1950 and 1982 by artists Maruki Iri and Akamatsu Toshiko. Together, they painted a series of fifteen pictures on large traditional Japanese panels that depict the tragic details of the atomic bombing in Hiroshima. The titles are: 1. Ghosts, 2. Fires, 3. Water, 4. Rainbow, 5. Boys and Girls, 6. Atomic Desert, 7. Bamboo Thicket, 8. Rescue, 9. Yaizu (the home port of the fishing boat Lucky Dragon 5 which was exposed to US hydrogen bomb testing in the Pacific), 10. Petition, 11. Mother and Child, 12. Floating Lanterns, 13. Death of American Prisoners of War, 14. Crows, and 15. Nagasaki. They established the Maruki Gallery for The Hiroshima Panels in 1967 to display the panels to the public.[3]

When the artist couple was painting the sixth panel in 1952, director Aoyama Michiharu visited their studio to capture their work in a documentary film. Aoyama and co-director Imai Tadashi planned to produce a short film to introduce the panels and record the terrible damage caused by the bomb. Aoyama and Imai's *Pictures of the Atomic Bomb* was released in 1953 with a running time of seventeen minutes. The film depicted Maruki and Akamatsu painting the panel, close examinations of the panels themselves, and the reception of the panels in nationwide exhibitions held in 1952. The filmmakers superimposed footage of other documentary films and pictures of Hiroshima to provide context for the painted panels. Their film was not only widely shown in Japan, but it was also screened to audiences

---

[2] Articles include: New Weapon of Propaganda for East Asia (Tōa e "Senden" no Shin-heiki), p. 2, 7 June 1943; Magic Lantern Exhibitions of War Paintings (Sensōga no Gentōten), p. 2, 14 February 1944; All 100 Million Citizens are Marching to Destroy the Enemy (Metteki e 1 oku Sōshingun), p. 3, 1 March 1944; From the Oath of Destroying the Enemy to Increasing Production (Metteki no Chikai o Zōsan e), p. 1, 10 March 1944; Natural Colored Magic Lantern Exhibition (Ten'nen-shoku Gentō Bijutsuten), 1 November 1944. All anonymous reports.

[3] Some of the pictures were shown in Washington D.C., Boston, and Brooklyn in 2016. The Brooklyn exhibition was selected to the "Best of 2015: Our Top 10 Brooklyn Art Shows" by the art magazine *Hyperallergic* (Hyperallergic 2015).

in Paris, Antwerp, and Brussels, where it was paired with Shindō Kaneto's *The Children of Hiroshima* (*Genbaku no Ko*) (Okamura 2015, pp. 181–82).

Establishing a reception history of this short documentary is somewhat difficult, but contemporaneous print media included reviews of the film. In 1952, an anonymous critic reviewed the film in the magazine *Soveto Eiga*. The reviewer's anonymity is problematic for researchers, but was typical of the time. Japanese magazines and newspapers often publish media reviews without identifying the author. The reviewer wrote:

> In the Soviet Union, introducing paintings through film began with the collected paintings of Repin and Surikov. There are some examples in France, also. But this work (*Pictures of the Atomic Bomb*) is successful because it captures not only a number of the paintings, but also the boundless growth of the artists as they evolve through their interactions with the masses. (Anonymous 1952, p. 84)

Maruki Iri and Akamatsu Toshiko also published a small illustrated book called *Pika-Don* in 1950.[4] "*Pika*" is a mimetic word that suggests a bright flash, while "*Don*" is an onomatopoeia of an explosion. This combination was widely used by the victims in Hiroshima to describe the atomic bomb, which was characterized by a sudden flash followed by the sound of a massive blast. *Pika-Don* was published in the style of a palm-sized Chinese picture book called a liánhuánhuà. Each page had a large illustration and a brief textual description. The story begins with a peaceful morning scene in the town of Mitaki northwest of Hiroshima City on August 6. When the narrator states "It was 8 o'clock. There was a light that flashed like *pika*", everything takes a turn for the worse. The protagonist, a woman based on Maruki's mother, is surprised that she can see the Ujina port, southeast of the city, because the buildings in between have vanished. Each page depicts various scenes of atom-bombed areas. The most famous page illustrates black, burnt trees with the description, "Nobody can tell the story of ground zero". The latter half of the book depicts the symptoms of illnesses caused by atomic-bomb radiation. The narrator describes the protagonist's actions after her husband dies; she starts to paint flowers and doves. The story ends with an illustration of two doves she has drawn. On the final page, the narrator states that after the Potsdam Declaration, the government tried to negotiate with the United Nations to save the position of the emperor. "If the people had known that this terrible thing would be dropped on August 6, all the people of Japan should have screamed out, 'Please stop the war!'"

The production company Seieisha produced the magic lantern version of *Pika-Don* in 1952 based on this illustrated book. The story and illustrations are essentially the same as the book, but the illustrations on 35 mm monochrome film are intricately hand-colored. Additionally, a separate production company, Kinuta Yokoshine, made a second magic lantern film in 1953. This version was named *Pictures of the Atomic Bomb*. Sculptor Hongō Shin was asked to create the order of pictures to be presented in this magic lantern and painter Uchida Iwao wrote the description for each image. Both were famous communist artists. Unlike Aoyama's documentary film, this magic lantern introduced the panel paintings in such detail that it could be used as a substitution for the actual exhibition of the panels. Uchida seemed to have recognized the magic lantern's potential as a proxy exhibit. His script contains the following directions: "When you project this film, pull it slowly as if you were walking in front of the picture in an exhibition" (Okamura 2015, p. 185).

In the case of *Pictures of the Atomic Bomb*, the documentary film and the magic lantern films played supplementary roles for each other. While the documentary film explained Maruki and Akamatsu's painting process and the effects of the bomb itself, the second magic lantern film showed the audience minute details of the paintings. The first magic lantern film, *Pika-Don*, depicted an additional story of the bomb using simple, yet beautifully colored pictures. Together, these media acted as an accounting of both Maruki and Akamatsu's creative process, as well as a historical record of the aftereffects of

---

[4] Maruki and Akamatsu published a reprint of this book with English translations in 1976. Maruki, Iri & Maruki, Toshi. Ed. by Suzuki, Haruhisa. Trans. by Matsumura, Ken'ichi. *Pika-Don*. Tokyo: Roba no Mimi sha. 1976.

atomic bombings. Audiences that viewed the film and both magic lanterns came to understand the tragedy which occurred under the mushroom cloud.

4. Voices from Students in the Deep Mountains: *School of Echoes* (1951)

The second example deals with students of a junior high school in Yamagata prefecture, located in Japan's rural northeast. In 1951, a collection of school compositions by these students was published in a volume called *School of Echoes* (*Yamabiko Gakkō*).[5] Muchaku Seikyō, a young teacher in Yamagata, encouraged his students to observe and write about their everyday lives for their writing assignments. The students wrote about problems like rural poverty and hardship. *School of Echoes* became a landmark text in democratic cultural production. The innocent voices of students in a poor, isolated village deep in the mountains roused children and adults to participate in independent publishing projects of their own. The volume was received as an ideal example of postwar democratic education put into practice (Sano [1992] 2005, p. 12). Teachers and students in other schools began following this text's example in their own classrooms. Workers in factories also began to chronicle their everyday lives in self-organized literary circles. They published small magazines by mimeograph, whereupon the publications were exchanged with other circles (Toba 2016, pp. 155–74).

At the pinnacle of the "echoes" (yamabiko) boom, director Imai Tadashi visited the original Yamagata village to shoot a narrative film *School of Echoes*. Imai brought Kimura Isao and other established actors with him from Tokyo, shooting scenes on location that reproduced episodes described in the book. Kimura acted in the role of the teacher Muchaku, playing the character as a young, passionate educator. Before the premiere screening, Imai described the film as follows:

> This film is not a so-called narrative film. Rather, it could be called a documentary film. To date, films dealing with schools have typically depicted the arrival of a new teacher, pressures from PTA (Parent-Teacher Association) bosses or feudal-minded principals, and love affairs between male teachers and a female student or teacher. After a series of conflicts, these movies tend to resolve all the problems peacefully. I tried, however, to portray the reality of the hard lives in Japanese villages, focusing on the teacher Muchaku and the children. The film's script, direction, and filming are dedicated to this aim. I hope that audiences contemplate this decision while watching the film, as well as appreciate the cooperation we received from the local people in Yamagata, the teacher's union, and the labor union. (Kanzaki 1952, pp. 43–44)

The film's plot emphasizes efforts by Muchaku and the students to relieve their classmates of hardship. When eight students could not afford the expenses of the school trip prior to graduation, their classmates worked in the mountains to pay the cost for them. After a student's mother dies of heart disease, the classmates worked his family's tobacco field so that he could graduate. Muchaku then encourages his students to chronicle poverty as they experienced it, publishing the first issue of the class magazine by mimeograph.

Imai's *School of Echoes* was based on real episodes in the everyday life of the village and shot on location. In this sense, it is unlike a narrative film produced in a studio. And yet, a contemporary audience would likely call the typical production process of documentary films of that time staged or fake. Unlike the contemporary conception of documentary filmmaking, in 1950s Japan a script writer or director wrote scenes for the documentary beforehand, then asked the crew to shoot the scenes as written. This is not to argue that documentary films of the time were produced without a concept of realism in mind. Rather, a documentary film's claim to realism was judged by different criteria. When director Kyōgoku Takahide's 1955 documentary film *A Record of a Mother* (*Hitori no*

---

[5] An English translation of this book was published three years later. Muchaku, Seikyō. Trans. by Caulfield, Genevieve & Kimura, Michiko. *Echoes from a Mountain School*. Tokyo: Kenkyūsha. 1954. The Government of New Zealand reprinted the English translation in 1965.

Haha no Kiroku) caused controversy over whether or not it could be called a documentary, the point of contention was not the production history of the film's scenario. The film was controversial because Kyōgoku invented a fictitious family for the film. He did not shoot the real family upon which the documentary was based, rather he selected interesting individuals from different families in the village and called them a family in the film. When Hani Susumu made *Children in the Classroom (Kyōshitsu no Kodomotachi)*, also in 1955, the audience was surprised by realistic portrayals of children's everyday actions. Children took pencils in their mouths like cigarettes, or patted the head of a friend from behind, generally acting as if there were no adults or supervisors watching over them. These actions and movements were unconventional at the time. Before writing the script, Hani had studied the arbitrary behaviors of children by shooting large amounts of film. Prior to this film's release, children in educational films were well-behaved and nervous about being filmed. The vast amount of filming in preparation for *Children in the Classroom* was only possible through the sponsorship of the Ministry of Education, which was at that time trying to establish a model of democratic education. Without this budget, Hani would have been forced to decide the contents of the scenes containing children before filming began, likely reproducing the acting tropes already established in the genre (Toba 2010, pp. 81–88).

When the documentary film based on *School of Echoes* went into production, Muchaku was eager to act as himself in the film, but Imai refused to allow his participation. The entire cast and crew went to Yamamoto village in Yamagata from Tokyo. While the film's production history suggests a significant degree of fictionalization, this does not preclude *School of Echoes* from being classified as a documentary film based on the conventions of genre categorization at that time. The episodes in the film were based on documented experiences of the actual students. Scenes from the film recreated these genuine events on location. In order to place the film in its historical context, we might compare it to *A Record of a Mother*, discussed above. It was generally accepted at the time that *A Record of a Mother* could be called a documentary film, despite an even greater degree of fictionalization. When considering the historical trends in documentary filmmaking in 1950s Japan, it seems logical that *School of Echoes* would be eligible for the same categorization.

Muchaku's dream of acting as himself on film came true when the magic lantern version of *School of Echoes* was produced by the Rural Culture Association of Japan. In the magic lantern film, Muchaku and the students appear as themselves. Like the movie, the story is based on episodes from the book. Given Muchaku and the children's inexperience with dramatic acting, it does not seem farfetched to argue that, had they in fact been cast as themselves in Imai's film production, the quality of acting may have been miserable. But for the magic lantern film, the amateur actors needed not speak or move for the camera. Without the need for extensive direction, the magic lantern successfully captures that which might be called genuine expression on the amateur actor's faces. What is more, the magic lantern version of *School of Echoes* reproduces beautiful landscape shots which convey the realities of a deep mountain village. The magic lantern also depicts the students' classroom in detail, as well as the actual home of a student. Shot on monochrome film, each frame of the magic lantern was carefully hand-painted in an effort to express to the audience the real environment where the students lived. While the movie depicted some of the troubles that students faced, the magic lantern film recorded the real faces and scenes of the village. In this sense, these two films and formats hold different values as documentary media. Taken together in their historical context, the original text, the documentary film adaptation, and the magic lantern demonstrate the complex interrelations of documentary and narrative, reality and fiction, monochrome and color—often in ways that complicate the seemingly dichotomous relationship between these characteristics.

5. Unearthing History: *The Tsukinowa Tomb* (1954)

The third example, a documentary and magic lantern about local archeologists uncovering ancient tombs, lays bare the entangled nature of history education, government control, and media history during both wartime and postwar Japan. From the Meiji Restoration in 1868 to the surrender in 1945, history education in Japan had a close relationship with the Emperor system. Japanese history textbooks traced the beginning of historical time from the mythical first emperor Jinmu, whose reign was supposed to have lasted from 660 BC to 585 BC. Students in elementary school were required to memorize the names of Japan's 124 Emperors, from Jinmu to the wartime Emperor Showa. The historical legitimacy of the Emperor was the core value in education, as well as in politics. The Emperor was fashioned a living god. This is why it was so shocking for Japanese people to see a picture of General McArthur and the Emperor standing side-by-side on the cover of newspapers on 29 September 1945. The Emperor declared his own humanity on 1 January 1946, publicly denying the concept of his being a living god.

Education changed drastically during the occupation era. GHQ (General Headquarters) banned the education of certain subjects in elementary schools, for example "Morals" (Shūshin), "National History" (Kokushi), and "Geography" (Chiri). Instead, they introduced the "Social Studies" (Shakaika) curriculum to replace these classes with the intention that students would learn the concept of democracy. One of the accomplishments of the new social studies curriculum was the book *School of Echoes*, discussed above. Muchaku Seikyō encouraged students to write their compositions not in the students' Japanese language class, but during the new social studies course. Muchaku recommended that students observe their home, school, and village, and to describe the problems they found. In higher education, the teaching of history courses could not be abolished outright, so Occupation authorities instituted specific curricular changes. The names of early Emperors—those thought to be mythical rather than historical rulers—were purged from textbooks. These new history textbooks now opened with archaeology lessons, rather than historical legitimizations of the Emperor's divine right to rule.

Occupation-era changes to history education, particularly the emphasis on archeology as the appropriate methodology of prehistorical investigation, inspired democratically organized historical societies. One example of the results of these studies is the extensive exploration of the Toro Remains (Toro Iseki), an archeological site in Shizuoka prefecture. The site consisted of a 1st century village, including many houses and large rice paddies. The ruins were discovered in 1943 when the government planned to build a munitions factory at the site. After a very limited excavational investigation, the government continued with construction and archeologists lost access to the site. In 1947, however, multiple universities formed an excavation team to explore the ruins. Many students from local high schools and junior high schools volunteered to help scholars and students of the university team. As mass media reported on the excavation nationwide, Toro became a symbol of novel archaeological and historical trends in newly democratic Japan.

In the 1950s, history was problematized in a different way by leftist scholars. Ishimoda Shō published *The Discovery of History and The People* (*Rekishi to Minzoku no Hakken*) in 1952. In this book, Ishimoda encouraged people to write their own histories. His slogan became: "Let us write the histories of our villages, of our factories". This historical movement came to be called "The Popular History Movement (Kokuminteki Rekishigaku Undō)", and took Ishimoda's book as the movement's core text.

The Tsukinowa Tomb (Tsukinowa Kofun), the tomb of a local political leader from the 5th century, sat at the top of a small mountain in Okayama prefecture. It also sat at the crossroads of these two historical trajectories: the resurgence of archeology under Occupation education reform and the development of local, democratic historical investigations. It was common knowledge among local residents that the small mountain in Yūka village was an ancient tomb. Before media coverage of the archeological excavations at the Toro Remains reached the town, however, residents of Yūka had never considered excavating the tomb. At the peak of the Popular History Movement, local residents determined that they could carry out excavation work by themselves.

In 1952, they organized a local history circle. They invited Professor Kondo Yoshirō of Okayama University to join their research of local history. The circle grew rapidly and soon formed plans to excavate the Tsukinowa Tomb in August of 1953, the off-season for farmers in the village who were participating in the history circle. Given that the timing of this project fell in the midst of summer vacation, students of all ages, from elementary schools to universities, joined the project. As concrete planning moved forward, the intersection of archeology and democratic historical societies converged with the climate of democratically produced media. As such, the Yūka history circle planned to produce a documentary film of the Tsukinowa Tomb excavation. Circle members visited Tokyo to recruit film production specialists to the project. Directors Arai Hideo and Sugiyama Masami, scriptwriter Yoshimi Tai, and film production staff agreed to produce the film. The filmmakers first visited the village in September of 1953. The successful collaboration between local historians and established filmmakers exceeded the original project timeline, with excavation and filming continuing until November of the same year (Kokuni 2007, pp. 100–24).

The documentary film *Tsukinowa Tomb* was released in 1954. It depicts the process of excavation during the daytime and the local history circle's courses in the evening. The film's narrator recites poetry penned by junior high school students participating in the project over shots of students working together on the excavation. One poem reads as follows:

> "Ancient Tomb" by Toyofuku Emiko, 1st grade of Fukumoto Junior High School.
>
> Ancient tomb on Mount Oji/Tearing the earth, little by little/The sweat stings when it gets in my eyes/My back hurts/Sunlight pierces through my gym clothes/Clay figures roll out from the soil/No matter how many times I dig there/Who buried so many?/Digging tree roots with scissors/Crouching to work my bamboo chisel/I study history with all my body/It must have been so hard/To bring these objects to this high place!

When the excavation discovers a smaller tomb at the bottom of the mountain, the film suggests a theory that structures of discrimination and class difference were already extant during the ancient era of the ruins. The narrator takes the opportunity to criticize the existence of discrimination then and now. The film also highlights the onsite visit of Prince Mikasa, the youngest brother of Emperor Hirohito. As an archaeologist himself, he demonstrated an interest in the excavation. But depicting his visit as a special event is one contradiction present in this film. The film criticizes discrimination on the one hand, while on the other hand praising the visit of a person possessing a social status similar to those buried at the site. The film relies on Prince Mikasa's comments regarding the importance of the project to justify the excavation.

The Ministry of Education's Council for Educational Films recommended designating *Tsukinowa Tomb* a "Ministry recommended film", but the Minister rejected the motion. This was due to the leftist nature of the film. Prince Mikasa's personal donations and recommendation did not sway the Minister's attitude toward the film (Anonymous 1954, p. 7).

The magic lantern film of *Tsukinowa Tomb* was released on color film in 1954 as a joint production between a local cultural circle and the Okayama prefectural teachers' union. The magic lantern version demonstrates clear connections to the documentary film—it cites the same poem by Toyofuku and depicts Prince Mikasa's visit to the site—but the material presentation varies. In the clearest sense, the magic lantern's use of color film presents an aesthetic difference from the monochrome documentary film. The vivid color of the sky, grass, and earth gives the audience tactile images of the excavation site. Furthermore, the closing remarks of the magic lantern script are more positive than the documentary film:

> The learning that occurred in Tsukinowa was founded on the members' cooperation. This in turn lit the hearts of the participants who were thinking seriously about how all people might find happiness. Children, teachers, scholars and villagers of Tsukinowa came to think: "It is up to us to make our new history". "Our power creates a peaceful society". Let us promote their works in our everyday lives!

In this closing statement, the democratic spirit of The Popular History Movement resonates with the viewers of the magic lantern version of *Tsukinowa Tomb*. History need not remain a distant endeavor, detached from the everyday lives of the people. Rather, each participant in the excavation of the Tomb approached the project with the expectation that they might learn a lesson from their own history. In the case of the magic lantern version of the film, the narrator suggests that participation in the intersecting trends in democratic history might bring improvement to one's own life, creating possibilities for new and better histories of tomorrow. The documentary film of *Tsukinowa Tomb* criticized social injustices of the ancient era. The magic lantern film of the same title, however, projected in vibrant natural color, attempted to capture and illuminate a bright future.

6. Conclusions

In Japan, magic lanterns not only survived until the 1950s, they also played a major role in postwar media and cultural movements. Due to lower production costs, magic lantern film production was widely used across Japan to deal directly with topics often covered by contemporaneous documentary films. As in the examples explored above, magic lanterns depicted artwork, highlighted social movements, and recorded local events. This understudied postwar Japanese media format could help unearth underlying complexities present in histories of media production, distribution, and aesthetics that have not yet been fully explored.

Drawing from the three examples highlighted in this paper, we might begin by recognizing that concepts of narrative film and documentary film in 1950s Japan differ from contemporary uses of the same terminology. The entangled histories of documentary film and magic lanterns contextualize postwar media in ways we might not expect. For example, what we might recognize today as independently produced narrative film often possessed cultural meanings close to those of documentary film. In a more direct relationship between the two forms, magic lantern films should be considered alongside documentary film in studies of postwar media history. The three cases observed in this paper demonstrate magic lanterns' distinct value to postwar media studies and their historical contexts.

Funding: This research was funded by Grants-in-Aid for Scientific Research, grant number 18K02022.

Acknowledgments: The titles of magic lantern films are based on the research by Hana Washitani. I would like to thank Eric Siercks for comments on a draft of this article.

Conflicts of Interest: The author declares no conflict of interest.

References

Anonymous. 1952. *Genbaku no Zu*. Soveto Eiga 3: 10. Also available in reprint: *Soveto Eiga [Fukkokuban]*. 5 vols. Tokyo: Fuji Shuppan.

Anonymous. 1954. Korede Sandome Bunshō no Suisen Tekkai: Kyōiku Eiga "Tsukinowa Kofun" ni. *Asahi Shimbun*. June 9. Available online: https://database.asahi.com/index.shtml (accessed on 15 May 2019).

Harada, Ken'ichi. 2012. CIE Eiga/Suraido no Nihonteki Juyō: "Niigata" toiu Jirei Kara. In *Senryō suru Me, Senryō suru Koe: CIE/USIS Eiga to VOA Rajio*. Edited by Yuka Tsuchiya and Yoshimi Shun'ya. Tokyo: Tokyo Daigaku Shuppankai.

Hyperallergic. 2015. Best of 2015: Our Top 10 Brooklyn Art Shows. Available online: https://hyperallergic.com/261439/best-of-2015-our-top-10-brooklyn-art-shows/ (accessed on 9 May 2019).

Jesty, Justin. 2018. *Art and Engagement in Early Postwar Japan*. Ithaca: Cornell University Press.

Kamiya, Makiko, and Hana Washitani. 2012. Post-war Social Movements Reflected through Gento. In *Quest for Vision Vol. 5: Spelling Dystopia*. Translated by Pamela Miki. Tokyo: Tokyo Metropolitan Museum of Photography.

Kanzaki, Kiyoshi. 1952. Yamabiko Gakkō. *Eiga Hyōron* 9: 5.

Kokuni, Yoshihiro. 2007. *Sengo Kyōiku no nakano "Kokumin": Ranhansha suru Nashonarizumu*. Tokyo: Yoshikawa Kōbunkan.

Okamura, Yukinobu. 2015. *"Genbaku no Zu" Zenkoku Junkai: Senryōka 100 Man-nin ga Mita!* Tokyo: Shinjuku Shobō.

Okudaira, Yasuhiro. 1986. Eiga no Kokka Tōsei. In *Sensō to Nihon Eiga: Kōza Nihon Eiga 4*. Tokyo: Iwanami Shoten.

Sano, Shin'ichi. 2005. *Tōi "Yamabiko": Muchaku Seikyō to Oshiego tachino 40 nen*. Tokyo: Shinchōsha. First published 1992

Toba, Koji. 2010. *1950 nendai: "Kiroku" no Jidai*. Tokyo: Kawade Shobō Shinsha.
Toba, Koji. 2016. Sākuru-shi Nettowāku no Kanōsei: "Jinmin Bungaku" to "Shin-Nihon Bungaku" kara Miru Sengo Gariban Bunka. In *"Sākuru no Jidai" o Yomu: Sengo Bunka Undō Kenkyū eno Shōtai*. Edited by Unoda Shōya, Kawaguchi Takayuki, Sakaguchi Hiroshi, Toba Kōji, Nakaya Izumi and Michiba Chikanobu hen. Tokyo: Kage Shobō.
Tsuchiya, Yuka. 2009. *Shinbei Nihon no Kōchiku: Amerika no Tainichi Jōhō, Kyōiku Seisaku to Nihon Senryō*. Tokyo: Akashi Shoten.
Washitani, Hana. 2013. Sengo Rōdō Undō no Media to shiteno Gentō: Nikkō Muroran Sōgi ni okeru Un-yō o Chūshin ni. *Engeki Kenkyu* 36. Available online: http://hdl.handle.net/2065/40368 (accessed on 15 May 2019).
Yoshihara, Junpei. 2011. *Nihon Tanpen Eizōshi: Bunka Eiga, Kyōiku Eiga, Sangyō Eiga*. Tokyo: Iwanami Shoten.

 © 2019 by the author. Licensee MDPI, Basel, Switzerland. This article is an open access article distributed under the terms and conditions of the Creative Commons Attribution (CC BY) license (http://creativecommons.org/licenses/by/4.0/).

Article
Legacies of Hani Susumu's Documentary School

Marcos P. Centeno Martín

Department of Cultures and Languages, School of Arts, Birkbeck, University of London, London WC1E 7HX, UK; m.centeno@bbk.ac.uk

Received: 14 May 2019; Accepted: 26 June 2019; Published: 3 July 2019

Abstract: This article seeks to cast light on some of Hani Susumu's theoretical and practical contributions to post-war Japanese documentaries. The article will also show how he created a documentary school at Iwanami Eiga based on authors' closeness to the filmed object. This is crucial in order to understand the tendencies that developed in non-fiction films from the late 1950s. Hani's influence can be seen in the leaders of militant cinema, Tsuchimoto Noriaki and Ogawa Shinsuke, who were trained at Iwanami Eiga. However, some of his theoretical writings, together with his documentary films *Hōryūji* (1958) and *Gunka Ken 2* (1962), reveal how his singular subjective realism is applied to unusual shooting objects, landscapes. This article assesses this lesser-known aspect of Hani's work and its links to certain developments in Japanese documentary films led by other filmmakers, such as Teshigahara Hiroshi and Adachi Masao, which have not yet been addressed.

Keywords: Hani Susumu; avant-garde documentary; new Left; Teshigahara Hiroshi; Adachi Masao; subjectivity; landscapes

---

1. Introduction

An approach to Hani Susumu's oeuvre is essential to understand the theoretical discussions and cinematic innovations that took place in postwar Japan. Hani became a leading figure of the Japanese New Wave and an internationally renowned filmmaker, mainly as a result of his feature films *Bad Boys* (Furyō shonen, 1960), which won the Director´s Guild Prize in 1961, *She and He* (Kanojo to kare, 1963), and, particularly, *Nanami: Inferno of First Love* (Hatsukoi: Jigoku-hen, 1968), which was nominated for the Golden Lion at the Berlin Film Festival. However, this research focuses on his work as a documentary maker and theorist in the earlier decade, which has been widely neglected by authors.[1] Hani was one of the five founding members of Iwanami Eiga, a production company that specialized in documentary films, for which he directed twenty-seven medium–length films, made between 1951 and 1962. Alongside this work as a filmmaker, Hani was a prolific author who simultaneously theorized about a singular film-making method and the possibilities of a new cinema through writings that, to date, have not received the attention they deserve.

This article seeks to illustrate how Hani created a documentary school based on the author's extraordinary commitment to the depicted object, which is crucial to understand certain developments in non-fiction film from the late 1950s.[2] Hani pioneered a kind of subjective realism in non-fiction by discovering a new kind of reality that is available for documentary makers, an inner universe existing in the outer world which could be explored through his method of shooting protagonists who did not act. Thus, Hani breaks with avant-garde authors of the time who prioritized the portrayal of directors'

---

[1] Although, the critic Satō Tadao noted that it was his precursor's character that laid the foundations for the renewal of the cinematic language of the 1960's (Satō 1973, pp. 174–87; Satō 1997, pp. 3–12).
[2] This pioneering nature of Hani for the creation of a postwar Japanese documentary school has already been noted (Satō 1970, pp. 373–74; Nornes 2006, pp. 56–89).

subjectivity, as well as departing from those exclusively concerned with the social reality of their characters. Hani opened up new avenues for the development of documentary practices which proved to be crucial for years to come. To tackle this question, this text first contextualizes Hani's theoretical framework and, secondly, interrogates how his ideas were put into practice, by himself as well as by subsequent documentary filmmakers. The final hypothesis is that the impact of Hani's school can be traced not only to Tsuchimoto Noriaki and Ogawa Shinsuke's works, based on an extreme engagement with the filmed objects, but also through the work of avant-garde documentary makers focusing on landscapes, such as Teshigahara Hiroshi and Adachi Masao. Hani's earlier usage of his filmmaking method to represent landscapes becomes one of the most innovative postwar attempts to develop cinematic subjectivity in unexplored directions.

2. Contextualizing Hani's Theoretical Contribution

Hani claimed that while filmmakers should not vanish, they should reduce their predominance and merge with the environment in order to penetrate into the inner universe of their characters. While the debates in which he was engaged from the mid-1950s had a significant repercussion in Japan, his texts have never been translated and are widely unknown in the West.[3] The first surprising aspect of Hani's work stance is the way it is shaped by multiple transnational references. First, British filmmakers of the 1930s and 1940s were significantly influential, as happened with many other Japanese filmmakers and theorists. Hani met Stuart Legg during his trip to Japan (Hani 1958, pp. 88–120) and praised Grierson, Rotha, Wright, Cavalcanti, and Arthur Elton's depiction of the working class (Hani 1958, p. 118). Second, while Hani does not follow their social concern, he is interested in their humanist tendency, which he also finds in other prior approaches to reality developed during the Spanish Civil War, such as Robert Capa's photography and André Malraux and Ernest Hemingway's literature (Hani 1960, p. 80). Third, Hani also admires the humanism displayed in the work of Robert Flaherty. While Hani acknowledges that he had been undermined by those who criticized that he had not been faithful enough to reality as a result of his staged sequences, it is his approach to the problems of the individual from a human, rather than social, angle where Hani finds a source of inspiration. He commends *Nanook of the North* (1922) as a pioneering work for its portrayal of the personal dimension of the Eskimo's world (Hani 1972, p. 36). Following the example of this American filmmaker, Hani claims that beauty is neither a result of imitating nature, as Kobayashi Hideo suggested, nor a calculated abstraction, as proposed by Mizuo Hiroshi, but what leads us to an emotional level (Hani 1969, pp. 25–36; 1972, pp. 3–40).[4]

In addition, the theoretical stance developed by Hani cannot be understood without taking into account the debates on realism led by the Iwasaki Akira and Imamura Taihei that had started before the war. According to Imamura, documentary making entails a selection of reality that he defines as *shiryō wo toru* ("taking a document") during which a non-subjective factual event is captured (Imamura 1954). Imamura's theory is articulated around the notion of "documentary quality" (*kirokusei*), which seeks to make cinema closer to a pure form of realism (Imamura 1952, p. 112) and revives certain practices from primitive cinema that reject any intervention over the filmed object (Imamura 1940, pp. 80–98). However, Iwasaki was opposed to that apparent capacity of cinema to mirror reality. He engaged in a discussion on the montage theory, criticizes the myth of cinematic objectivity, and raises the problem of fallacy in cinema even stating that "films lie deliberately" (Iwasaki 1956, p. 26).[5]

---

[3] Among those who drew on Hani's ideas are Matsumoto and Matsumoto and Noda (1964), Iijima (1960), and, particularly, Satō (1971, 1977, 1997, 2010).

[4] In the discussions about the links between image (*eizō*) and reality proposed by Hani in late 1960s, Kobayashi claimed that beauty is taken from the external reality, while Mizuo argued that is an artistic construction whose origin is inside the human mind. Kobayashi's text is included in Hani (1999, pp. 164–77) and Mizuo's text in Hani (1969, pp. 113–32).

[5] According to Iwamoto Kenji (Iwamoto 1974), Iwasaki introduced the term 'montage' in Iwamoto, Japan.

Hani's stance inherits Imamura's understanding of cinema as a valid witness to reality, however, he also joins Iwasaki Akira's criticism of Grierson's pretension of objectivity and Rotha's blind confidence in dramatization (Hani 1959a, p. 9; Hani 1972, pp. 33–75). Hani certainly rejects the employment of actors, settings, rehearsals, and scripts in order to film the spontaneous and unpredictable reality. Therefore, despite sharing a background in realism with the British documentary makers, Hani's filmmaking method was not exactly the same. To a great extent, the spread of lighter cameras, such as the Arriflex, allowed filmmakers to implement a new style and gave them further freedom to work without detailed planning.

Indeed, these technical improvements in the second half of the 1950s allowed for the development of new documentary formats, such as the North American *direct cinema* and the French *cinéma vérité*, emerging as a response to dramatization in documentary film. One may be tempted to link Hani to these movements, as he shared their naturalist techniques, such as shooting on location with non-professional actors and natural lighting, with them, as well as their necessity to be constantly vigilant about the predetermined judgements and common sense fostered by mainstream cinema. However, none of these Western developments are suitable to accurately define Hani's style. As Nornes (2006, p. 58) stated, they never had an equivalent in Japanese documentary film, as Japanese writers and directors were reluctant to follow them.

Japanese avant-garde documentary linked to the new Left was significantly different from the stance proposed by *direct cinema*. Japanese authors generally agreed about the need for a filmmaker's presence and self-conscious attitude, understanding that a documentary is merely the shooting of what is observed (Matsumoto [1963] 2005, pp. 66–79). However, Hani's method does not fit completely in a *cinéma vérité* approach. According to Erik Banouw, while *direct cinema* brings the camera to a situation of tension and waits for a crisis to happen, Rouch's *cinéma vérité* triggers a crisis (Banouw [1974] 1996, p. 223). Hani certainly shares Rouch's understanding that a filmmaker's participation entails a subjectivity that is not only unavoidable but also necessary (Hani 1959b, p. 49; 1959c, p. 45). However, his goal is not highlighting the presence of the filmmaker. On the contrary, his method is based on a discreet attitude not aimed at exploring the author's own subjectivity, but that of the characters before the camera (Hani 1956, p. 211). By doing this, Hani inverts the focus in the postwar discussion of subjectivity, shifting the attention from the filming subject (director) to the object (profilmic world).

Hani's writings originated in fact before the *direct cinema* and *cinéma vérité* movement. His publications, including film theory, criticism, reviews and interviews, appeared from 1955 until 1967.[6] His theoretical developments must be contextualized within the discussions taking place within the culture circles that had proliferated in the aftermath of World War II and have been studied recently (Toba 2010, pp. 19–47; Key 2011, pp. 7–34). Avant-garde artists, including Teshigahara Hiroshi, Kōbō Abe, Okamoto Tarō, and critic Hanada Kiyoteru, engaged in a quest for new ways to capture reality and sought a renewal of the concept of *kiroku*—which can be translated as "document" or "documentary" in a wide sense—in literature and other arts.[7] At the end of the 1950s, these explorations expanded into the film scene, when documentary makers Hani Susumu and Matsumoto Toshio joined the group Genzai no Kai (Contemporary Society). As a result, the group was reorganized into the Kiroku Geijutsu no Kai (Documentary Arts Society) in May 1957 with the notion of documentary as part of the visual culture (Key 2011, p. 13).[8] The increasing importance of documentary film in these debates is also noticed by Nornes (2006, p. 58), who asserted that Japanese documentary production

---

[6] Although Hani also published on the television (1959–1960), the nature of image, art, and means of communication (1969–1972).

[7] As Key (2011, p. 7) noted, realism was at stake from the early literary discussions around artistic innovation of the 1950s, not only because forms unavoidably evolved but also because the understanding and perception of "the real", of which realism is supposed to represent, also changed.

[8] For an account on the documentary groups that proliferated in the 1950's and Matsumoto's role in the discussion about subject (*shutai*) and object (*taisho*) also see Key (2011, pp. 7–34); Nornes (2007, pp. 19–27), and Raine (2012).

had increased more than 1000% from 1946 and that vitality demanded a fresh critical approach to this medium.

To a great extent, this discussion of the avant-garde documentary film was shaped by an ideological and aesthetical rupture in the Left, especially as a result of artists' and intellectuals' rejection of the Soviet repression of the Hungarian Uprising in November 1956.[9] The result was illustrated by a 1957 debate that Hani Susumu held with the veteran documentary maker Kamei Fumio, published in *Kinema Junpō* (Hani and Kamei 1957, pp. 40–47). Hani became a representative filmmaker of that "new Left" (*shinsayoku*), alongside other authors such as Teshigahara Hiroshi and Matsumoto Toshio, who resisted old forms of realism, which were seen as a mark of authoritarianism typical of fascism as well as of Stalinism (Matsumoto 1963, p. 64). Hani criticized Stalinism and the restoration of János Kádár's government throughout several articles written for the journal *Chūō kōron* after his visit to Hungary and Poland in the end of the 1950s. It is precisely within the Iron Curtain where Hani finds an inspiring reaction against socialist realism. He wrote extensively on Polish directors, such as Andrzej Wajda, Andrzej Munk (Hani 1961a, 1961b, 1961c), and Jerzy Kawalerowicz, (Hani 1959a), whose films surprised him for their personal approach as well as for the way the dealt with political issues (Hani 1961c, p. 245). Throughout these films, Hani finds a "personal criticism", *jiko hihan*, that anticipates the notions of subjectivity and authorship on which the debates around the new cinemas would be based (Hani 1963, p. 132).

However, the concept of subjectivity (*shutaisei*) can be quite misleading as its meaning varied depending on who used it.[10] Even within the new Left, there was no consensus. To Matsumoto, the narrative tradition of documentary film had failed to interrogate the cinematic medium as such, neglecting other potential ways to perceive reality. As a result, backed by Hanada Kiyoteru and Abe Kōbō's theories, he proposed an avant-garde documentary whose aim was to dismantle automatisms of perception through defamiliarizing techniques (Matsumoto [1963] 2005, pp. 253–61). As can be seen in his early shot documentaries *Bicycle in Dream* (Ginrin, 1955), *Security Treaty* (Anpo jōyaku, 1960), and *The Song of Stone* (Ishi no uta, 1963), Matsumoto challenges the apparent image's testimonial nature by dismantling impressions of reality and engages in a discussion about the subject (*shutai*) and in opposition to the world as *taishō* (object), although as Raine (2012, p. 146) notes, Matsumoto does not employ the widely used concept of the time, *shutaisei*, in his essay.

Unlike in Matsumoto, Hani's will for a breakthrough was not incompatible with cinema's role as a witness of reality. After all, if cinema moved away from reality, the chance to discover, which was an essential task for filmmakers, would be neglected (Hani 1958, p. 49). Hani devotes a large number of texts to defending how documentaries should explore the circumstances of the filmed individuals. However, rather than focusing on their external appearance, films should interrogate their internal dimension, often leading to an emotional level. Ironically, this approach to realism does not reject fantastic and imaginary aspects, since they are part of the human being. Like Matsumoto, he does not reduce the reality available to documentary makers to the factual world but also expands their scope to a subjective world, a field that had been considered exclusive to fictional avant-garde up until that point. However, unlike Matsumoto, this interior world portrayed in documentary films should not belong to the author, but rather to the individuals featured on the screen (Hani et al. 1956, pp. 45–52).

Thus, Hani's filmmaking style is grounded on the improvisation of characters who play themselves. Nevertheless, while Hani proposes closeness to reality in which he rejects any absolute control over the filmed object, his works cannot be categorized as observational cinema either. According to Hani, the best way to explore the inner universes of the characters before the camera is to become familiar with them. To that end, documentary makers should work with three kind of "protagonists who do not act" (Hani 1958). The first two are children and animals, who's spontaneous behaviour would

---

[9] Discontent had started to crystallise from the Sixth Congress of the Japanese Communist Party in July 1955, but it intensified as a result of the Soviet intervention in Hungary.
[10] Also noted by Nornes (2006, pp. 56–89).

allow privileged access to instincts, anxieties, and desires alien to filmmakers. This is why Hani spent weeks visiting schools and observing children in his most outstanding works, *Children in the Classroom* (Kyōshitsu no kodomotachi, 1954) and *Children who Draw* (E wo kaku kodomotachi, 1956), but also the lesser-known *Sōseiji gakyū* [*Twins Study*] (1956) and *Gurūpu no shidō* [*Group Direction*] (1956). After that, Hani embarks on an even more daring enterprise, seeking to interrogate the inner universe of animals in *Dōbutsuen nikki* [*Zoo Diary*] (1957), for which he spent one year and a half visiting Ueno Zoo in Tokyo.[11] It is in these documentaries where we can find the hallmarks of a style that Hani developed in the following decade, including improvisation, shooting on location with non-professional actors, rejection of scriptwriting, psychoanalysis, and traumatic pasts. These are the main traits that epitomise not only Hani's most renowned feature films internationally, such as *Bad Boys* (1960), *She and He* (1963), *Nanami: Inferno of First Love* (1968), and *Aido: Slave of Love* (1969), but also the early developments the Japanese New Wave in the 1960s.

During the following years, a sort of radical version of Hani's documentary was somehow developed by two leading figures of the Japanese militant documentary cinema, Tsuchimoto Noriaki and Ogawa Shinsuke, who were trained at Iwanami Eiga in early 1960s.[12] Both followed Hani's stance based on familiarizing with the portrayed objects on screen, but also added an extreme commitment to the topics they depicted. Tsuchimoto, who joined Iwanami Eiga in 1956 after watching *Children Who Draw*, caused a great impact on him (Gerow and Noriaki 2014) and became Hani's assistant director for *Bad Boys* (Furyō shōnen, 1960). For almost a decade, between 1965 and 1974, Tsuchimoto visited Minamata village, where he made a series of documentaries on Minamata disease, following peasants seeking compensation for the poisoning of thousands of people by mercury spilled into the water. The close relationship between Minamata victims and Tsuchimoto is illustrated by Inoue (2019) and the way Tsuchimoto adopts Hani's theoretical and methodological framework is assessed by Jesty (2019), both in this Special Issue.

However, Ogawa is an even a more radical example of this closeness between filmmakers and environment, to the extent that they merge in his films and become indissolubly linked. In 1968, Ogawa founded Ogawa Productions and travelled to Sanrizuka with his team, where they ended up living collectively for six years. During this time, they followed the peasants' uprising against the construction of Narita Airport throughout seven films, made from the viewpoint of farmers, between 1968 and 1973.[13] They are the so-called Sanrizuka series, in which the weight of Hani's documentary school is evident in a number of traits, such as improvisation and the lack of scripts, but particularly in the familiarization with the lives of protagonists. Ogawa's team shared the farmers' lifestyle and concerns and the portrayed struggle became their own struggle. The film crew participated in the construction of barricades and joining the fight against the riot police—the cameraman Koshiro Otsu was even arrested during the shooting of *A Summer in Narita* (1968). The limits between the concepts of subject (*shutai*) and object (*taishō*), discussed by Nornes (2007), become increasingly blurred. Ogawa and his crew turned out to be inseparable elements of the filmed reality when the collective moved to Magino village in Yamagata Prefecture and ended up living as farmers for the following thirteen years while making documentaries about rural life.

3. Hani's Method on Films of Landscapes

3.1. The Inner World of a Temple

Going back to Hani's theoretical framework, he proposes a third possibility for exploring subjectivities alien to that of the filmmaker, temples (Hani 1958, pp. 158–213) or, in other words, architectural landscapes. But what kinds of inner world could be captured from an inanimate structure?

---

[11] For an account on these lesser known works see Centeno Martí (2016, pp. 33–54).
[12] Both, Ogawa and Tsuchimoto left Iwanami Eiga together with Hani in 1964 and became independent filmmakers.
[13] For an extensive account on this film see Nornes (2007, pp. 54–128).

This proposal of making films without ("living") characters becomes a courageous attempt to explore subjectivities in the 1950s documentary. Hani crystalises this idea in his enigmatic *Hōryūji* (1958), a middle-length film about the eponymous temple in Nara, the country's oldest wooden structure and a World Heritage Site since 1993. Surprisingly, the film keeps great consistency with Hani's method developed in his earlier works, including shooting on location, non-professional actors, rejection of scriptwriting, and adaptation to the changing circumstances of the environment, e.g., Hani and his cameraman Junichi Segawa took advantage of changes in natural light to capture different tints on the coloured wood as well as the reddish walls.

More than a decade before, the same temple had been filmed by Kenji Imamura in his documentary, *Hōryūji* (1943), which is depicted from outside to inside. However, Hani focuses on the interiors. His earlier scenes, shot in classrooms and zoo cages, are replaced with hidden corners in the temple. In addition, instead of children and animals, we find wooden sculptures, which are portrayed through a variety of camera angles and movements, making viewers forget that they are inanimate figures. Segawa's thorough camerawork depicts the temple by playing with lighting and volumes and experimenting with a long focus lens and different compositions. The camera reaches unseen details of the temple, revealing beautiful aspects of the figures, such as wood wear, traces of gold upon the sculptures, twists imitating clothes, veins in their hands, and wrinkles on their faces.

While *Hōryūji* was financially a failure (Kudō 2018), the film succeeded in exploring a new kind of subjective approach, giving the impression that the temple had come to life. Satō (2010) highlighted its ability to create the illusion of movement between the building shapes and structures. More recently, Tsutsui (2012, p. 73) pointed out that its brilliance was a result of the rhythmic montage that became a sort of poetic expression of the temple's energy. The existing accounts on this film share that impression. According to which, what is represented in *Hōryūji* goes beyond the physical appearance of the carved wooden figures. Hani reaches an internal dimension transcending the materiality of the filmed object. Editing becomes a mosaic of paintings, reliefs, and sculptures of demons, Buddhas, and old emperors, portrayed with a lyricism that provides the temple with a living and anthropomorphized nature. As Satō noted, "the content is full of multiple sentiments and human emotions hiding a sympathy towards sculptures that have virtually become men. Hōryūji is alive" (Satō 2010, p. 274).[14]

According to Hani, monks of the temple asked him to keep a respectful attitude towards those sacred figures and not to see them as simple objects (Hani 1958, p. 167). Hani certainly projects a special aura over the objects, however, he moves away from mere veneration. Above any religious belief, the sculptures on screen seem to be animate figures. The statuettes of musicians playing the flute seem to perform the piece composed by Akio Yashiro, which is simultaneously heard on screen. This cinematic phenomenon of using the soundtrack as a device to present a living temple gains prominence in the room, representing the Buddhist scene of Shūmisen or Mount Sumeru.

The jarring voices of torment are played by a choir over close-ups of disturbing faces sculpted with enigmatic expressions of ire, awe, and suffering. Thus, Hani finds unusual marks of subjectivity in the filmed environment, throughout which inanimate figures seem to invite viewers to an inner and mysterious world. The sculptures present a hidden universe that somehow was linked to the people that had carved them in the seventh century. The abundant extreme close-ups reveal a refined technique with which they had been created but also something about the spirit of those anonymous people who left upon wood messages about their fears, pleasures and desires. In this way, *Hōryūji* presents an unusual display of emotions throughout these perturbing faces, which seem to contain the beliefs and daydreams of those who had built it.

---

[14] Author's translation.

3.2. Humanising the Rural Landscape

Hani had started exploring the depth of the filmic environment in his first work at Iwanami Eiga, a series of photographic reports on the country's prefectures, called *Shin Fūdoki* (New Geographic Chronicle). It was published between 1954 and 1958 as a result of collaboration with the publisher Iwanami Shoten. A few years later, Hani directed the television documentary *Gunma-ken 2* (broadcast on 27 May 1962). This was the 49th episode of *Nihon Hakken* [Discovering Japan], a series produced between 1961 and 1962, for which Tsuchimoto Noriaki and Ogawa Shinsuke had also worked. It was produced by Iwanami Eiga for NET channel and found inspiration in *Shin Fūdoki* printed reports. In January 1962, Kuroki Kazuo made the first part of a documentary on Gunma prefecture and in May, Hani made the second part. This was a region that Hani knew well, as it was the homeland of his father and they summered there during his childhood (Hani 1973, p. 181). *Gunma-ken 2* is based on the photographic report "Gunma ken", a volume published in 1956, whose editor was the renowned photographer Natori Yōnosuke.

According to Hani, this way of capturing reality proposed by Natori was opposed to his own.[15] As a consequence, comparing *Gunma ken 2* with Natori's "Gunma ken" becomes an enriching exercise to explore Hani's singular style in depicting landscapes. While Natori (1963, pp. 55–65) seeks a rational and even scientific description of landscapes, rejecting any ambiguity on images, Hani is not only interested in the physicality of the rural environment, but also in the people living in it. This difference materializes at the formal level too. Natori privileges middle and long shots, moving away from the human presence and focusing instead on its geography, and the characteristics of its rivers, mountains, wetlands, gardens, and hot springs. On the contrary, Hani makes wide use of close-ups and extreme close-ups and gives the landscape a subjective dimension through the interaction with its inhabitants.[16] As Karatani Kōjin asserted, the analysis of the landscape, which was discovered in Japan through European painting and photography in the 19th century, helped to produce an understanding that subject and object are not prior to the landscape, but emerge within it (Karatani 1993, p. 34). Thus, rather than a mere objective representation of its materiality, the landscape in Hani is only the result of the interactions with other subjects depicted in this external environment. The film evolves in relation to the weight and importance that the landscape has for the people living in it.

3.3. Applying the Method to an Urban Landscape

Hani participated in a cinematic experiment on the representation of landscape in *Tokyo 1958*. This is a collective film made alongside Teshigahara Hiroshi and the other seven members of the group Cinema 58.[17] This work focuses on the urban space of Tokyo and was made in order to be sent to the Brussels World Fair of 1958 (Ogi 1958, p. 72). *Tokyo 1958* is a documentary that is difficult to categorize. Each collaborator applied their personal gazes to portray the Japanese metropolis, resulting in a heterodox work comprised of an amalgam of styles and genres. The portrayal of Tokyo's geography begins with the representation of figures about its population, birth and death rates, and the number of cameras and cinemas per inhabitant. However, this expository format is quickly followed by a succession of satiric and humoristic experimentations employing overprints of *ukiyo-e* engravings, sound effects taken from the classical Noh theatre, such as *taiko*, drums, and *kakegoe*, drummers' utterances, or classical music such as *gagaku*. Other scenes combine television reports and commercial formats with an avant-garde style, featuring eccentric camera angles, framing, and movements.

The material coexistence of diverse modern and premodern formats in the film also serves to highlight its main theme, the coexistence of modernity and tradition in the city. The filmmakers bring the viewer to Ginza district, where one finds a diverse depiction of the Japanese economic miracle,

---

[15] Hani interview in Centeno Martin (2015, p. 774).
[16] For examples on these differences between Hani and Natori's style see Centeno Marti (2016).
[17] I have previously written a more detailed analysis of *Tokyo 1958* in Centeno Martin (2019a, pp. 41–62).

including boutiques that specialize in Shinto weddings as well as bustling department stores full of advertisements from the new cosmetic industry. Japanese modernity seems to have been "prettied up" as a false appearance. This urban space is represented as having been rebuilt by modern citizens who keep repeating folk practices, such as *hatsumode*, who visit Shinto shrine in New Year, and who keep consuming eroticism that can be traced back to the old *shunga* art of woodblock prints. The authors also find contradictions related to the endogamy of the economic and political structures in the Tokyo landscape where the elites, including the emperor, have perpetuated their power for centuries. The faces of businessmen and politicians are portrayed with premodern paintings of feudal figures.

4. Impact on Subsequent Avant-Garde Documentaries

4.1. Recovering the Fascination for the Architectural Environment

The aforementioned examples about films of landscapes illustrate a lesser known facet of Hani's documentary method, whose impact can be traced through disparate filmmakers such as Teshigahara and Adachi Masao. Hani's approach to documentary film clearly had a great impact on Teshigahara. He was exposed to Hani's practices through their activities as members of Kiroku Geijutsu no Kai from 1957 and their collaboration in *Tokyo 1958*. However, Teshigahara was also aware of Hani's theoretical developments and defended his stance before that represented by Matsumoto and Noda (see Hani et al. 1961; Matsumoto and Noda 1964).

Hani's impact is evident in a cinematic experiment Teshigahara embarked on only one year after filming *Tokyo 1958*, the documentary *Antonio Guadí* (1984), which focuses on the architectural landscape of Barcelona. Teshigahra travelled to Barcelona in 1959 to make a documentary on the buildings designed by the Catalan architect, Antonio Gaudí. He travelled to Spain together with his father, Sofu Teshigahara, a renowned ikebana master and filmed footage on 16 mm film, including a visit to Salvador Dalí's home in Port Lligat village.[18] The project was eventually abandoned, only to be taken up again by Teshigahara a quarter of a century later as a homage to his father, who had passed away a few years earlier. Thus, Teshigahara not only returns to the same city, but also revives the interest for renewing documentary cinema that had been developed in the 1950s. He draws on the discussion developed by the post-war cultural circles about the necessity of redefining the document through a "synthesis of arts" or *sōgō geijutsu*. The film combines scenes of modernist architecture created by Guadí with empty shots of Barcelona's Gothic Quarter, medieval frescos, Joan Miró's paintings and sculptures, and traditional dances performed at Spain Square.

Gaudí contains some black and white footage and photos that Teshigahara took in 1959 and shows this architectural landscape using a filmmaking method similar to that employed by Hani in Hōryūji temple. All sorts of technical resources, shot scales, and camera movements are deployed to capture the details of colour and shapes of Gaudí's buildings. The same interest that Hani had in filming impossible corners of the temple is developed through close-ups featuring craftwork, glasses, mosaics, twisted shapes in windows, floors, ceilings, and columns.[19]

As was the case in *Hōryūji*, some high shots were taken from scaffolding and cranes, and it has been suggested that some of them may have even been filmed by operators lowering themselves using ropes (William 2009, p. 10). Another stylistic trope resembling Hani's *Hōryūji* is the entrance to the Casa Milà building through opening gates while the camera comes in and shoots the interior. Last but not least, similarly to *Hōryūji*, the soundtrack, composed by Toru Takemitsu alongside Kurodo Mori and Shinji Hori, plays a dominant role in *Gaudí* and, as has been noted (Holden 1998, p. 23), it contains a hypnotic power aimed at projecting fascination as well as bewilderment on the screen.

---

[18] This footage *Gaudí, Catalunya, 1959* has been edited recently in Criterion's DVD *Hiroshi Teshigahara. Antonio Gaudí*.
[19] For a closer analysis of *Gaudi* see Centeno Martin (2019b).

4.2. Interrogating Japanese Enigmatic Landscapes

The influence of Hai's exploration of inner universes hidden in the environment is not only visible in Teshigahara. One decade after Hani's *Hōryūji*, Masao Adachi recovered the interest in urban and rural landscapes through his enigmatic documentary film *A.K.A. Serial Killer* (Ryakusho: renzoku shasatsuma, 1969). This is another collective film made by Adachi and the members of the *Nichidai Eiken* film club at Nihon University. They follow thirty-three places in which the 19 year old boy Norio Nagayama lived before perpetrating multiple murders in 1969, for which he was sentenced to death. This case gained notoriety among intellectuals and artists and became a symbol against the death penalty in Japan. Nagayama had been born in poverty to a broken family in Hokkaido. As a young boy, he travelled and worked across the country until he stole a gun at the American military base in Yokosuka and killed two guards and two taxi drivers. Before being executed for these crimes, Nagayama spent three decades on death row where he learned to read and wrote several novels, including his autobiography *Tears of Ignorance* (Muchi no namida, 1971), donating any profits to the families of his victims. Kaneto Shindō adapted Nagayama's story for the big screen in *Live Today, Die Tomorrow* (Hadaka no jūkyūsai, 1970). However, Adachi and *Nichidai Eiken* members took a different approach and decided to focus on the relationship between this case and the landscape. As Furuhata (2007, p. 349) has explained, the film is closely linked to the *fūkeiron* ("the theory of landscape") led by the film theorist Masao Matsuda, who had also participated in the film, from the late 1960s. The theory of landscape, in which Adachi had also participated, channeled a growing skepticism towards the prominence of the "subject" (*shutai*) and was accompanied by criticism of the documentary genre and political and aesthetical resistance to the commercial cinema of the time.

A.K.A. Serial Killer presents an unconventional experiment that echoes Hani's proposal of finding inner worlds hidden in the external world. The authors of the film invite the viewer to see Japan through the eyes of the murderer by exploring an internal dimension of the Japanese landscape that could explain the crime. Similar to Hani's stance, the scarce voice-over and lack of narrative structure shift the focus from the filmmaker to the profilmic world. In other words, the authorial subjectivity is replaced with that of the filmed environment. Adachi and his peers include sequences of factories, working-class neighborhoods, trains and markets, barely featuring people on screen, while those who are shown are mostly reduced to uniformed schoolchildren and the Self-Defense Forces. This portrayal becomes a claustrophobic and strangely homogeneous setting in which there is a strong presence of economic, political, and military structures of power (Matsuda 1971, p. 16).

5. Conclusions

Hani's films on landscapes and the theoretical discussions that have accompanied them since the 1950s constitute a fundamental cornerstone for understanding some of the most relevant aspects that characterised the documentary avant-garde in post-war Japan. Hani's contribution emerges from a context of ideological and aesthetical rupture among documentary makers, triggered by a growing interest in promoting subjective approaches to reality. Therefore *Hōryūji* comes to illustrate a singular kind of film, made with "protagonists who do not act". Hani proposes to interrogate an invisible but also authentic universe, free from filmmaker's prejudices. This reveals the applicability and consistency of Hani's documentary method in films featuring no characters, a topic that has not been studied to date.

Surprisingly, Hani finds inner universes existing in different kinds of landscapes, obtaining similar results to those of earlier documentaries on animals and children. He discovers that landscapes are a deep rather than a flat environment, in which cameras can penetrate and discover hidden realities. This is possible because the landscape is not a mere abstract space that merely projects author's perceptions, interests, and concerns. For Hani, it is rather a lived space that has been carved, shapped, inhabited, and even designed by other people, and the marks of these alien inner words are subject to be explored by filmmakers. These ideas are also articulated in discussions that undoubtedly reveal the existence of a rich theoretical production in Japan. Hani's theoretical and practical contributions mark the inception of a documentary school based on filmmakers' extraordinary engagement with the topics and characters they depicted. This filmmaking style was followed not only by Ogawa and Tsuchimoto's militant cinema, but was also adapted by filmmakers such as Teshigahara and Adachi, who were involved in making films on different kinds of architectural, rural, and urban landscapes. As a consequence, we should not assess all these directors as isolated authors since they became key figures of a true Documentary School in post-war Japan. They reconceptualized cinema with a groundbreaking approach to reality that raises fascinating questions about subjectivity, the engagement of filmmakers in the filmed reality, and authorship.

Thereby, the documentaries of landscapes assessed in this article constitute some of the most unusual and the boldest attempts to explore the possibilities of subjectivity in Japanese non-fiction and show how the documentary avant-garde of the time moved in multiple and unexpected directions. Through a close gaze deployed on the environment, Hani and subsequent filmmakers, such as Teshigahara and Adachi, reveal something intimate that trascends the materiality of the filmed objects. The examples demonstrate how documentary cinema is only partially limited by the materiality of the external world. They interrogate details that evoke a human presence which makes documentary film expand beyond the physical appearance of its objects.

Funding: I hugely appreciate the financial support provided by the Daiwa Foundation (ref: 197/13307) and GREGAL Research Project (SGR 2017–2019) particularly to its IP, Blai Guarné.

Acknowledgments: I am really grateful to Michael Raine for his enriching discussion on Matsumoto and Hani following Kinema Club Symposium at Sainsbury Institute in 2017 and for his extraordinarily effective work co-editing this special issue. I am also indebted to Iwanai Eizō, particularly to Michiko Nakai, for helping me find Hani's documentaries used in this article and Jinshi Fujii who, years ago, introduced me to the *Kiroku Eiga Ākaibu Projekuto*, whose seminars at Todai were extremely useful.

Conflicts of Interest: The author declares no conflict of interest.

References

Banouw, Erik. 1996. *Documentary: A History of the Non-Fiction Film*. Gedisa edition. Barcelona and Nueva York: Oxford University Press. First published 1974.

Centeno Martín, Marcos P. 2015. Susumu Hani (1950–1960): The Theoretical and Practical Contribution to the Japanese Documentary and Youth Cinema. An Approach to Hani's Case as a Precursor of the New Wave. Ph.D. thesis, Universitat de València, València, Spain.

Centeno Martí, Marcos P. 2016. Imágenes del «espíritu de reconstrucción». Hacia el redescubrimiento del documental japonés a través de la obra olvidada de Susumu Hani. In *El Japón Contemporáneo. Una aproximación desde los Estudios Culturales*. Edited by Lozano Artur. Barcelona: Ed. Bellaterra, pp. 33–54.

Centeno Martín, Marcos P. 2019a. Post-war Narratives through Avant-garde Documentary: Tokyo 1958. In *Media and the Politics of Memory in Japan*. Edited by Lozano Artur, Martínez Dolores and Guarné Blai. New York and Oxford: Berghahn Books, pp. 41–62.

Centeno Martín, Marcos P. 2019b. Crónicas de Paisaje. Nuevas formas de subjetividad en la vanguardia documental japonesa. In *Memoria y paisaje en el cine japonés de posguerra*. Edited by Pedro Iacobelli. Santiago de Chile: Pontificia Universidad Católica de Chile.

Furuhata, Yuriko. 2007. Returning to Actuality: Fūkeoron and the Landscape Film. *Screen* 48: 345–62. [CrossRef]

Gerow, Aaron, and Tsuchimoto Noriaki. 2014. Tsuchimoto Noriaki. Documentarists of Japan No. 7. *Documentary Box*. Available online: http://www.yidff.jp/docbox/8/box8-2.html (accessed on 5 April 2019).

Hani, Susumu, Donald Richie, Teizō Kanda, and Tatsuhiko Matsugi. 1956. Avan garudo eiga ni tsuite: Donald Richie shi ni kiku (On avant-garde: Asking Donald Richie). *Eiga Geijutsu* No. 6: 45–52.

Hani, Susumu, Noda Shinkichi, Matsumoto Toshio, and Teshigahara Hiroshi. 1961. Kiroku eiga to gekieiga. Dokyumentarī no hōhō o megutte (Documentary Film and Fiction Film. About the Documentary Method). *Shin Nihon Bungaku* 16: 125–37.

Hani, Susumu. 1956. Satsuei shinagara manabukoto (What One Learns While Shooting). *Gunzō* 11: 211–14.

Hani, Susumu. 1958. *Engi shinai shuyakutachi (Protagonists Who Do Not Act)*. Tokyo: Chūō Kōronsha.

Hani, Susumu. 1959a. Zenei eiga no koto (On Avant-garde Film). *Ongaku geijutsu* No. 8: 69–70.

Hani, Susumu. 1959b. Eizō de wa kangaerarenaika (Can't We Think With Images?). *Mita bungaku* 2: 47–50.
Hani, Susumu. 1960. *Kamera to maiku (Camera and Mic)*. Tokyo: Chūō kōronsha.
Hani, Susumu. 1961a. Gendai pōrando no eiga (Contemporary Polish Cinema). *Ongaku Geijutsu* 19: 24–25.
Hani, Susumu. 1961b. Teikō no enerugī to hiroizumu. Higashi yōroppa de kangaeta koto (2) (The Resistance's Heroism and Energy. What I Thought in Eastern Europe (2)). *Chūō Kōron* No. 3: 175–79.
Hani, Susumu. 1961c. Kenryoku to taiwa suru mono. Higashi yōroppa de kangaeta koto (3) (People Speaking with Power. What I Tought in Eastern Europe (3)). *Chūō kōron* No. 4: 53–261.
Hani, Susumu. 1963. Atarashi eiga (New Cinema). *Scenario* No. 1: 122–32.
Hani, Susumu. 1969. *Bi no shisō (The Idea of Beauty)*. Edited by Hani Susumu. Tokyo: Chikuma shobō.
Hani, Susumu, and Fumio Kamei. 1957. kiroku eiga no uso to shinjhitsu (Truth and Lie in Documentary Fim). *Kinema junpō* 15: 40–47.
Hani, Susumu. 1959c. Gijutsu no ninmu (The Technique's Duty). *Mita bungaku* 49: 45–50.
Hani, Susumu. 1972. *Ningenteki eizōron (Theory of Human Image)*. Tokyo: Chūō kōronsha.
Hani, Susumu. 1973. Boku ga dōbutsu ni mananda koto [Lo que aprendí de los animales]. Tokio: Bunka Shuppan kyoku.
Holden, Stephen. 1998. Film Review: A Musical Tour of Architecture as an Ode to Fertility. *New York Times*, February 27, p. 23.
Iijima, Kōiji. 1960. Hani Susumu to 'Furyō shōnen' (Susumu Hani and *Bad* Boys). *Eiga hihyō* 17: 24–28.
Imamura, Taihei. 1940. Eiga kirokuron (Documentary Film Theory). In *Kiroku eigaron*. Tokyo: Daiichi Geibunsha, pp. 80–98.
Imamura, Taihei. 1952. *Eiga no sekai (The World of Cinema)*. Tokyo: Shinhyōronsha.
Imamura, Taihei. 1954. *Eiga riron nyūmon (Introduction to Film Theory)*. Tokyo: Itagaki Shoten.
Inoue, Miyo. 2019. The Ethics of Representation in Light of Minamata Disease: Tsuchimoto Noriaki and His Minamata Documentaries. *Arts* 8: 37. [CrossRef]
Iwamoto, Kenji. 1974. Nihon ni okeru montāju riron no shōkai (Introduction to Montage Theory about Japan). *Hikaku bungakunenshi* 10: 67–85.
Iwasaki, Akira. 1956. Kiroku eigaron (Theory of Documentary Film). *Eiga hyōron* 12: 26.
Jesty, Justin. 2019. Image Pragmatics and Film as a Lived Practice in the Documentary Work of Hani Susumu and Tsuchimoto Noriaki. *Arts* 8: 41. [CrossRef]
Karatani, Kōji. 1993. *Origins of Modern Japanese Literature*. Durham: Duke University Press.
Key, Margaret S. 2011. *Truth from a Lie. Documentary, Detection and Reflexivity in Abe Kōbō's Realist Project*. Lanham: Lexington Books.
Kudō, Mitsuru. 2018. Documentarists of Japan No. 10. *Documentary Box*. Available online: http://www.yidff.jp/docbox/10/box10-2-e.html (accessed on 4 April 2018).
Matsuda, Masao. 1971. *Fūkei no shimetsu (The Extinctionof Landscape)*. Tokyo: Tabata shoten.
Matsumoto, Toshio. 1963. Eizō no hakken. Avangyuarudo no dokyumentari. Tokyo: Seiryū Shuppan.
Matsumoto, Toshio. 2005. Zenei kiroku eigaron (Theory of Avant-garde Documentary). In *Eizō no hakken. Avangyuarudo no dokyumentari*. Tokyo: Seiryū Shuppan, pp. 59–61, Originally published in 1963, Tokyo: San'ichi Shobō.
Matsumoto, Toshio, and Shinkichi Noda. 1964. Sengo dokyumentarī eiga hensenshi V. Hani Susumu no kanōsei to sekai (History of the Transformations of postwar documentary film. V. The possibilities of Susumu Hani's World). In *Kiroku to eizō*. Tokyo: Eizō Geijutsu no Kai.
Natori, Yōnosuke. 1963. *Shashin no yomikata,(The Way of Reading Photography)*. Tokyo: Iwanami Shoten.
Nornes, Abé Mark. 2006. El Rastro del cine documental japonés de posguerra: A tientas en la oscuridad. In *El cine de los mil años. Una aproximación histórica y estética al cine documental japonés (1945–2005)*. Edited by Carlos Muguiro. Pamplona: Colección Punto de Vista.
Nornes, Abé Mark. 2007. *Forest of Pressure: Ogawa Shinsuke and Postwar Japanese Documentary*. Minneapolis: University of Minneapolis Press.
Ogi, Masahiro. 1958. 'Tōkyō 1958 to Shinema 58'. *Eiga Hihyō* 15: 72–74.
Raine, Michael. 2012. Introduction to Matsuoto Toshio: A Theory of Avant-Garde Documentary. *Cinema Journal* 51: 144–47. [CrossRef]
Satō, Tadao. 1970. *Nihon eiga shisōshi (History of Japanese Cinema Ideas)*. Tokyo: Sanichishobō, pp. 373–74.
Satō, Tadao. 1971. *Nūberu bāgu igo. Jjiyū o mezasu eiga (After the New Wave. Cinema Aspiring to Freedom)*. Tokyo: Chūōkōronsha.

Satō, Tadao. 1973. *Nihon eiga hyakusen*. Tokyo: Akita Shoten.
Satō, Tadao. 1977. *Nihon Kiroku Eizōshi (History of the Japanese Documentary Image)*. Tokyo: Hyōronsha.
Satō, Tadao. 1997. Hani Susumu. Geki eiga no kanosei wo kakudai shita 'Furyō shōnen' (Susumu Hani. Bad Boys the film that expanded the possibilities of cinema"). In *Nihon Eiga no Kysoshō tachi III*. Tokyo: Gakuyō Shobō, pp. 3–12.
Satō, Tadao. 2010. *Shirīzu Nihon no dokyumentarī [Series de cine documental japonés]*. Tokio: Iwanami Shoten.
Toba, Kōji. 2010. *1950 nendai: 'Kiroku' no jidai (1950s: The Documentary Age)*. Tokyo: Kawade Shobō Shinsha.
Tsutsui, Takefumi. 2012. Nūveru vāgu toshite no Iwanami Eiga: Hani Susumu no sakuhin o chūshin ni (Iwanami Eiga as New Wave: Fosucing on Susumu Hani's oeuvre). In *Iwanami Eiga no 1-oku furēmu (Images of Postwar Japan. The Documentary Films of Iwanami Productions)*. Edited by Niwa Yoshiyuki and Yoshimi Shunya. Tokyo: Tōkyō Daigaku Shuppankai, pp. 59–83.
William, Johnson. 2009. On Broadmindness. *Film Quarterly* 62: 10–12.

© 2019 by the author. Licensee MDPI, Basel, Switzerland. This article is an open access article distributed under the terms and conditions of the Creative Commons Attribution (CC BY) license (http://creativecommons.org/licenses/by/4.0/).

Article

Image Pragmatics and Film as a Lived Practice in the Documentary Work of Hani Susumu and Tsuchimoto Noriaki

Justin Jesty

Department of Asian Languages & Literature, University of Washington, Seattle, WA 98195-3521, USA; jestyj@uw.edu

Received: 11 February 2019; Accepted: 21 March 2019; Published: 27 March 2019

Abstract: This paper focuses on two discrete bodies of work, Hani Susumu's films of the late 1950s and Tsuchimoto Noriaki's Minamata documentaries of the early 1970s, to trace the emergence of the cinéma vérité mode of participant-observer, small-crew documentary in Japan and to suggest how it shapes the work of later social documentarists. It argues that Hani Susumu's emphasis on duration and receptivity in the practice of filmmaking, along with his pragmatic understanding of the power of the cinematic image, establish a fundamentally different theoretical basis and set of questions for social documentary than the emphasis on mobility and access, and the attendant question of truth that tend to afflict the discourse of cinéma vérité in the U.S. and France. Tsuchimoto Noriaki critically adopts and develops Hani's theoretical and methodological framework in his emphasis on long-running involvement with the subjects of his films and his practical conviction that the image is not single-authored, self-sufficient, or meaningful in and of itself, but emerges from collaboration and must be embedded in a responsive social practice in order to meaningfully reach an audience. Hani and Tsuchimoto both believe that it is possible for filmmakers and the film itself to be fundamentally processual and intersubjective: grounded in actual collaboration, but also underwritten by a belief that intersubjective processes are more basic to human being than "the individual," let alone "the author." This paper explores the implications for representation and ethics of this basic difference in vérité theory and practice in Japan.

Keywords: documentary film; film theory; documentary film theory; postwar Japan; post-1945 Japan; Hani Susumu; Tsuchimoto Noriaki; cinéma vérité; direct cinema; observational documentary

1. Introduction

It is generally agreed that a new mode of participant-observer, small-crew documentary appeared around 1960 and was greeted as revolutionary in its time.[1] Its appearance has been well-studied in relation to France and the U.S., enshrined in terms, like cinéma vérité and direct cinema and linked to foundational texts such as *Chronicle of a summer* (*Chronique d'un été*, 1961) and *Primary* (1960). Its emergence in Japan is less well-known. This is a shame because, as Bruce Elder points out in his evaluation of the Canadian Candid Eye movement, the theory and practice of these supposedly similar forms of documentary are actually quite different (Elder [1977] 2016). Japan's case affirms Elder's observation and, in offering an alternative articulation of the rhetorics, practices, and aesthetics of documentary realism, it can bring greater clarity to the assumptions at work in each case. One major difference to note at the outset is that cinéma vérité in Japan is not strongly linked to technological

---

[1] Participant-observer is a term proposed by Charles Musser. I also follow Musser in using cinéma vérité as a general term that encompasses a variety of new approaches (Musser 1996).

change: Synchronized sound—which many have been taken to be indispensable to vérité—is absent or erratic, not only in early examples, but for many small-crew social documentaries through the early 1970s. Exploring these differences may provide ways to understand certain key features of social documentary in Japan, particularly as practiced by Ogawa Shinsuke and Tsuchimoto Noriaki in the 1960s and 1970s. A full account of that history is beyond the scope of this paper. What I do instead is sketch out one set of episodically-recurring problematics that might be relevant to the broader field, by focusing on two discrete and thematically different bodies of work: Hani Susumu's films of the late 1950s and Tsuchimoto Noriaki's Minamata documentaries of the early 1970s.

The new approach to documentary appeared in Japan in 1954, six years earlier than in France and the U.S. (see Nornes 2002, p. 43). Hani Susumu (b. 1928) pioneered it in *Children of the classroom* (*Kyōshitsu no kodomotachi*, 1954), a short film that examines the behavior of children in a functioning second-grade class. The film was greeted as opening a new horizon in the look and feel of documentary. Although it does not seem remarkable today, its impact at the time was clear: Tsuchimoto Noriaki, for one, talked about it as life-changing: The spark that kindled his desire to try his own hand at filmmaking (Tsuchimoto and Ishizaka 2008, p. 41). As a film theorist, Hani himself also played an important role in cementing his early films' reputation, by interpreting them in accordance with a well-developed theory of the moving image. While there are limitations to letting Hani—a prolific filmmaker, author, and public figure—dominate the narrative, the first half of this essay examines two of his early films alongside his theoretical and methodological writings. The account can and should be complicated, but the goal here is to show how Hani's emphasis on duration and receptivity in the practice of filmmaking, along with his pragmatic understanding of the power of the cinematic image, establish a fundamentally different theoretical basis and set of questions for social documentary than the emphasis on mobility and access, and the attendant question of truth that tend to afflict the discourse of cinéma vérité in the U.S. and France.

The second half of the paper will argue that Tsuchimoto Noriaki (1928–2008) critically adopts and develops Hani's theoretical and methodological framework. Like Hani, Tsuchimoto emphasizes the importance of sharing the life-world of the subjects he is filming, although Tsuchimoto extends this to the scale of a lived practice.[2] His films about the effects of environmental mercury poisoning—which number at least 17 in all, shot between 1965 and 2004—are the products of a lifelong engagement with the victims. The films' meaning is inseparable from the extreme duration of the filmmaking. Also like Hani, Tsuchimoto is centrally concerned with processual complexity and implicitly argues that film has a special capacity to register the material, ecological interdependence of people and their environment. Finally, although Tsuchimoto does not share Hani's faith in the power of the uncut shot, he approaches the image with similar pragmatism. Just as Hani's theory emphasizes the effectivity of the image, the importance of communicating the feeling of the subjects' life-worlds, and the contingent nature of both filmmaking and viewing, Tsuchimoto demonstrates a practical conviction that the image is not single-authored, self-sufficient, or meaningful in and of itself, but emerges from collaboration and must be embedded in a responsive social practice to meaningfully reach an audience.

---

[2] Film as a lived practice is a reference to the phrase *"eiga wa ikimono no shigoto de aru,"*, which Tsuchimoto used to title his first book of essays (Tsuchimoto [1974] 2004). I have previously translated the phrase as "film is a work of living things" (Jesty 2011), while Adam Bingham translates it as "filmmaking as a way of life" (Bingham 2009). Tsuchimoto explains the phrase's multiple meanings this way. It references: How each new project is already in motion by the time he conceives of it as a film project, that he feels like a craftsman who loses himself in the process of his work (as opposed to the more individuated concept of artist or author), how his films emerge from the richness, dynamism, and contradictions of the lives of the people who become the subjects of the film, how those subjects are living bare lives outside the mainstream social system, the collective and collaborative nature of film production, the need to represent the damage pollutions wreaks upon the ecosystem and all living things, and finally, his disinterest in taking this or that side in debates about film form and his greater concern for how film can become part of the broader project of human life, like revolution (Tsuchimoto [1974] 2004, pp. 377–80). I adopt the idea of art as a lived practice from the book *A Lived Practice* (Jacob and Zeller 2015).

2. An Image of Eternal Youth: Redemption by Rejuvenation

Hani Susumu is from an elite background. His grandmother was Japan's first female journalist and a leading social reformer, his father a world-class Marxist historian and critic, and his mother a prominent advocate for women's and children's rights (Hani Motoko, Gorō, and Setsuko, respectively). As a boy, Hani attended the private school founded by his grandmother and headed by his mother, which bore the emphatic name Freedom Academy (Jiyū Gakuen) and taught self-reliance and personal responsibility. At a time when his peers were receiving an imperial education or, in the desperate final years of the war, being mobilized to work in military supply factories, Hani had access to books, and schooled himself in much of the Western literary and philosophical canon (Hani 1984, 2007). When he graduated just after the war ended, his experience and intellectual horizon were quite different from most others around him. He remained a maverick through the 1950s and 1960s: an innovative filmmaker and a prominent intellectual but never closely identified with a particular cohort, school of thought, or artistic movement.

He was, however, recognized as one of the leading young filmmakers at Iwanami Film, a company that produced non-fiction films primarily for educational and public relations (PR) markets. Iwanami was well-regarded as a hothouse for innovative filmmaking in the 1950s, aided in part by a theatrical distribution agreement with Nikkatsu (from 1955), which brought in audiences beyond its sponsors. Abé Mark Nornes observes that it provided a training ground for some of "the best directors and cinematographers in Japan: Ogawa Shinsuke, Tsuchimoto Noriaki, Kuroki Kazuo, Higashi Yoichi, Tamura Masaki, Iwasa Hisaya, Suzuki Tatsuo, and a couple dozen more" (Nornes 2007, p. 17), and Takuya Tsunoda argues that Iwanami Film "institutionally fostered [the development of] cinematic modernism" in postwar Japan (Tsunoda 2015, p. iii). Hani joined Iwanami in 1950, soon after it was founded, and *Children of the classroom* (*Kyōshitsu no kodomotachi*, 1954) launched him into prominence.[3]

Up until *Children of the classroom* children's documentaries—and documentaries generally—used scripts, actors, and highly-staged filming and editing techniques that differed little from fiction films. But the children in *Children of the classroom* had no script and they were not acting for the camera.[4] It was filmed in an actual, functioning classroom, but rather than hiding their presence, Hani and his crew introduced themselves to the class and set up their camera in full view. Then they waited, and, within a few days, the children began to ignore it. They wrapped a quilt around the camera to muffle its noise and hung additional lighting over the whole room so that they could start and stop filming without distracting the class. When class was in session the crew was forbidden to move around or switch lenses. They shot most of the classroom scenes using a telephoto lens (150 mm)—a key decision that enabled close-up shots of individual facial expressions and behavior in small groups. While the camera does not move, the children themselves fill the frame with motion, creating the impression of having been thrown into the middle of a churning classroom.

Children of the classroom had been commissioned by Japan's Ministry of Education to be a teacher training film about problem children. The framing narrative (which is scripted) begins with a trainee teacher on her first day. She has much she wants to teach, but does not understand how to connect with actual children. As we hear her voice on the soundtrack, a series of shots shows a boy exploring his mouth with his finger, another karate-chopping a book in the back row, and another absorbed in balancing a piece of wire on the end of his pencil. The remainder of the film is narrated by the character of the host teacher. One could interpret the visual narration as presenting the classroom as it appears to this more experienced teacher's eyes. What she and we see are individual children, each living different lives. As the film progresses, the image track becomes gradually less chaotic and the film

---

[3] *Children of the classroom* won the top prize in the general education category at the Educational Film Festival (Kyōiku Eigasai), and was 3rd place in *Kinema Junpo*'s top 10 list of short films that year. It was also the first Iwanami film to be distributed to Nikkatsu theaters (Kusakabe 1980, pp. 50–51).

[4] This account of the film's production comes from Hani (1958, pp. 6–46) and Kusakabe (1980, pp. 55–57). See Centeno (2018b) for more information regarding Hani's ideas about the role of scripting in documentary.

ends with the class's choral performance at the school festival. The chorus functions as a metaphor for each individual finding their respective role in a productive whole and it was widely criticized as hackneyed, even by the film's supporters (Hani 1958, p. 46). The film as a whole, therefore, was not seen as revolutionary. It is the unstaged shots that were new and fresh.

The surprising complexity and fluidity of children's behavior would be difficult to track without the intervention of the camera, and the telephoto lens in particular. It establishes a perspective sympathetic to each child's embodied struggle with their environment. As Nornes argues, the film "used observation to approach the subjectivity of the individuals involved" (Nornes 2002, p. 43). The boy balancing the strand of wire on his pencil goes through incredible expressive changes in the space of a single take. He balances it once then suddenly looks up, eyes wide and forehead creased (it is the middle of Japanese class). Seeing the coast clear, he returns to balancing and then begins flying the assemblage like a helicopter before he suddenly drops it and snaps his eyes forward to check on the teacher again. Hani writes:

> [As I was shooting the film], I understood that the overflowing fresh curiosity and vitality fairly bursting out from inside the children, even if it was expressed in mischief, was something that people in the teaching profession shouldn't ignore. Guidance that could grasp the bodily and physiological condition of children, would be able to raise that energy into an actual power to seek things out. The telescopic lens turned out to be very effective in creating an index to show that. If we had shot the scenes in the usual scale, [the activity] would have simply looked like mischief. In close up though, something *from inside of them* came through in their expressions. [Original emphasis.] (Hani 1958, pp. 24–25).

Though the boy sailing his wire through the air might have been a troublemaker from the stand-point of Japanese class, the problem was not that he lacked concentration or curiosity.

Children of the classroom features many such redemptive moments. One sequence focuses on children vying to be called upon. One boy with his head on his desk raises his hand excitedly but when someone else is called upon he slumps back down. A student named Aoki raises his hand, but struggles to answer. In the end, Aoki is overwhelmed by a chorus of other students, but the film continues to focus on his face as he processes the experience. Later in the film, we meet another student who is diligent and conscientious, but, the teacher/narrator feels, is holding herself back in reserve. The problem comes out on the playground when the camera, stationed some distance away, observes Tanigawa as she hovers near a group of other girls playing. She looks on and seems eager to join them but wavers, physiologically, about how to make the move. She hovers just on the edge, but cannot quite bring herself to jump in. The sequence ends with a long shot of her standing in the middle of the playground by herself.

These passages concentrate on a single child for long enough that they go through major changes of bodily and emotional attitude. Because they are not aware of the camera, their bodies and faces are extremely expressive, alive in the precariousness of an experience that does not know its future. The effect is amplified by the way the framing brackets off each child's surroundings: In many cases, the viewer is only aware of events in the environment as they appear suddenly within the child. By portraying the struggles of individual children so intently, the shots complicate a summary or synoptic view of classroom behavior. One boy is not paying attention, one raises his hand, but is not called upon, one who is called upon cannot answer the question, and a girl on the playground fails to join in a game. All of these children are portrayed in a vivid fullness that, partly because they are children, elicits a powerful sympathy while ultimately facing the viewer with the extended experience of children as they move within their own dynamic worlds, not satisfying pedagogical desires and, indeed, not satisfying their own desires, but passionately absorbed in trying.

Many of Hani's films are concerned with growth, individuation, and socialization. After *Children of the classroom*, he directed *Children who draw* (*E o kaku kodomotachi*, 1956), which documents a class of first grade students together with their artwork, to show how they use art and fantasy to apprehend and explore the world. *Twin class* (*Sōseiji gakkyū*, 1956) examines sets of twins attending a special school for twins set up by Tokyo University, investigating resemblances while also arguing for the formative role of environment in their development. *Bad boys* (*Furyō shōnen*, 1960/1961) is usually categorized as a fiction film, but it also used non-professional actors, location shooting, and, as will be discussed, problematizes not only the characters' growth but also the actors'.[5] Outside of his filmmaking, Hani was a lifelong student of psychology and advocate of child-centered experiential learning.[6] He wrote over a dozen books on child-rearing and the family. One example, *The hands off approach* (*Hōnin shugi*), captures his convictions with section headings such as, "Children have the right *not* to be educated," "Treat your children like roommates," "Let them explore sex," "Don't teach them about right and wrong," "Parents all die one day," and "Life is a gamble" (Hani 1972a).

The significance of childhood, however, goes beyond children per se. As Bianca Briciu argues, Hani's attention to the perspective of women and children entails a "[critique] of Japanese society through his alliance with the powerless" and the most "vulnerable to oppression" (Briciu 2013, p. 60). I would add that Hani positively valued the qualities of life that tend to be most visible in children. His theory of filmmaking and the moving image is motivated by the project of liberating people's chaotic, creative energies, in other words, of making them young again. Although some of the advice in *The hands-off approach* is clearly meant to provoke the reader, the phrase "life is a gamble" captures something at the core of Hani's thinking. The individual organism always finds itself in the midst of a world that is ongoing. It cannot refuse the world. It must act and react with no guarantee of the outcome. Adults empower themselves by claiming to know what the world has in store, but, for Hani, that self-assurance is fundamentally wrong. "Living, insofar as one is reciprocally engaged [*aikakawatte iru*], does not admit of any truth that can be pinned down and stopped. Because [that truth] only ever presents itself in the already living moment" (Hani 1972b, p. 123). For Hani, play and experiment are truer to life as an unpredictable intersubjective process than anything a teacher or parent might appeal to in the name of safety and stability.

The term Hani uses to denote the activity by which "humans subjectively engage with the moment" is performance (*engi*): a usage that goes beyond the word's usual meaning in Japanese or English (Hani 1972b, p. 123). Performance is often a struggle, and Hani's films concentrate on moments of hesitation, of performative "stuttering" as he calls them (Hani 1972b, p. 79). These are moments when the individual is attempting to engage with their environment in an unfamiliar way—a way that remains faithful to the reality that they are not fully in control—by deploying hypothetical forms (*kari no sugata*) (Hani 1972b, pp. 105–6). Automatic, habitual activity cannot be considered performance and, for Hani, is not true to life as a contingent process of reciprocal engagement. He recognized that modern, adult society is built upon principles of stability and universality that devalue performance as inauthentic and untrue (*uso*) and insist each individual maintain a basic character (*hontai*). But he argued in opposition that "hypothetical form should not be taken lightly because in life there can never be anything more than hypothetical personae." (Hani 1972b, pp. 105–6).

For Hani, film (i.e., the recorded moving image) is special because it can capture performance in real time and make it observable in a way not possible in other media or by recollection. This capacity of film comes through most powerfully in the uncut shot. The uncut shot is where reality's dynamics push into the film with their greatest force and directness and for this reason the shot has a resistant power (*teikōryoku*) (Hani 1960, p. 67). The dialectic engine of film works not between shot and shot, but through "the force exerted by the fragments upon the process of montage itself" (Hani 1960, p. 68). Giving maximum play to the tension between the motion of the world and the internal motion of the filmmaker (and audience), could make the film "a firm joint (*kansetsu*) between human being and reality," a "dynamic balance within the historical situation" (Hani 1960, p. 48).

---

[5] The first review of *Bad boys* appears in 1960, but it was released to cinemas in early 1961.
[6] For Hani's relationship to progressive education movements in the late 1950s, see Jesty (2018).

This position sets his theory and practice in opposition to filmmakers who advocated montage: something he shared with cinéma vérité advocates elsewhere.[7] But Hani's idea of where the power of the uncut shot comes from, and what it implies for filmmaking and viewing, differs from those of cinéma vérité pioneers in France and the U.S. (Edgar Morin and Jean Rouch and the Robert Drew Associates filmmakers, respectively).[8] When Hani claimed that film could establish a joint between viewer and reality, he was not appealing to the indexical/material nature of the film image or the spatio-temporal integrity of the uncut shot serving as evidence of a scene having been recorded as it really happened (as was common in the U.S.). Nor was he claiming that the mobile camera and synchronized sound made new immersive, intimate qualities possible (as Morin did). Hani contended the shot appears as a moment of rupture, in both the film and the life space of the viewer. It is fragmentary and its impact is episodic. It does not function as a kind of visual evidence in the rational/legal sense of the word (as often claimed in discourse in the U.S.), nor as something that bears witness to unstaged confessions (as for Morin). The shot, rather, is important to Hani for its affective impact, what he calls its capacity for sensual expression (*kankakutekina hyōgen*) (Hani 1960, p. 96). The most precious connection with reality the shot establishes is the *feeling* of being profoundly interconnected with others and the *sense* of a world much wider and more dynamic than one's habituated sphere of (self-)control.

Although Hani's theorization of the shot's power is scattered, an important passage is his discussion of Nakai Masakazu's well-known theory of how the audience's emotion creates continuity at the points of rupture between shots. To paraphrase Nakai, the shot catches the historical moment just as it leans into the future, thus provoking a directionality in the desire of the audience (in Hani 1960, pp. 88–90). Hani then connects this concept of directionality to the work of the psychologist, Kurt Lewin, who developed a field theory of human behavior, which employs topological analysis to understand the attractions and repulsions at work across the territory of the individual. For Lewin, individual behavior is best understood by mapping out the transindividual psychic and social forces that an individual is subject to, the sum of which comprise the individual's "environment," or "life space" (Lewin 1936). No action, thought, or psychological state exists in a vacuum: An individual's psychological state forms part of the environment that envelopes others, just as that individual is subject to the forces created by everyone around them. Much like affect theory, field theory understands human behavior to be preconscious and transindividual in its basic orientations. It can illuminate how individuals or groups get "stuck" in patterns of repeated failure (individuals are not conscious of all the forces affecting them) and how changes in environment can change individual behavior and group dynamics. The passages imply that Hani believed film could preserve the power of the directional forces in and among the subjects being filmed: The unresolved nature of the shot referenced in Nakai's theory left the viewer open to the field dynamics unfolding in a moving image.[9] Thus, the intensity of the children's engagement with their environment in *Children of the classroom*—especially presented at such a large scale—pulls the audience into their world alongside them to experience the tensions of their life space, the intersubjective ebb and flow of their situation.

Even though the moving image has the power to displace the viewer, Hani believed that familiarity and convention usually blocked that potential. By bracketing off the moving image with categories like, "it's just a movie," or "just something on TV," the adult horizon of experience insulated itself from any involvement the image might otherwise provoke (Hani 1972b, pp. 6–11). It was therefore important to defamiliarize moving imagery in ways that would weaken viewers' perceptual frameworks and create slippage between their life space and that of the image. This idea also imagines a rejuvenation

---

[7] For further information on Hani's position within contemporary debates in Japan on filmmaking and documentary see Centeno (2018a, 2018b), Jesty (2018), and Tsunoda (2015).
[8] For a brief introduction to cinéma vérité and direct cinema, see Musser (1996).
[9] In the same passage, Hani also cites the work of developmental psychologist, Hatano Kanji, as showing that viewing is not passive, but requires the viewer to actively process the tensions in what is being depicted.

(even infantilization) of the viewer's relationship with the moving image. Such rejuvenation could be hard to achieve. Pure duration risks triviality, while the reality effect of fiction films and expository documentary produce powerful conventions in expectation. Hani wrote a great deal about the technical work necessary to capture such powerful shots. His 1960 collection of essays, *Camera and microphone*, argues that the titular camera and mic be understood as the principle creative tools of the filmmaker, not passive receptors. Like paint and brush would be for a painter, they represent the sometimes arbitrary material disciplines where potentiality condenses into actuality. The shot, therefore, is not an unmediated registering of reality, but a space where the given recording technologies and the skill of the filmmaker make aspects of reality visible in an image that might not have been visible with other cameras or with the naked eye.

Ultimately, however, the shot's power is a question of its effect: something not entirely under the filmmaker's control. Writing about the television documentary, for instance, Hani praised the work of the amateur producers from radio backgrounds who, notwithstanding their lack of experience with film, had been pressed into service making documentary programming in the early days of television in the late 1950s. As Hani puts it, they did not know even the "ABCs" of filmmaking (Hani 1960, pp. 196–97). Nevertheless—or perhaps because of that—their work had "a fresh effect." They filmed "impressive," "unconsciously successful" imagery and often failed to bring closure to the narratives they opened (Hani 1960, p. 197). Their work had "the power to startle viewers" (Hani 1960, p. 198), something lost in the hands of professionals with film backgrounds who were—at the time Hani wrote the essay—being brought in to replace them. "Whether we like it or not," Hani wrote, "reality exists and is always moving." Television had the potential to be a "window" into that reality—right from everyone's living room—but its professionalization threatened to turn it into another "mirror" that simply "reproduces the world we choose to believe in" (Hani 1960, pp. 202–3). The shot must almost necessarily be beyond the control of any single individual (including the filmmaker) in order for it to be effective and to remain true to reality, which, as Hani characterizes it, is not a particular thing to be discovered or exposed but change in and of itself: things in the state of being "unresolved" and "in process" (Hani 1960, p. 201).

The fluidity of intersubjectivity is prominent in the thematics of Hani's films as well. Towards the end of *Children of the classroom* the children do some group work. The film takes this an opportunity to briefly but prominently introduce the sociogram—an analytical tool developed by the influential group psychologist, Jacob L. Moreno—by means of an animated diagram. At this point in the film, the viewer can recognize about 10 characters whose behavior has been described and/or shown. During the sequence, the narration describes how group dynamics significantly alter their behavior. Children who were shy or lethargic actively contribute, a sunny outspoken girl and a more serious child form an effective leadership combination, while a bright but domineering boy proves unable to work with others. The sequence breezily reframes many of the "problems" that had emerged to that point in the film: A changed environment can bring out a whole new person. The refreshing potential of a changed environment is the key to reform in *Bad boys* as well. The reform of the main character—his rediscovery of his ability to grow and change—is achieved not by deep psychological excavation but by transfer to a different work unit, whose environment affords him the space to form his own relationships. Notably, the final stage of his growth comes by listening to his friend's story, not telling his own. Both thematically and in the theorization of the documentary image, Hani's work centers on reintroducing intersubjective instability as a practice of liberation.

The psychological assumptions in these works are thus different from what we see in cinéma vérité in France and the U.S. Although *Chronicle of a summer* also creates new situations as a way to provoke psychosocial discoveries among its protagonist-participants, Morin and Rouch's theorization of the process assumes a model of depth psychology. Through comfortable conversation—which Morin likens to confession, psychotherapy, and psychodrama at various points—the film sets the stage for something to be expressed which is usually hidden (Morin [1962] 2016). Though the conversations may be unscripted, they are used as a pretext, a tool, to reveal what is assumed to be an already-existing (but as-yet unexpressed) truth. The film itself, meanwhile, operates almost entirely through dialogues, monologues, and conversations: Speech is the primary vehicle of whatever truths are to be found. Hani's depiction of psychosocial change, by contrast, is not language dependent, but relies on minute observation of facial expressions, bodily movement, group interactions, and—we must not omit—attentive voice-over explanation.[10] Behaviors and their causes are horizontally complex and closer to the surface, while change is less cathartic and more fleeting. It happens not by revelation of something inner or deeper, but by opening out the viewer's sensitivity to the ever-present transformations at play in overlapping intersubjective fields of action and reaction. The ultimate goal, however, is openness to ongoing intersubjective processes itself.

This being the case, the filmmaker does not have to infiltrate private spaces to lay in wait for the film's subject to expose their true character (as in Drew Associates' rhetoric). Neither is the filmmaker like a diver: an explorer of unfamiliar depths, both enabled and encumbered by bulky equipment (Morin [1962] 2016, p. 462). In both French and U.S. varieties of cinéma vérité, access to what is usually hidden is the touchstone of new documentary meaning, and mobility is fundamental to the feel of the image and claims about its authenticity. In Hani's filmmaking and theory, however, mobility is not required. To the contrary, reality is already moving. The task of the filmmaker is to become aware of it: a practice that requires time and receptivity. Hani reflected on shooting *Children of the classroom* that, "When we became aware of the psychological waves that were constantly rippling through the classroom, all the different behaviors necessarily began to register in our own feelings. Or rather, whatever it was within us that responded dynamically to this calling began to move of its own accord, becoming happy, disappointed, anxious, distracted. . . . When we became participants in the class, suddenly things that we hadn't been able to see became visible" (Hani 1958, pp. 33–34). Documentary filmmaking is thus a process of immersing oneself in the world(s) of the subjects of the film, surrendering one's senses to them in order to understand what and when to film. Rather than by penetration or exploration, the filmmaker accesses the world they hope to film by opening themselves to its dynamics. As opposed to Morin's metaphor of the diver, Hani likens filmmaking to predicting the weather: operating by means of heightened receptivity to the winds and tides of psychosocial fields (Hani 1958, pp. 33–34).

Language also works differently. Before we write off the different emphasis on language as a result of Hani's lack of access to synchronized sound equipment, we should note that the "inauthenticity" of overdubbed language corresponds well with Hani's theory of performance (*engi*). Given that Hani believes the idea of a basic character (*hontai*) is false and that "there can never be anything more than hypothetical personae," it follows that he would also see language as situationally complex, but unconnected to a presumed psychological depth.[11] Writing about *Bad boys*, a film which, like *Chronicle of a summer*, features non-professional actors performing a version of themselves, Hani argued that it was the slippage between two life-spaces and life-times introduced by the process of overdubbing that marked how the actors in the film had changed and grown in the process of making it. As he describes it, the mismatch between the image track and sound track marks a difference between the actor acting and the actor speaking, thus demonstrating in a single sound-image how the "same" person is not actually the same across space and time. The faith that Morin and Rouch put in the power

---

[10] Jeanne Hall has written an excellent critical analysis of *Primary* (1960), showing how the discourse surrounding direct cinema/cinéma vérité in the U.S. diverges significantly from what one can see in the actual films (Hall 1991). She shows that the films are far more conventional in their form than either advocates or critics allow. A similar analysis could be undertaken with Hani's films, which only episodically deviate from standard practices of documentary filmmaking. Rather than overturning all prior filmmaking practices, Hani adds significant new ones, while taking on many of the others. But I ultimately disagree with Hall's logic. Discursive interpretation of films—which is first and foremost a selection of salient elements in them—is unavoidable, and is equally part of Hall's own critical analysis and her historical and institutional circumstances. Her implied claim that she has accessed the real films by viewing them in a more objective manner seems to replicate the rhetoric of realism she finds problematic in others.

[11] Hani critiques the naïve understanding of language as an expression of the subject's internality in his discussion of stuttering (Hani 1972b, pp. 78–82).

of synchronized sound to reveal individuals' hidden experience of daily life shuts down that opening by insisting that there is some persisting reality to be found. For Hani, reality is non-identity, change, and difference itself.

To expand on this, *Bad boys* is a fictional narrative that follows the character of Asai Hiroshi, who is arrested for robbing a jewelry store, but who is able to transform himself through friendship and supportive collaboration in the juvenile detention center he is sent to. Hani provides a supplementary account of the non-fictional process of making the film in his writing about it.[12] The young men playing the roles of the juvenile delinquents were non-professional actors who themselves were recently juvenile delinquents. Although Hani wrote a script for the film, the young actors did not like reading it. He accommodated this by letting them improvise scenes as they thought best. To draw them into the process, he and his assistant, Tsuchimoto Noriaki, would act out a scene and then let the young men show them how to do it properly. Although the story was fictional, the young men were acting roles that resembled their former selves. Hani claimed that the film's production offered an object lesson in the way performance could empower people vis-à-vis their own behavior. The process of re-enacting their delinquent behavior—as an enactment—opened a social space for their behavior by loosening it from "reality." Hani recalled the breakthrough that occurred when the actor playing Asai was assured that he could do the jewel robbery sequence (which was shot on location at a real store) with no fear of arrest. The boys could fight off bullies with no fear of getting hurt and muscle their way into movie theaters with no fear of reprisal. In a way, it was a bad boy's dream. But rather than encourage further bad behavior, the loosening of the bonds of basic character allowed the performance to come to the fore and be played through as what it always actually had been: hypothetical.

Film was important to Hani's claim of redemption because it made it possible to reanimate a unique, indeterminate moment. He relates how, when the boys were faced with the image of their own actions when they were doing the overdubbing for the soundtrack, they began to comment on their behavior rather than voice it. In one of the mugging scenes, the boys were critical of their behavior, which they were now able to see from outside the momentum of their former position within it. Film alone can provide this feedback, this doubling of perspective that demonstrates so clearly that the individual is not the same through time. Experiencing the "same" moment beyond identity reopens the reality of each moment as something without closure, without final resolution, so that behavior can become performance once again. With *Bad boys*, the rejuvenating power of the film was literal, at least according to Hani's account of its significance to the actors. The film made their performances available yet again: capturing actions that were of that moment and no other, while at the same time demonstrating in the very distance between image (of them acting) and viewer (when they watched themselves acting) that that was not the only possible playing out. Filmmaking and the moving image can catalyze change in the world, but the mechanism works through a demonstration of non-identity and non-necessity, not the discovery of a deeper or more complete picture.

Hani Susumu's approach constitutes a major deviation from the U.S. and French discourses of realism around cinéma vérité. The theory is interesting in that it is highly reflexive about the contingent and partial nature of mediation: Hani was deeply hostile to claims of neutrality and objectivity, once arguing that they "present nothing more of people ... than their subjugation" (Hani 1960, p. 91). In order to capture reality, the filmmaker has to understand it, which means they have to be in it, in an actual time and place. Taking a position—adopting a prejudice (*henken*), as Hani advocates—is necessary for the film to work as a sensual expression of the inextricably and irreducibly embedded struggles of the film's subjects. One could argue that the theory is still realist, based on the claim that reality is so intensely productive, creative, and fascinating that there is no way to capture or cover it in the form of a conclusive image, regardless of the technology employed.

---

[12] This account of the film's production comes from Hani (1972b, pp. 102–17). For more detailed accounts of this film's production and reception, see Centeno (2018a) and Tsunoda (2015).

But Hani's position is better described as pragmatic. His image theory is concerned with how moving images mediate processes. He attempts to theorize what images do, in a way that parallels pragmatic linguists' concern with how words do things (in contrast to what they mean semantically). Hani's consideration of that question is necessarily contextual. The moving image did something very specific for the actors in *Bad boys* viewing it during overdubbing. But more typically, Hani imagines the context of viewing (particularly in the case of television) in more general terms: as daily life in its state of being colonized by ideologies of stability, predictability, and productivity. That sets the stage for disruption as the image reintroduces reality as an unforeclosed process. Hani's theory of filmmaking likewise insists that the actions captured on film be treated as integrally interconnected with the context of their happening. He pushed back against defenders of Eisensteinian montage, who assumed each shot to be almost meaningless until the filmmaker combined them with other shots (Hani 1960, pp. 51–70). Treating a shot in this manner reduced its unique contextual density to a general, stereotypical sign (Hani 1960, p. 54). Hani treated the shot as an utterance: something integral to and effective in an actual context, in the time-space of both its recording and its viewing.

Hani's theory of the documentary image is less concerned with how the image is (or is not) truthful or faithful to a particular picture of reality than with how the image's movement succeeds (or fails) in reanimating the life space of the viewer by transporting the affective dynamics of the subjects and their situation into it. We might even say that the implied vector is diametrically opposite the one imagined by Morin and Rouch. Rather than the filmmaker prodding the subjects of the film into unfamiliar situations in order to film *them* rediscovering the non-necessity of the current disposition of everyday life, Hani's ideal filmmaker pushes the viewer out of the false equilibrium of comfortable uninvolvement by casting them into the precariousness of others' struggles, as they play out in the present tense of viewing the recorded image.

3. Film as a Lived Practice

Tsuchimoto Noriaki acknowledges *Children of the classroom* as the inspiration that attracted him to documentary. He did not initially have any ambition to become a filmmaker. He entered Iwanami Film because his background as a radical activist blocked him from finding steady employment elsewhere. In his student days in the late 1940s, he had risen to the level of vice-president of Zengakuren, the radical national student organization, and he was arrested and jailed for Communist Party activism in the early 1950s (Tsuchimoto and Ishizaka 2008, pp. 20–39). The Iwanami producer, Yoshino Keiji, was an old friend, and found a way to hire him as a contract worker in 1956. Although Tsuchimoto and Hani have written about each other's work admiringly on many occasions, it would be wrong to imply that Hani had a linear influence on Tsuchimoto. Tsuchimoto was part of a large cohort of up-and-coming filmmakers, who incessantly discussed their ideas and experiences, eventually forming an informal but intense study club called the Blue Group (Ao no Kai) that convened at a bar after work a few nights a week to discuss work, ideas, and films they had seen (Tsuchimoto and Ishizaka 2008, pp. 61–74). Trying to trace Tsuchimoto's development amid that ferment would be a daunting task, and Tsuchimoto's style changes a great deal over time. Discussing their commonalities, therefore, is not to claim a strict historical lineage. The commonalities are remarkable enough, however, that I believe they warrant consideration. Especially because they also resonate with the work of other prominent filmmakers, such as Ogawa Shinsuke and Satō Makoto.[13]

The commonalities are most apparent in Tsuchimoto's first feature-length film about mercury pollution, *Minamata: the victims and their world* (*Minamata: kanjasan to sono sekai*, 1971), which remains his best-known film. First-time viewers are often surprised that there is relatively little information about the history or science of mercury poisoning or the Minamata victims' movement. The film's

---

[13] Abé Mark Nornes also speculates on the connections among these filmmakers (Nornes 2013, pp. 190–97). For more information on Ogawa, see Nornes (2007).

framing is much closer, intently focused on bringing the viewer into the embodied and environmentally enveloped experience of the victims' situation. The camerawork of Ōtsu Kōshirō (also an Iwanami graduate) is both creative and attentive to the textures and rhythms of the people's lives, finding ways to admire their sensitivity and knowledge while also showing the ways the damage caused by mercury has infiltrated every connection and relationship in them.[14]

Tsuchimoto and his crew clearly located themselves at a particular place and time, in alliance with a particular community. That position is not only the enabling condition of *Victims and their world* in a logistical sense, but is inextricable from its voice and rhetoric. The position was not something given or planned. The crew developed it over many months working with the people they filmed and it changed over time. The crew shared the filmmaking process, and both sound and image register the presence of the filmmakers in the events. The film is therefore a document of the filmmakers' participation in the life-world they are recording, and vice versa. One of Tsuchimoto's juniors remembers this practice as "symbiotic" (Suzuki 1993, p. 14), and the ecological metaphor is apt. The filmmakers did not melt into the world of the subjects to become one with them (Tsuchimoto never claimed to be one of the local people): The filmmakers remained a different kind of entity within the situation. But while the people filmed and the film crew were irreducibly different entities, their meeting and interaction produced a meaning of an order different from any one of them.

Tsuchimoto was also highly focused on the viewers of these films. If the film was something that emerged from an actual, unpredictable process of filmmakers sharing in and learning about the life world of the subjects of the film, then the distribution had to be equally attuned to the fact that viewers were not an abstract entity, but specific people who came to screenings with particular needs. Whereas Hani's invocation of the viewer of the moving image is usually abstract, Tsuchimoto ceded priority to viewers' needs in a more practical sense, by planning subsequent films based on audience feedback. Tsuchimoto's overriding emphasis on the effects of his films in fact led away from Hani's investment in the uncut shot. Tsuchimoto was willing to sacrifice such formal restrictions in order to maximize the practical impact of his work.

Tsuchimoto first met people in the Minamata victims' movement in 1970, when he was arrested for participating in a protest at the Tokyo headquarters of Chisso, the company responsible for the mercury pollution in Minamata. Following from that connection, he and his crew arranged to go to Minamata that summer to begin filming what would become *Victims and their world* (Tsuchimoto [1974] 2004, pp. 69–70). There was no script for the film at the time they arrived. Its content and narrative grew out of the experiences of the filmmakers over their five months shooting. The most important enabler of this practice was a position among the patients. The crew lived at the family home of Hamamoto Fumiyo, located in one of the fishing hamlets hardest hit by the disaster. Both of Fumiyo's parents had died of acute mercury poisoning in the 1950s, leaving her with the house. She and her brother, Tsuginori, both suffered the effects of mercury, and their homestead had become a meeting place for the victims' group that was pursuing a court case against Chisso for compensation.

Tsuchimoto and the crew slept and bathed there, shared meals with Fumiyo, and after a day of shooting, they viewed the rushes there, together with anyone from the neighborhood who cared to drop in. From that starting point, the crew met other families, and went to film people who invited them. Eventually they filmed 46 victims or their relatives, and 22 children who had been poisoned in utero. The film's structure reflects the method: The people and events appear in the film in the same order that they were shot. The one-share movement—which creates a narrative arc that culminates in an unforgettable climax when Fumiyo confronts the president of Chisso with the tragedy of losing both her parents—is something that emerged by chance during the filming (Tsuchimoto [1974] 2004, pp. 36–40, 61–76; Tsuchimoto and Ishizaka 2008, pp. 137–59). Although the film is undeniably a social

---

[14] For an account of the Minamata mercury disaster, its history, and significance, see George (2001). For a more detailed account of Tsuchimoto's engagement with Minamata, see Jesty (2011).

movement film, Fumiyo's expression of grief also indicates a problem that lies beyond restitution: She screams into the president's face that no amount of money is enough, that all she wants is her parents back. Significantly, the film does not end with the confrontation, but takes us back to Minamata for a short closing segment, where we see the fishing boats going out again, continuing their round of work. The political movement is important, but the victims must always return to their world, and the film is, at its core, an attempt to portray that world.

Most live in difficult circumstances, suffering from mercury-related disability, or having lost relatives in the disaster. We meet them person by person, family by family, in a series of portraits where the people speak about their experiences and the camera portrays them in their everyday surroundings, sitting at home, fixing nets, and working out at sea. Apart from a few doctors, and the occasional interjection of Tsuchimoto himself, the voices on the soundtrack are those of the patients describing their struggles. An older man remembers how, when his daughter died in the late 1950s, he had to carry her body home from the hospital on his back because no taxis would take him. A young woman relates how she was forced to divorce her beloved husband when his family found out she had the disease. A fisherwoman reminisces about how much her father knew about the sea and the weather, saying she's lost without his knowledge.

But the lives of the "victims" are not defined by their tragedy. The filming invites us to appreciate the complexity of their continuing way of life and the sensitive interconnection with the environment that it rests upon. One sequence introduces a family preparing bait. The camera does not focus much on the people, but on the bait itself: Hands drop in the ingredients, and a giant ladle stirs the cauldron. When the mixture has cooled, a chorus of busy hands molds it into shape to be used. A man's voice explains that the fish love it: It's delicious, nutritious, fit for human consumption. Anyone can catch a fish that's already there, he confides, the real skill is in getting the fish to come to you. The scene portrays an intimate and highly attuned form of knowledge. The family lives by understanding how to entice the fish they mean to catch.

In another scene, the camera follows a man wading in chest-deep water, catching octopus. The sequence is poetic, set to gentle music. On the soundtrack, the man explains how he lures them out, snags them on a stick, and then quickly kills them by biting a particular "vital spot" between their eyes. As his voice explains the technique, the camera observes in close-up as he demonstrates, bringing a squirming octopus up to his face and biting, essentially kissing it in order to kill it. In this and similar scenes, we understand the specific, visceral link between the fisher families and their environment. They must learn the ways of their world in order to be able to live as part of it. Their knowledge is finely tuned, embodied as a "sense" or "feel" for how to operate.

The film gives great attention to small things, to everyday ideas and habits. Ōtsu's camerawork is instrumental in this: His extreme close-ups and remarkable use of deep space illuminate the complexity of everyday competence. Habit and familiarity tend to dissolve everyday interdependence into invisibility, but the filming brings the substance and grammar of those connections into the foreground, closely studying the coordinated actions that comprise select moments in the lives of the victims and their world. The knowledge and competence thus portrayed rest on terribly sensitive interrelationships, and in that they are also vulnerable.

The film celebrates the ingenuity of the victims and fishermen in their relationship with the world, but it never lets the audience forget that that relationship has been forever altered by mercury. In one fleeting example, a man who had once been incapacitated demonstrates how he is finally able to hold a glass of water again after years of rehabilitation. The camera frames his face and hand in turn, and then there is an unusual shot, which keeps the shaking cup of water in the foreground while looking up the man's arm to his face. On the one hand, we have a great achievement. The old man is able to establish the sensory feedback loop necessary to steady the muscular impulses that mercury had destroyed.[15] But at the same time, this relationship is called into question. The hand and head are separated from each other, their distance emphasized. Holding a cup of water is one of the most trivial forms of understanding. It might as well be invisible. But the film emphasizes how, after the poisoning, even this most banal relationship is no longer stable or given. The film never tires of documenting the small marvels of daily life, but at the same time calls them all into question.

The visual "testimony" of *Victims and their world* is composed of this kind of minute observation of people and their surroundings, and it often forms a counterpoint to the tragic verbal testimony on the soundtrack. One woman tells the story of her young daughter's death, and how the autopsy revealed extensive brain damage that was the result of mercury poisoning. As she does so, the camera concentrates on her hands as she uses an ashtray on the floor in front of her to illustrate which portion of her daughter's brain was destroyed. In another scene, the grandmother of a teenage boy with cognitive and physical deficits from being poisoned in utero, relates how the boy sleeps most of the day, does not eat much, and needs help going to the bathroom. Unconcerned by this, the boy reaches out his hand and begins to play with the camera while it is filming.

The visual details accrue to create a sense of the victims and their world that works at a liminal register, similar to preconscious level of fascination that the behavior of the children in *Children in the classroom* elicits. The details in the victims' surroundings seem undermotivated, random, not entirely in tune with their speech. But in their density they are recognizable as the idiosyncratic, irreplaceable substance of people's lives. The sense of fragility in *Victims and the world* is not the fragility of evanescent moments that Hani believed the shot could capture, but the fragility inherent in the unique intimacy of small things that have been invested with familiarity over a long-shared life by the people who live among them. Through the slow, uneven observation of the victims, their homes, their work, and all of the minutia that make up their world, the viewer can glimpse something of the scale of the damage, and its absolute irreversibility. Mercury has not shattered the world but infiltrated and reshaped it—all of it, at a scale both much larger and much smaller than we can readily imagine, "shallower" in the sense that it takes shape in extremely recognizable objects and scenes (an ashtray, stickball, a family dinner, etc.), but vertiginously broad in its extension, through all of these most familiar objects and daily activities that hold amongst them the feeling of home.

The achievement of *Victims and their world* was also a shortcoming. As Tsuchimoto screened the film around Europe on the occasion of the United Nations Conference on the Human Environment in 1972, one critique he kept hearing was that it contained little information about the medical or environmental science of mercury (Tsuchimoto [1974] 2004, pp. 139–80). To answer that need, Tsuchimoto and his producer, Takagi Ryūtarō, decided to make three one-hour documentaries about the science of mercury (Tsuchimoto [1976] 2004, pp. 18–29). By the end of the project in 1975, they had produced four films totaling 420 min.

Although these films lack much of the formal uniqueness and explosive political confrontation of *Victims and their world*, they might be considered a more remarkable achievement. Tsuchimoto and his crew needed to move out of their comfort zone—they were no longer immersing themselves in the world of a specifically located group of people and none of them had expertise in medicine or science. Stylistically also, the films adopt many of the conventions of the expository documentary, such as voice-over narration, diagrams and visuals aids, and interviews with experts. The films are remarkable, finally, because they make a unique statement about science. For many of the intellectuals who supported the Minamata patients in the 1970s, science was inextricably bound up with the extractive and destructive habits of industrial modernity. These films, however, take a more nuanced view, in which the problem is not science itself, but the way that science so often intersects with state

---

[15] Some important context to this scene is that an early television documentary about the Minamata poisoning (*In the shadow of a mysterious disease* (*Kibyō no kage ni*), 1959) features a scene with this same man, when he was suffering the throes of acute poisoning, which manifest in symptoms such as uncontrollable jerking and shaking, difficulty walking, and slurred speech. One shot shows how he is unable to hold a glass of water. This scene in *Victims and their world* answers that earlier image.

power as a tool to disenfranchise local knowledge. They document how local researchers had been, and still were, on the forefront of knowledge about the disaster.

Dr. Harada Masazumi, who narrates the final film in the medical trilogy, *Clinical field studies* (*Igaku toshite no Minamatabyō—sanbusaku dai sanbu: rinshō ekigaku hen*, 1975), is one such scientist, whose approach to his work resembles that of the films themselves (Tsuchimoto [1976] 2004, p. 55). Harada is well-known for having spent his career treating and studying the victims of Minamata. He discovered and established congenital Minamata disease almost single-handedly and has written many books about it. While the camera follows him in his research around the Shiranui Sea, he introduces his theory of the disease and how it must be studied. His first insight is that Minamata disease is not yet fully understood. A new and distressing case has appeared that none of the current accounts of mercury poisoning can adequately explain; for Harada, it is evidence that the theories should be thrown into question, not the victim. He argues also that Minamata disease affects the whole body (not just the sensory neurons), and that its diagnosis must consider epidemiological factors, such as the residence and dietary habits of the patient. He visits families whose members received different diagnoses from the certification board in charge of compensation benefits because of small differences in the expression of symptoms. Harada's location on the ground among the patients made it impossible to endorse the black-and-white approach of official diagnosis. Across the fabric of behaviors and environments, the disease itself appears differently, and that complex variation can only be understood through extended, ongoing research. It is ultimately Harada's view of science that underlies the trilogy's view, as an unending practice of inquiry that gives priority to the emergent variety of the world rather than the desire to tidy it up.

Shiranui Sea (*Shiranui Kai*, 1975) is in some sense the crowning achievement of Tsuchimoto's first five years of engagement with mercury poisoning. It is a long and powerful meditation on the depth and breadth of the tragedy, and brings together the issues raised in the films made since *Victims and their world*: the complex integration of natural patterns and human habit in the formation of community and ecosystem, the vulnerability of these systems in the face of pollution, appreciation for the spirit of people coping with adversity, the difficulty of many patients in finding proper recognition, and the conviction that the extent of the disease was not yet known.

The film extends Tsuchimoto's area of research beyond Minamata, to the entire Shiranui Sea, a body of water about 40 miles long and 10 miles wide, bounded on one side by the mainland and on the other by a string of closely grouped islands. It exposes the fact that although fishing had stopped in Minamata Bay, it continued basically unchanged on the wider sea. Remarkably, this film is the first to give sustained attention to the great natural beauty of this ever-calm inland sea. Shot almost exclusively on brilliant sunny days, it introduces the viewer to a variety of traditional fishing methods, the ingenuity of which is almost as stunning as their setting. The viewer is treated to shots of the fishermen preparing a feast of fish they have caught and, thanks to Tsuchimoto's unerring empathy, it comes across as less shortsighted than it might otherwise. For people whose lives and communities have taken shape around fishing, and who have enjoyed a daily bounty of fresh fish since childhood, it is simply impossible to give it up. It is the fabric that ties them to the world. Yet symptoms of mercury poisoning continue to spread around the sea and further inland. As happened with so many before them, the people affected usually go undiagnosed, because of a combination of ignorance about the disease, the incompetence of local doctors, and the social pressures to keep quiet in order to protect the local fishing industry.

In addition to portraying the geographic spread of the poisoning, *Shiranui Sea* shows how its effects continue to develop over time. It revisits many patients familiar from previous films. The children born with congenital Minamata disease are growing up. They are now entering their teenage years, and with that their lives grow more complicated. One scene records a long conversation between a young woman with congenital Minamata disease and Dr. Harada. The camera is set at a respectful distance behind them, where they sit on a rock facing the sea. The young woman begins by asking Dr. Harada if she can have a brain operation that will make her better. She realizes that she is different from people around her, and breaks into tears as she tries to explain how when she looks at things, like the sea or a flower, nothing comes to mind. She knows something should. She sees other children making progress each day at school, but she seems to stay in the same place. It is heart-rending testimony, that she cannot see a place for herself in the world. The effects of the mercury poisoning continue to be very real in the lives of these young adults and, as they grow up, the way it affects them continues to change. The film gives us access to many of the patients speaking in their own time, but it also gestures to the lifetimes ahead.

Tsuchimoto revisited Minamata many more times, but always remained a visitor, someone whose work lay in connecting these experiences to others. Mercury pollution was an ongoing problem and Tsuchimoto knew that the people who most needed to see his films were often those with least access to them. In December 1973, the photographers, W. Eugene and Aileen M. Smith, received a letter sent to them in Minamata from two private citizens in Canada who were fighting a battle against mercury in the English-Wabigoon River in northern Ontario (Smith and Smith 1975, p. 141). The mercury was being dumped upriver by a paper mill, while downstream there was the same mixture of economic self-interest and disregard for marginalized populations—the Cree Nation were bearing the brunt of the pollution. In the face of government inaction, members of the Cree Nation formed an interlocal alliance with people of Minamata. In spring 1975, a group of Minamata researchers visited them and in July of that year, five members of the Cree Nation travelled to Minamata. Tsuchimoto accompanied the Cree during their visit, making a short documentary about it for Japanese television.

The collaboration laid the groundwork for his own trips to Canada. With the help of local activists, Tsuchimoto and a group of assistants made two tours of First Nation reservations across Canada, the first from September to December, 1975, the second from May to July, 1976. Over the course of the two trips, they exhibited a combination of Minamata films in over 110 screenings involving over 12,000 people.[16] There were sometimes communication problems: Not everyone could read the English subtitles and there were often empty seats by the end of a show. But the screenings were flexible. As director of all the films, Tsuchimoto had the leeway to re-edit them in the process of projection, to concentrate on the segments that seemed most effective for the audience. They regularly stopped the films for translators to speak and to take questions. After Tsuchimoto returned to Japan, he re-edited footage from his previous films based on his experiences with the audiences in Canada. The result is a much shorter introduction to Minamata disease, *Message from Minamata to the world* (1976, produced in cooperation with Radio Quebec), that includes some of the most harrowing footage of mercury's effects. It could hardly be more different from *Victims and their world*.

Tsuchimoto also brought his films to audiences around Japan, especially those who lived in the shadow of mercury, but lacked the knowledge to protect themselves or seek redress. To the people living on the small islands that were only reachable by boat across the Shiranui Sea, the news about Minamata seemed to come from a different world. It was a big city problem, not something that they had to worry about. The isolation of the communities favored local power holders just as it had in Minamata. Local fishing cooperatives could not afford to lose their market in a pollution panic, which meant people applying for official certification as a Minamata disease sufferer risked ostracism.

Much as they had done in Canada, Tsuchimoto and a group of supporters brought the Minamata films on a tour of these islands, with the goal of screening them in every village on their coasts. They eventually succeeded, holding screenings and information sessions at 76 locations over the late summer and fall of 1977. Sleeping in local community halls and men's clubs, often holding screenings outdoors, they brought the films to approximately 8500 people. Tsuchimoto collected many anecdotes in his record of the trip that suggest the screenings helped people understand that loss of sensation, tremors, and birth defects might have causes other than what their doctors told them, and gave courage to those who had considered applying for recognition or had tried and failed (Tsuchimoto [1979] 2000).

---

[16] These numbers refer only to the first, longer trip. Numbers for the second trip are unknown (Tsuchimoto [1979] 2000, p. 87).

4. Conclusions

Tsuchimoto continued to be involved with Minamata for the rest of his life.[17] But we have already come a long way from Hani's *Children of the classroom*. As argued, Hani and Tsuchimoto share certain ideas and commitments. They both believe that it is possible for filmmakers and the film itself to be fundamentally intersubjective. This is grounded in actual collaboration in most of their filmmaking, usually by sharing rushes and keeping up ongoing discussions with people appearing in the film. But it is also underwritten by a belief that intersubjective processes are more basic to human being than "the individual," let alone "the author." It is interesting that in the discourse of Euroamerican social documentary, the relationship between filmmaker and filmed subject is a territory that produces deep anxiety. It is possibly the most intensely theorized aspect of documentary ethics. And indeed, this scrutiny is probably justified insofar as cinéma vérité, as we have seen, operates according to a model wherein the director arrogates the empowered role of an investigator (an observer or "diver") seeking a truth conceived to exist apart from themselves, within the personal, private lives of their subjects. The filmmakers' positioning raises questions about the viewers' positioning as well: Does the viewer identify with the filmed subjects or do the films (re)affirm the viewer's superiority over them by encouraging identification with the filmmaker or camera?

Japanese small-crew social documentary of the 1960s and 1970s has not been as centrally concerned with these questions. Rather than being a mark of the filmmakers' ethical naiveté, however, I would argue that the reason may lie in a fundamentally different understanding of social reality—as intersubjective and fluid, and a different investment in the image—as something effective rather than revealing. From the outset, there is no explicit or implicit claim that a particular film reveals an objectively valid deeper truth. Hani urges that documentary aspire to being a sensuous expression of a specifically located (and therefore not universal) intersubjective context that evolves incessantly through time, with the aim that viewers come to the end of the film with an altered sense of their own life space, one more complexly interconnected with the subjects on the screen and their struggles, not as a way to gain objective knowledge or in the mode of identification, but as an expanded and therefore more exposed and precarious sense of interrelation. These ideas are closely imbricated with filmmaking and film exhibiting practices, especially for the filmmakers who emerged a few years after Hani. If Hani was responsive to people appearing in his films over spans of a few months, Tsuchimoto, Ogawa, and Satō extended that engagement into lived practices, producing series of films over decades that shift and adjust according to the dynamics of the worlds being filmed, and exhibition practices similarly sensitive to the life-worlds of their viewers (on Ogawa, see Nornes 2007). For the most part, Hani's viewer remains an abstract, bourgeois audience while for Tsuchimoto and his cohort, viewers were specific individuals in need of particular forms of knowledge presented in particular ways. For both, the intended effect of film viewing was to upset the status quo by connecting the viewer to different (not necessarily deeper or more universally valid) perspectives and positions.

Funding: This research received no external funding.

Conflicts of Interest: The author declares no conflict of interest.

---

[17] In the late 1970s, he co-directed *My town, my youth* (*Waga machi, waga seishun*, 1978), which followed a group of young people with congenital Minamata disease as they organized a public concert featuring the popular female vocalist Ishikawa Sayuri. In 1981 he made *The Minamata mural* (*Minamata no zu monogatari*, 1981), about the artists Maruki Iri and Toshi, well-known from their murals depicting the atomic bombings, as they completed a mural about the tragedy of Minamata. In the 1980s, Tsuchimoto's interests expanded: He directed two films about nuclear power and its dangers, *Tsuchimoto Noriaki's nuclear scrapbook* (*Genpatsu kirinuki cho*, 1982), and *Umitori—Robbing the sea at Shimokita Peninsula* (*Umitori—Shimokita Hantō, Hamasekine*, 1984), and an ambitious work on Afghanistan during the Soviet occupation, *Afghan spring* (*Yomigaere karēzu*, 1989). In his final works, however, he returned to the subject of Minamata with *Memories of Kawamoto Teruo—Minamata: The person who dug the well* (*Kaisō—Kawamoto Teruo, Minamata ido o hotta otoko*, 1999) and *Minamata Diary—Visiting resurrected souls* (*Minamata nikki—yomigaeru tamashii o tazunete*, 2004).

References

Bingham, Adam. 2009. Filmmaking as a way of life: Tsuchimoto, Ogawa, and revolutions in documentary cinema. *Asian Cinema* 20: 166–75. [CrossRef]

Briciu, Bianca. 2013. Love and power: The objectification of the adolescent body in Hani Susumu's *Hatsukoi jigokuhen/Nanami, inferno of first love* (1968). *Journal of Japanese and Korean Cinema* 5: 59–76. [CrossRef]

Centeno, Martín Marcos P. 2018a. The limits of fiction: Politics and absent scenes in Susumu Hani's *Bad boys* (*Furyō Shōnen*, 1960). A film re-reading through its script. *Journal of Japanese and Korean Cinema* 10: 1–15. [CrossRef]

Centeno, Martín Marcos P. 2018b. Method directors. Susumu Hani and Yasujirō Ozu: A comparative approach across paradigms. In *Yasujirô Ozu and the Aesthetics of His Time*. Edited by Andreas Becker. Frankfurt: Goethe-Universität Frankfurt, Darmstadt: Büchner-Verlag, pp. 125–52.

Elder, Bruce. 2016. On the candid eye movement. In *The Documentary Film Reader: History, Theory, Criticism*. Edited by Jonathan Kahana. New York: Oxford University Press, pp. 492–500. First published 1977.

George, Timothy S. 2001. *Minamata: Pollution and the Struggle for Democracy in Postwar Japan*. Cambridge: Harvard University Press.

Hall, Jeanne. 1991. Realism as a style in cinema verite: A critical analysis of *Primary*. *Cinema Journal* 30: 24–50. [CrossRef]

Hani, Susumu. 1958. *Engi Shinai Shuyakutachi*. Tokyo: Chūō Kōronsha.

Hani, Susumu. 1960. *Kamera to Maiku*. Tokyo: Chūō Kōronsha.

Hani, Susumu. 1972a. *Hōnin Shugi*. Tokyo: Kōbunsha.

Hani, Susumu. 1972b. *Ningenteki Eizōron*. Tokyo: Chūō Shinsho.

Hani, Susumu. 1984. *Jiyū Gakuen Monogatari*. Tokyo: Kōdansha.

Hani, Susumu. 2007. Interview with author, recorded. Tokyo, May 23.

Jacob, Mary Jane, and Kate Zeller, eds. 2015. *A Lived Practice*. The Chicago Social Practice History Series; Chicago: School of the Art Institute of Chicago and University of Chicago Press.

Jesty, Justin. 2011. Making mercury visible: The Minamata documentaries of Tsuchimoto Noriaki. In *Mercury Pollution: A Transdisciplinary Treatment*. Edited by Michael C. Newman and Sharon Zuber. Abingdon: Taylor and Francis, pp. 139–60.

Jesty, Justin. 2018. *Art and Engagement in Early Postwar Japan*. Ithaca: Cornell University Press.

Kusakabe, Kyūshirō. 1980. *Eizō o tsukuru hito to kigyō: Iwanami Eiga no sanjūnen*. Tokyo: Mizuumi Shobō.

Lewin, Kurt. 1936. *Principles of Topological Psychology*. New York: McGraw-Hill.

Morin, Edgar. 2016. Chronicle of a film. Translated by Anny Ewing and Steven Feld. In *The Documentary Film Reader: History, Theory, Criticism*. Edited by Jonathan Kahana. New York: Oxford University Press, pp. 461–72. First published 1962.

Musser, Charles. 1996. Extending the boundaries: Cinéma vérité and the new documentary. In *The Oxford History of World Cinema*. Edited by Geoffrey Nowell-Smith. New York: Oxford University Press, pp. 527–37.

Nornes, Abé Mark. 2002. The postwar documentary trace: Groping in the dark. *Positions: East Asia, Culture, Critique* 10: 39–78. [CrossRef]

Nornes, Abé Mark. 2007. *Forest of Pressure: Ogawa Shinsuke and the Postwar Japanese Documentary*. Minneapolis: University of Minnesota Press.

Nornes, Abé Mark. 2013. The crux. *Concentric: Literary and Cultural Studies* 39: 189–202.

Smith, W. Eugene, and Aileen M. Smith. 1975. *Minamata: Words and Photographs*. New York: Holt, Rinehart and Winston.

Suzuki, Shiroyasu. 1993. Documentarists of Japan (second in a series): An interview with Suzuki Shiroyasu. By Mark Abé Nornes. *Documentary Box* 2: 9–16.

Tsuchimoto, Noriaki. 2000. *Waga eiga hakken no tabi*. Ningen no Kiroku 128. Tokyo: Nihon Tosho Sentā. First published 1979.

Tsuchimoto, Noriaki. 2004. *Eiga wa ikimono no shigoto de aru*, new ed. Tokyo: Miraisha. First published 1974.

Tsuchimoto, Noriaki. 2004. *Gyakkyō no naka no kiroku*, new ed. Tokyo: Miraisha. First published 1976.

Tsuchimoto, Noriaki, and Kenji Ishizaka. 2008. *Dokyumentarī no umi e: Kiroku eiga sakka Tsuchimoto Noriaki to no taiwa*. Tokyo: Gendai Shokan.

Tsunoda, Takuya. 2015. The Dawn of cinematic modernism: Iwanami Productions and postwar Japanese cinema. Ph.D. dissertation, Yale University, New Haven, CT, USA.

 © 2019 by the author. Licensee MDPI, Basel, Switzerland. This article is an open access article distributed under the terms and conditions of the Creative Commons Attribution (CC BY) license (http://creativecommons.org/licenses/by/4.0/).

Article

The Ethics of Representation in Light of Minamata Disease: Tsuchimoto Noriaki and His Minamata Documentaries

Miyo Inoue

Independent Scholar, El Cerrito, CA 94530, USA; miyo@berkeley.edu

Received: 28 January 2019; Accepted: 15 March 2019; Published: 20 March 2019

Abstract: In this paper, I will examine how Japanese documentary filmmaker Tsuchimoto Noriaki (1928–2008) tackled the issue of visual ethics through the representation of Matsunaga Kumiko and Kamimura Tomoko—two young female patients known for the symbolic roles they each played in the history of Minamata disease. I will introduce the ethical challenge Tsuchimoto encountered upon his first visit to Minamata in 1965—especially how he grappled with the question of filming subjects (*shutai*) who were unconscious and/or unable to express whether they approved the act of filming or not—and how such conundrums were reflected into his representation of Kumiko in her hospital bed. For the analysis of the representation of Tomoko as seen in Tsuchimoto's documentary, I will bring in W. Eugene Smith's photograph "Tomoko and Mother in the Bath" as a point of comparison to explore what could be an ethical representation of Minamata disease patients, including the issue of photographs that seem to beautify the tragedy. Based on the above examinations, I will argue that the challenges Tsuchimoto faced upon representing unresponsive subjects and the very struggle to find a way to capture them as humans, not as patients or victims, altered his manner of artistic and political involvement with Minamata disease. And in the current post-Fukushima era, the issue of ethical representation that he kept exploring carries even more significance upon representing disasters.

Keywords: Minamata disease; Tsuchimoto Noriaki; W. Eugene Smith; Ishimure Michiko; ethics of representation; *The Children of Minamata are Living*; *Minamata: The Victims and Their World*

Prior to Tsuchimoto's first visit to Minamata in 1965, numerous journalists and artists covered this strange disease, but only a handful continued their lifelong engagement with Minamata.[1] One of them was Kuwabara Shisei (1936–present), who started photographing patients in 1960. Kuwabara strived to find a way to present patients without repelling the audience, as he argues that "[t]he more shocking the subject is, the more effective it might be [to use] a soft photograph."[2] One example of this soft photograph is his best known work—the close-up photograph of Matsunaga Kumiko's eyes. The most notable artist who worked on Minamata disease, however, would undoubtedly be the local author Ishimure Michiko (1927–2018). Ishimure's novel, *Paradise in the Sea of Sorrow* (Ishimure 1969), brilliantly described life in pre-modern, pre-disaster Minamata and Shiranui Sea in stark contrast to the chaos and tragedy brought on by the disease, and also presented the lives and voices of patients

---

[1] Minamata disease is a pollution-triggered disease which was first officially confirmed on 1 May, 1956. Methyl mercury contained in the waste water discharged from the Chisso Minamata factory was consumed by fish and shellfish in Minamata Bay, which were then consumed by humans, and the consumption of mercury-contaminated fish and shellfish triggered damage to their central nervous systems. Common symptoms included sensory impairment of the extremities of all four limbs, lack of bodily control, constriction of the visual field, and hearing disorders triggered by damage to the central nervous system. While the degree of severity varied among patients, those with the fulminant form (*gekishōgata*) of this disease developed symptoms very rapidly and often met quick physical deterioration and abrupt death.

[2] (Kuwabara 1989, pp. 38–40). My translation.

who were often rendered voiceless. As a result, Minamata disease, and especially its unresolved status, attained renewed awareness nationwide. This socially active author often collaborated with other journalists and artists, including Kuwabara and Tsuchimoto.

Through his 45-year career, Tsuchimoto Noriaki explored many social issues in his documentaries, but it is unquestionable that his name is most closely associated with Minamata—the place where he was "reborn" as a filmmaker. The questions of how to capture Minamata disease patients without objectifying them or putting them on display, and also from what position to represent them, were the issues Tsuchimoto encountered when he visited Minamata for the TV documentary, *The Children of Minamata are Living* (*Minamata No Ko Wa Ikiteiru* 1965).[3] For this documentary, Tsuchimoto followed Nishikita Yumi, a female college student and a volunteer case worker, as she visited the Minamata Municipal Hospital and the areas considered as the disease's epicenter. Despite his initial enthusiasm for reporting the state of Minamata disease almost ten years after its official confirmation, the rejection by villagers that he encountered left him emotionally devastated. He recalls his experience in the article, "Document in Adversity" (*Gyakkyō No Naka No Kiroku*):

> [O]n the first day I entered Yudō, the area with the large number of patients, I was bitterly informed that its residents regarded [me] with loathing. It was February 1965, when Minamata disease [patients] were treated like aftereffects and secluded inside the area. While we were shooting the panoramic view of the area with the wide lens, housewives who were gathered at one of the houses started to raise a clamor. I was unaware of a child patient among them, but they harshly blamed us, complaining that we filmed [the child] without permission. I listened in without a word of justification. After that incident, both my cognitive faculty and speech completely ceased to function. In short, I was destroyed. Torn apart by the intuition that "I do not have the right to film Minamata disease," I heard my own internal voice, "You don't have the energy to shoot a film, so just quit," endlessly. Unable to turn the camera to anywhere, I just stood on top of the stone wall by the wharf ...
>
> Eventually, I saw a fragment of translucent and shiny tea cup at the bottom of the sea ... "Can we focus [the lens] on it?" With this as a cue, we filmed several shots of the china at the bottom of the sea for a long time in silence ... Filming it was the only way for us to start again. Namely, it was merely "a document at a standstill" (*ashibumi no kiroku*). But only by doing so, I could barely endure the profound sense of setback as a filmmaker. Without this experience, my relationship with Minamata until today would not have been born.[4]

After years of suffering discrimination from Minamata citizens at large and even neighbors, patients and their family members grew very sensitive to the presence of the media, particularly of the camera. In their eyes, the media in 1965 were mostly curious bystanders who "snatched" their images for a use which, though potentially well-meaning, might make their lives even harder. Hence, distrust and rejection of men with the camera and other recording devices was nurtured. Even though Tsuchimoto considered himself as an outsider to the established media, villagers would have registered him as "one of those media people" all the same. He took the rejection to heart, to the point that he even doubted his profession as a filmmaker, especially because he imposed on himself a policy of always asking for permission to film his subjects prior to actually filming them.[5] This moment of standstill, however traumatic it might have been, allowed him to take steps forward in a form of independent documentary making five years later, namely without any connection to the mainstream

---

[3] This documentary was produced for Nihon TV's program "Non-fiction Theater" (*Non Fikushon Gekijō*; 1962–1968), which is often considered as the pioneer of TV documentary on social issues. Film director Ōshima Nagisa's *Forgotten Imperial Army* (*Wasurerareta Kōgun;* aired on 16 August 1963) is arguably the most known documentary it produced.

[4] (Tsuchimoto 1976, p. 93). My translation. This article was first published in the 31 January, 1975, issue of *Tōkyō Shimbun*.

[5] (Tsuchimoto 2005, p. 89). My translation.

media. Moreover, it strongly urged him to contemplate further on the role of documentary film and the issue of privacy, particularly in relation to Minamata disease.

Tsuchimoto's encounter with, or rather "witnessing" of, Matsunaga Kumiko, was exactly in line with this ethical question that he was struggling with, as he writes in "Minamata Note" (*Minamata Nōto*):

> It is easy to film her because she is unresponsive and thus unable to reject [her being filmed]. I was supposed to simply film her just as many other visual media professionals did. Certainly, I felt pain against her being compelled into gradual oblivion due to the indifference of Minamata citizens, and filmed her with anger while branding onto myself what the act of capturing (*toru*; とる) her image means. However, ever since the moment when she endured the close-up without blink, rejection, and pain, I could neither suppress nor appease inexpressible bewilderment until I completed the piece. Why, for what, and from what position am I filming? Kumiko compelled me to ask myself this question.[6]

As Tsuchimoto points out with an implied sense of cynicism toward the existing media coverage of Minamata disease patients, the physical or technical ease of capturing the image of an immobile Kumiko marks a sharp contrast with the psychological difficulty of executing it. This is because the act of filming, according to him, should be a form of mutual interaction between image-makers and their subjects. Alternatively, if Tsuchimoto found it easy, he would be no better than the Minamata citizens whose "indifference" compelled Minamata disease patients into oblivion. In the fourth sentence, he uses the verb "capture" (*toru*; とる) in *hiragana* instead of "film" (*toru*; 撮る) in *kanji*, with the implication that image-makers and their act of "capturing" could lead to "taking" (*toru*; 取る) something away from subjects, or even "stealing" (*toru*; 盗る) something from these subjects by force. Here, his finger points at Minamata citizens as the indifferent bystanders, and also at himself as a filmmaker. "Why, for what, and from what position am I filming?" This is Tsuchimoto's self-questioning toward his act of filming a subject who neither blinks nor rejects the camera—that is, the subject with whom he cannot interact, the one who cannot "speak for" herself. And this self-questioning leads to a larger question of how one should address such a subject.

Indeed, posing questions on issues related to the ethics of filmmaking is an essential part of Tsuchimoto's career as a filmmaker-theorist, and he often examines the position of filmmakers in his writing. In the article, "Film is a Work of Living Beings" (*Eiga Wa Ikimono No Shigoto De Aru*), he states:

> That I chose filmmaker as a profession means that I am not bare-handed and bare-faced as I am armed with the camera, and I impose on myself a deepened awareness of how to remain bare as a human being while retaining the functions of such a recording device.[7]

> The condition where the camera is present is not normal, and even if it is, it creates the relationship between the ones filming and the ones being filmed, resulting in a mutual sense of tension.[8]

> Documentary film steals people, cuts out and shoots portraits, and collects their words ... As long as I singlehandedly monopolize such physical weapons as lens, film and tapes, and possess them as power, my "subjects" (*hishatai*) and I would never be equal.[9]

Tsuchimoto's profession as a filmmaker makes him inseparable from the camera, which can also become a weapon figuratively depending on the context, and he is keenly aware of the danger that the camera as a weapon imposes on his subjects. Furthermore, the power of the camera as a weapon comes

---

[6] (Tsuchimoto 1974, p. 15). My translation. This article was first published in the November, 1970, issue of *Shin Nihon Bungaku*.
[7] (Tsuchimoto 1974, p. 115). My translation. This article was first published in the June, 1972, issue of *Tenbō*.
[8] Ibid., p. 117.
[9] Ibid., p. 136.

with the ability to not only "steal people, cut out and shoot portraits, and collect their words," but also publicly exhibit what it captured—the ability to document a subject's life as a power that could be used and/or *ab*used. He is also sensitive to how the presence of the camera changes the ordinary into the extraordinary, as well as the position of the one who possesses it and the one who does not. There are always spaces *in front of* and *behind* the camera, and people *in front of* the camera are rendered in the passive term of *hishatai* (subject), which literally means "the body exposed to the gaze of the camera." Tsuchimoto's physical presence within his film, therefore, might be as much the manifestation of the constructed-ness of documentary films as his intention to also expose himself to the gaze of the camera, which indicates his urge to be on equal terms with his *hishatai*, if only momentarily.

Based on the above-discussed incident of standstill and also the inherent psychological difficulty of filming unresponsive patients, how did Tsuchimoto deal with the potential harm the presence of the camera poses to his subjects in *The Children of Minamata are Living*? This TV documentary features two main types of voiceover: that of a female narrator explaining the overall situation from the protagonist Yumi's perspective and Yumi's own voice that is interwoven between the narrator's voice. Approximately two minutes into the documentary, the image of Yumi with her voiceover explaining how a young patient is like a wax doll (*rō ningyō*) and unable even to recognize her own parents is abruptly intercut by the medium shot of a little girl's frail right arm popping out of the *futon* (Figure 1). The arm then slowly lowers and hides beyond the *futon*. After this ten-second shot, the extreme close-up of Kumiko's blinking right eye cuts in (Figure 2). This six-second shot is then followed by a series of still images before the location of the scene shifts from the city of Kumamoto to Minamata. Who the arm belongs to remains uncertain, yet I assume it belongs to Kumiko's judging from the order of shots as well as the somewhat ironic shot-voiceover pairing. Yumi's voiceover does not specify which patient she is referring to, and whether she is speaking of a single patient or multiple patients is unidentifiable due to the fragmentary nature of the voiceover as well as the structure of the Japanese language. However, considering that Kumiko's byname is *ikeru ningyō*, I think it likely that the term "wax doll" is used to refer to Kumiko, or at least someone in a condition similar to hers. Then, the pairing of the term "wax doll," namely a lifeless and immobile object, with the images of Kumiko's moving arm and eye is rather poignant. There are two ways to describe these subtle movements: an arm and an eye that do indeed move if only slightly, and an arm and an eye that only move slightly. Whichever the viewer's take might be, this subtle shot-voiceover pairing already begins to challenge the common tendency of putting these patients under fixed categories. The inserted image of the arm, while a gesture of invitation to Minamata, already encapsulates the tragedy that happened to human bodies by presenting the involuntary (and, most likely, unconscious) body movements patients exhibit. And the close-up of Kumiko's eye, instead of emphasizing her beauty, speaks to her status as an object of gaze who cannot gaze back; that is, as the being who lost touch with her surroundings.

Figure 1. A right arm raised in the air. Still from *The Children of Minamata are Living* (1965), director Tsuchimoto Noriaki.

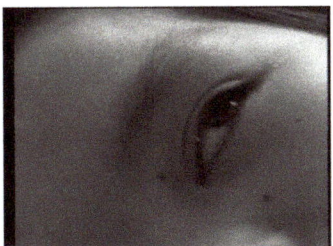

Figure 2. The extreme close-up of Kumiko's right eye. Still from *The Children of Minamata are Living* (1965), director Tsuchimoto Noriaki.

Another shot of Kumiko is included at the very end of the two-minute handheld tracking shot, in which the camera traces the path from the Minamata Municipal Hospital's main entrance to its Minamata disease ward. The sheer distance traveled by the camera reveals how deep inside the hospital building the patients were hidden away. As Tsuchimoto recalls, this special ward, which was located next to the mortuary and the contagious disease quarantine ward, was "the space for death and contagious disease where hospital visitors would not step in under any circumstances."[10] Indeed, while the entrance and the general waiting room are busy with the flow of visitors, past the waiting room the corridors are quiet, and once in the Minamata disease ward there are only doctors, nurses and patients. This distance is physical as well as psychological since, as the narrator reveals, both in the town of Minamata and the hospital, the presence of Minamata disease has faded and people no longer talked about it.

The hospital also plays a crucial role here for this process of concealment. Being part of the municipal government, this hospital is a shelter as well as a prison for patients, particularly due to the secluded location of this special ward, which underlines the undeniable symbolism of its being a place of no return. To battle against this general inclination to undermine the significance of Minamata disease, the unintended underexposure and overexposure included in the shot provides unexpected effects. The long tracking shot covers both the exterior and interior of the hospital. As a result, the section of the general waiting room crowded largely with Minamata citizens—those "indifferent" citizens Tsuchimoto criticizes—is underexposed and mostly veiled in darkness, as if to embody their not-so-laudable deeds to their neighbors. On the other hand, at the Minamata disease ward, the well-lit sections with the windows and other openings nicely illuminate the subjects, including Kumiko. Through this natural lighting, Minamata disease patients are brought out as those who deserve to be in the spotlight and be treated with respect, not contempt. While the natural light helps to soften the impression of the severely-ill Kumiko, capturing her image is no easy matter psychologically. Upon facing her, both Tsuchimoto and his cameraman backed off, revealing the conflicting emotions of being unable to turn the camera to her while finding it even harder to face her without it.[11] In this shot, Kumiko is in bed but not sleeping, unlike in the director's cut of *Minamata: The Victims and Their World* (*Minamata: Kanja-San to Sono Sekai* 1971) in which she is captured asleep, as I will discuss shortly. Is there be any difference between filming a patient asleep and one not fully conscious but neither asleep?

What is suggestive is not only Kumiko's on-screen presence but also her absence. As a matter of fact, she does not appear in the wider-circulated 120-min version of *Minamata: The Victims and Their World*; however, she does appear in the 167-min director's cut version.[12] The scene begins with the

---

[10] (Tsuchimoto 1988, p. 47). My translation.
[11] Ibid., p. 48.
[12] In 1969, the major Minamata disease support group, named the Mutual Aid Association for the Family of Minamata Disease Patients (*Minamatabyō Kanja Katei Gojokai*), was divided into the arbitration group (*Ichininha*) and the trial group (*Soshōha*) depending on their stance toward the Japanese government's response to the plea for compensation. The former largely avoided media exposure, while the latter, which brought the company Chisso and the government to the court, actively

establishing shot of the building, with the sign "Rehabilitation Center."[13] The tracking shot through the corridor that follows is reminiscent of the one in *The Children of Minamata are Living*, though shorter this time, and after passing by one young male patient in a wheelchair, the camera finally stops to capture the arithmetic lesson for some congenital Minamata patients. After this sequence, the camera focuses back on the male patient captured earlier, Yamamoto Fujio, and then shifts to the short sequence of Kumiko in bed sleeping. While the scene up to Fujio remains largely the same between two versions of *Minamata*, Kumiko's shots are deleted from the shorter version. The sequence with these two patients appearing after one another is actually significant, since Tsuchimoto was particularly intrigued by them, as he writes in "Minamata Note":

> I would especially like to see Matsunaga Kumiko, who has been confined to bed for more than a decade in the adult Minamata disease ward on the fourth floor, and Yamamoto Fujio, who is in the congenital patients' ward on the second floor. They are typical Minamata disease patients at the cruelest this disease can be ...
>
> I go to "witness" Kumiko and Fujio at the Rehabilitation Center because I want to meet human beings that live alone in the psychologically distant world that defies and rejects any interaction. I approach them to face the origin of Minamata disease. Their horrifying existence unsettles the life with Minamata disease that I grew accustomed to.[14]

For Tsuchimoto, both Fujio, who barely ceases to move, and Kumiko, who barely moves, are the symbols of Minamata disease at its bleakest since they represent "absolute disconnect" (*tetteitekina danzetsu*) as human beings. In other words, this disease damages and challenges the very aspects of what makes humans *human* by disabling their interaction with others.[15] Fujio's family largely abandoned him, and thus his shot was kept in the shorter version. However, Kumiko, whose family remained as attentive caretakers, disappeared altogether.

In the short sequence of Kumiko, she is filmed in the medium shot while sleeping with her eyes closed, from the left and then from the right (Figure 3). Without her signature big open eyes, and also without explanation of who she is (her byname *ikeru ningyō* had been well established by the time of Tsuchimoto's filming) other than her name and patient number, it might be rather difficult to recognize her just by this image. Two medium shots that both last a few seconds maintain the sense of comfortable distance, allowing the audience to observe her without getting too close to her, if through the non-immediacy of screen. The fact that she is visibly sleeping, instead of laying down barely responsive as in *The Children of Minamata are Living* (Figure 4), might also make the act of witnessing her feel a little less guilty. At the same time, however, filming her asleep gives Tsuchimoto a different sort of mental qualm from filming her awake but not responsive, again reverting to the question of how to capture a subject who does not return the gaze to the camera. Compared to the image of 15-year-old Kumiko in *The Children of Minamata are Living*, that of 20-year-old Kumiko in *Minamata* does not reveal much change at a glance. Yet, Tsuchimoto senses her early decrepitude, already starting to shrink and emitting an odor of old age after the lifelong battle, she has lost the power to thrive and is about to rush away her short life.[16] Taking this "aging" factor into consideration might enable a more sensitive reading of the different level of Kumiko's responsiveness along with the environmental factor. In *The Children of Minamata are Living*, as the ending point of the long tracking shot, the camera comes

---

engaged with the media to appeal their dire situations to the larger public and allowed photographers and filmmakers to capture them both at home and at street demonstrations. I assume the main reason for this sequence's deletion from the wider circulated version is the position of Kumiko's father as the arbitration group's leader and Tsuchimoto's connection with the trial group. In addition, Kumiko's photographs taken by Kuwabara Shisei were often used at demonstrations without the permission of Kuwabara and Kumiko's family, which Kumiko's family was not content with.

[13] Yunoko Rehabilitation Center opened in March 1965 as the region's first rehabilitation facility, and all the Minamata disease patients at the municipal hospital's Minamata disease ward were transferred to this center.

[14] (Tsuchimoto 1974), pp. 13, 15

[15] Ibid., p. 17.

[16] Ibid., p. 16.

to stop to focus on her nicely-lit face, eventually framing her face in the close-up. The youthfulness of an adolescent girl that is sensible through her appearance makes up for her lack of response and movement. In *Minamata*, the still camera simply frames her in the stable medium shots from both sides; along with the darkness of the room, the fast-asleep Kumiko seems to be almost beginning a gradual process of implosion, thus rejecting the external world even more categorically than before. When facing this rapidly aging woman in a secluded hospital ward, Tsuchimoto might have felt a sense of relief, or felt less guilty, that she is asleep and thus does not return the gaze—aside from the fact that even if she were indeed awake, it would be nearly impossible to tell whether she is returning the gaze or having her eyes open aimlessly. The deletion of Kumiko's sequence from the wider-circulated version deprives the audience of the opportunity to witness the person who symbolically embodies the ordeal of being a Minamata disease patient, of the life consumed by the darkness of an incurable, man-made (or corporate-made) disease, and awaits her slow death in silence.

Figure 3. The medium shot of Kumiko asleep in bed. Still from *Minamata: The Victims and Their World* (1971), director Tsuchimoto Noriaki.

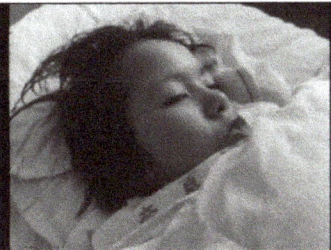

Figure 4. The medium shot of Kumiko awake in bed. Still from *The Children of Minamata are Living* (1965), director Tsuchimoto Noriaki.

While Matsunaga Kumiko was known for her beauty *despite* being a Minamata disease patient, Kamimura Tomoko was identified by the opposite reason—as the embodiment of all the ordeals this disease could possibly impose on a human body. What contributed to her symbolic status was W. Eugene Smith's photograph "Tomoko and Mother in the Bath," which shocked and awed the world outside Minamata. Smith and his wife, Aileen Smith, stayed in Minamata from 1971 to 1973 in order to capture the daily lives and moments of political encounters.[17] The photograph "Tomoko and Mother in the Bath" was taken at the Kamimura residence's bathroom in December 1971, and published as part of the eight-page feature story of Minamata disease, entitled "Death Flow from a Pipe" in the 2 June 1972 issue of *Life*. Out of the eleven photographs included in this story, this photograph is

---

[17] As the encapsulation of their three-year stay in Minamata, they published the photobook, Minamata, first in the US in 1975 and later in Japan in 1980. As a result of the discussion with Kamimura Tomoko's parents in 1999, Aileen Smith, who holds the copyrights to Smith's Minamata photographs, decided to withhold this photograph from further exhibition and distribution. I discussed this issue extensively in Chapter 1 of my dissertation (Inoue 2018).

the concluding, and most dramatic, image. While this photograph triggered heated reactions from artists and critics alike, Japanese photographers and filmmakers working in Minamata around the same time raised strong voices of opposition, including Tsuchimoto who criticized it based on Smith's photographing a naked teenage girl. Although Tomoko could not verbally communicate her feelings, Tsuchimoto claims that her discomfort upon being photographed in such a condition was manifested by her unusually tightened body in the photograph. Tsuchimoto even cites Smith's photograph when pointing out that young, speech-impaired patients often appear angry and their faces are twitching in many photographs because photographers are unaware that these patients do not want to get photographed. According to him, "[Tomoko's] body [in Smith's photograph] is stiffened up. A close look at the photograph reveals how much this girl, who barely entered puberty, is reluctant [to get photographed]."[18] In his view, it is ethically wrong to capture the image of a subject who is unwilling to be photographed—the view which reflects his belief of *torasetemorau*, namely his subjects allowing him to film them, instead of him filming them irrespective of their reactions. As his contemporary, Ōshima Nagisa points out, "[f]or Tsuchimoto, film production is always built upon the principle in which his subjects have to allow him to film them (*torasetemorau*). And this process of *torasetemorau* means, on the one hand, to discover a person, company or organization that gives him a material base to produce a film, and on the other, to have his subjects allow him to film them."[19] As the earlier discussion of how the accusation of filming a young patient without permission left him emotionally devastated reveals, Tsuchimoto was a firm believer of establishing communication with his subjects, of getting to know them, before filming them. That is also why subjects such as Matsunaga Kumiko, with whom he could not achieve such communication, posed great challenges to his ethics as a filmmaker. Based on this belief, Smith's act of exposing an unconsented subject to the gaze of a camera was unthinkable and unethical to Tsuchimoto.

How, then, did he deal with Tomoko as a subject to be filmed? To begin with, Kumiko and Tomoko created a fascinating contrast. While the infantile patient, Kumiko, retained her body relatively undeformed, the congenital patient, Tomoko, born with deformed feet, could never support her own body and her entire body suffered deformation as she aged. On the other hand, unlike largely unconscious Kumiko, Tomoko was conscious, responsive, and "cried out" to express her emotions, as her parents listened to her and "interpreted" her cries to guests on her behalf. The following is how Tsuchimoto, whose lodging was near the Kamimura residence, describes her:

> Sometimes, among the boisterous voices of ... innocent children of the Kamimura family that live across the street, I hear the inarticulate, voiceless voice—shall I call it a groan or the emotional expression of the vocal cords ... Kamimura Tomoko has already turned fourteen. Despite that her period had started early, her eyes glare at empty space and are rolled up into her head, her fingers have bent inward like a crane and been hardened, and her legs are too wilted to even seat herself. The characteristic action of organic mercury poisoning melts and perishes brain cells, robbing humans of what make them humans. However, the activities of stomach, bowel and heart are exempted from direct poisoning. Therefore, while I can still observe the remnant of humanness from the chest and stomach parts, when I compare them with the small-scale skull, bony legs and the twisted waist, [Tomoko's entire body] appears to us as an indescribable, cruel human body. Yet, though not entirely certain, this girl follows human voices and reacts to them with the slightest sway of facial expressions. Seating her on their laps, her mother and father acknowledge the faintest clues of her emotional swings, interpret them with attentiveness characteristic of parents, cradle and talk to her ... I seat

---

[18] (Tsuchimoto and Ishizaka 2008, p. 143). My translation.
[19] (Ōshima 1978, p. 74). My translation.

myself among visitors and other children and witness such an interpretation of the soul, and thinking of the day when I might be able to talk with her loosens my hardened heart.[20]

The above quote contains disclosure of very private information, which could lead to a violation of the patient's privacy. Tsuchimoto's intention behind violating Tomoko's privacy in such a manner, however, is to communicate the loss of basic human functions, which is hard to visually represent and thus could otherwise go unnoticed. In that sense, his method of political appeal is similar to that of Tomoko's parents—to present her body in front of the camera to let it speak for its tragedy. However, this position does not imply that he regards patients' bodies as mere objects to be captured. It is particularly clear considering the ways in which he includes the sequences of interaction between patients and himself as another subject captured on screen, such as when the filmmakers wait outside until getting invited, signaled by a patient's gesture of beckoning, to enter the house, and another patient enjoys the moment of interviewing Tsuchimoto instead. Tsuchimoto is sensitive to his communication with these patients, and this is again indicative of his *torasetemorau* stance. But to what extent such communication is possible is uncertain. The third-to-last section of the above quote does begin with the expression "though not entirely certain," that is to say, casting a slight shadow of uncertainty about whether Tomoko really understands her surroundings. But Tsuchimoto is evidently inspired by Tomoko's parents as "interpreters of the soul" and how they make the seemingly impossible interpretation of and communication with Tomoko possible. Therefore, his filming of patients might be torn between inquiry into the interpretations of patients' inner states provided by their family members, namely the inaccessibility to these patients, and his urge to understand and access their interiority despite the seeming impossibility.

To gain further insight into this conundrum, I shall introduce how Ishimure Michiko describes Tsuchimoto's first impression of Tomoko:

> It is scary to look at Tomoko. At the beginning it was just too painful to bring out the camera. However... while I was talking, I realized that the voice of Tomoko in [her mother's arms], which I initially thought expressed her anger, instead expressed happiness for the visit of a person she is familiar with. At such a moment, Tomoko's face looks very beautiful, almost breathtakingly beautiful. Gradually, [her face] came to look that way. It is only when she appears beautiful to me that I can turn the camera to her.[21]

Such an image of Tomoko, with the impression she leaves in the hearts of beholders, is what Tsuchimoto aims to capture in the scene at the Kamimura household in *Minamata*. In the first shot, the camera frames Tomoko's younger siblings and her father and then pans to the left to show her in the arms of her mother, being fed. Throughout the scene, the camera alternates between the image of Tomoko and that of her siblings, sometimes through pan shots and at other times in separate shots. The comparison with her healthy siblings accentuates her helpless state. Furthermore, the degree of physical destruction she suffered due to mercury poisoning is highlighted by their facial semblance and physical differences, which are made visible especially through two sets of pan shots that first show the entire body of Tomoko's youngest sibling and then frame Tomoko.

The first close-up of her face, which shows her inability to swallow the liquid food at once and her mother scooping the overflowing liquid and putting that back into her mouth is, in a sense, a dehumanizing, exploitative image of Tomoko being put on display for the audience. However, it is not only the tragedy that Tsuchimoto tries to communicate visually, but also the attention and affection that Tomoko receives from her family. The linking of Tomoko with the rest of the family members through the pan shots also indicates her inclusion within the family circle, which was often difficult

---

[20] (Tsuchimoto 1974) Emphasis is mine, pp. 14–15.
[21] (Ishimure 2008) My translation, pp. 274–75.

for the severe congenital patients to retain.[22] And this is where Tsuchimoto inserts Tomoko's "happy" voice as part of the soundtrack, along with her mother's explanation on the way she reacts to the presence of someone she knows with such a voice. Overlapped with such a "happy" voice is the close-up of Tomoko in her mother's arms (Figure 5). Their posing is almost exactly the same as Smith's "Tomoko and Mother in the Bath," with her mother slightly lowering her chin and looking into her face. The difference, though, is that instead of the darkness that frames their solitary figures in the bath, they are surrounded by the light and the chattering voices of Tomoko's siblings. In other words, the public nature of the living room and the private nature of the bathroom are symbolically indicated by the degree of darkness. Moreover, unlike photography, which necessarily captures one frozen moment, Tsuchimoto's film, being a moving image, is capable of capturing even subtle changes in her facial expressions and, therefore, of presenting to the audience the non-dramatized face of Tomoko in the continuing (unstopped) historical time. And the way the audience gradually gets to know Tomoko and her surroundings through this sequence parallels, if temporarily condensed, Tsuchimoto's own experience with her—from the initial fear to the eventual admiration.

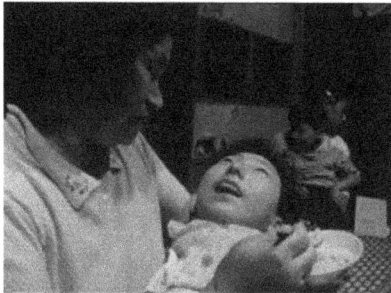

Figure 5. The medium shot of Tomoko. Still from *Minamata: The Victims and Their World* (1971), director Tsuchimoto Noriaki.

Tsuchimoto's involvement with Minamata lasted for the rest of his life, and between the TV documentary in 1965 and the video piece, *Minamata Diary: Visiting Resurrected Souls* (*Minamata Nikki: Yomigaeru Tamashii O Tazunete*, 2004), four years before his death, he worked on more than a dozen Minamata documentaries. The encounter with subjects who forced onto him the question of what is an ethical representation of the persons incapacitated of self-expression enriched his thoughts and experiences as a filmmaker, making his devotion to this disaster even more meaningful. In the wake of the earthquake and tsunami in northern Japan and the Fukushima nuclear plant disaster ("3.11"), Minamata disease has received renewed interest as one of Japan's first and worst environmental disasters. A growing number of artistic and journalistic representations about 3.11 has been produced, and for instance, a couple dozens of films, both documentary and fictional, have been produced with 3.11 as their main subject. And that is why it is essential for artists and journalists involved in this disaster to challenge themselves with the very question Tsuchimoto grappled with. The power of the media should be a catalyst for empowering subjects, and in the age of media proliferation, such power needs to be exercised with caution, with greater mindfulness to the ethics of representation and to the fact that there might only be a thin threshold between the use and *ab*use of images.

Funding: This research received no external funding.

Acknowledgments: I would like to express my gratitude to Michael Raine, Daniel O'Neill, Aaron Kerner, and my colleagues Marianne Tarcov and Soo Mi Lee for their continued support.

---

[22] Due to the difficulty of proper care and the lack of equipment, most severely ill and congenital patients were sent to hospitals, which became their final home.

Conflicts of Interest: The author declares no conflict of interest.

References

Inoue, Miyo. 2018. Exhibition, Document, Bodies: The (Re)presentation of Minamata Disease. Ph.D. dissertation, University of California, Berkeley, CA, USA.

Ishimure, Michiko. 1969. *Kugai Jōdo: Waga Minamatabyō*. Tokyo: Kōdansha.

Ishimure, Michiko. 2008. Eiga 'Minamata' (Tsuchimoto Noriaki Kantoku) (1). In *Ishimure Michiko Zenshū, Shiranui*. Tokyo: Fujiwara Shoten, vol. 14.

Kuwabara, Shisei. 1989. *Hōdō Shashinka*. Tokyo: Iwanami Shoten.

Minamata No Ko Wa Ikiteiru. 1965. Directed by Noriaki Tsuchimoto. Tokyo: Siglo, 2006. DVD.

Minamata: Kanja-San to Sono Sekai, Kanzenban. 1971. Directed by Tsuchimoto Noriaki. Tokyo: Siglo, 2006. DVD.

Ōshima, Nagisa. 1978. *Dōjidai Sakka No Hakken*. Tokyo: San'ichi Shobō.

Tsuchimoto, Noriaki. 1974. *Eiga Wa Ikimono No Shigoto De Aru: Tsuchimoto Noriaki Shiron Dokyumentarī Eiga*. Tokyo: Miraisha.

Tsuchimoto, Noriaki. 1976. *Gyakkyō No Naka No Kiroku*. Tokyo: Miraisha.

Tsuchimoto, Noriaki. 1988. *Minamata Eiga Henreki: Kioku Nakereba Jijitsu Nashi*. Tokyo: Shin'yōsha.

Tsuchimoto, Noriaki. 2005. Kiroku Eiga Sakka No 'Genzai' Ni Tsuite. In *Minamatagaku Kōgi*. Edited by Masazumi Harada. Tokyo: Nihon Hyōronsha, vol. 2, pp. 81–112.

Tsuchimoto, Noriaki, and Kenji Ishizaka. 2008. *Dokyumentarī No Umi E: Kiroku Eiga Sakka Tsuchimoto Noriaki Tono Taiwa*. Tokyo: Gendai shokan.

© 2019 by the author. Licensee MDPI, Basel, Switzerland. This article is an open access article distributed under the terms and conditions of the Creative Commons Attribution (CC BY) license (http://creativecommons.org/licenses/by/4.0/).

Article

Record. Reenact. Recycle. Notes on Shindō Kaneto's Documentary Styles

Lauri Kitsnik

Graduate School of Human and Environmental Studies, Kyoto University, Yoshida-nihonmatsu-cho, Sakyo-ku, Kyoto 606-8501, Japan; kitsnik.lauri.84z@st.kyoto-u.ac.jp

Received: 24 December 2018; Accepted: 15 March 2019; Published: 22 March 2019

Abstract: In his work, the filmmaker Shindō Kaneto sought to employ various, often seemingly incongruous, cinematic styles that complicate the notions of fiction and documentary film. This paper first examines his 'semi-documentary' films that often deal with the everyday life of common people by means of an enhanced realist approach. Second, attention is paid to the fusion of documentary and drama when reenacting historical events, as well as the subsequent recycling of these images in a 'quasi-documentary' fashion. Finally, I uncover a trend towards 'meta-documentary' that takes issue with the act of filmmaking itself. I argue that Shindō's often self-referential work challenges the boundaries between fiction and non-fiction while engaging in a self-reflective criticism of cinema as a medium.

Keywords: authorship; documentary film; hibakusha; Japanese cinema; Mizoguchi Kenji; non-fiction; semi-documentary; Shindō Kaneto

1. Introduction

An already established screenwriter, Shindō Kaneto (1912–2012) spent most of the 1950s struggling to make his name as a film director. After debuting with the autobiographical *Story of a Beloved Wife* (Aisai monogatari, 1951), he mostly worked as an independent, with brief stints of being hired by major studios. An amalgam of melodrama and social realism that soon became a defining feature of his works puzzled critics and it was not until the experimental semi-documentary, *The Naked Island* (Hadaka no shima, 1960), that he was able to gain a reputation for directing. Although this trend became clearer in his later work, from early on, Shindō sought ways to mix fiction and documentary styles, recording as well as reenacting, especially when making films based on true events.

In his influential study on 1950s Japan, Toba Kōji characterized it as the age of *kiroku* (record, document). Toba (2010, p. 9) points out five closely related cultural phenomena that were part of the 'kiroku boom': amateur writing about everyday life, news reportage, documentary film, photography and *kamishibai* shows. This was also when young filmmakers such as Hani Susumu (1928) and Tsuchimoto Noriaki (1928–2008) joined Iwanami Productions (Iwanami Eiga), a major vessel for subsequent developments in Japanese documentary film. It is against this background that Shindō began his long directing career that comprises both fiction and non-fiction works. The aim of this paper is to examine how and why Shindō employed a variety of documentary styles in his films, whether it was for attaining heightened realism, forging and reusing images of historical events, or pursuing a (self-)critique of the act of recording and reporting in visual media.

2. Semi-Documentary

In *Kiroku eigaron* (On Documentary Film, 1940), one of the first studies on the subject in Japan, the seminal film theorist, Imamura Taihei, discusses and provides examples on how documentary style is beginning to emerge in Japanese cinema. 'What can be found ... is the stripping of the usual fictional [*kakōteki*] elements and simple but deep-rooted yearning *towards documentary film*. (Imamura 1940, p. 43)' He singles out recent works by major directors such as Kumagai Hisatora, Shimazu Yasujirō, Shimizu Hiroshi, Tasaka Tomotaka and Uchida Tomu. Imamura pays particular attention to the latter's *A Thousand and One Nights in Tokyo* (Tōkyō sen'ichiya, 1938).

> Uchida Tomu shoots the movements of a gravel-collecting machine for an almost involuntarily long time. The actors are looking at the machine from a far-away riverbank. People looking at a machine from afar are actors who have retreated from being in front of the camera. Along with the final scene depicting gymnastics, here is clearly a strong dislike towards drama. Also, the film's plot is entirely devoid of necessity. This is an expression of resistance to story, stage drama and fiction. (Imamura 1940, p. 43, author's translation)

I have previously examined (Kitsnik 2018) how the over-long and repetitive sequences in Shindō's *The Naked Island* relate to earlier works such as Uchida's next film, *Earth* (Tsuchi, 1939), shot over a period of one year and simultaneously to *A Thousand and One Nights in Tokyo*. Shindō's first substantial assignment as a screenwriter had actually been with the elder director, although the project that included taking a trip to Manchuria and going through a number of rewrites ultimately came to nothing. However, Shindō's employment of long scenes of repeated gestures that continued to the point of meaninglessness should be considered as a defining feature of his work and this 'semi-documentary' style can be delineated to the trend Imamura is describing in prewar Japanese cinema. Perhaps the most notorious example of this approach can be encountered at the beginning of *The Naked Island* (See Figure 1), where a peasant couple (Otowa Nobuko and Tonoyama Taiji) living on a small island without a clear water source is repeatedly going through the slow and tedious process of carrying buckets up a steep slope in order to water sweet potato plants at the summit.

Figure 1. *The Naked Island* (Shindō Kaneto, 1960).

Physical labor and its representation through the images of routinely repeated gestures can be seen in almost all of Shindō's films. In *Mother* (Haha, 1963) (See Figure 2), a middle-aged couple, once again played by Otowa and Tonoyama, runs a small printing house in Hiroshima. Their everyday chores include operating a number of machines in the shack and then delivering the product in a shabby three-wheeled van. In summer heat, their perspiring bodies are caught by the black-and-white camera as suggestively as in *The Naked Island*. In the autobiographical *Tree Without Leaves* (Rakuyōju, 1986) the whole peasant family (in contrast to *The Naked Island*, a wealthy one) is engaged in various acts of processing agricultural products (See Figure 3). Their New Year's Eve is spent preparing rice cakes (mochi), whereby cooked rice is pounded into paste and then molded into smaller buns. This takes place in a large open space of the family house, with all members except the patriarch participating. When autumn comes, we find them sitting in the same room, peeling one basket of persimmons after another. Approaching ethnofiction, these images present both the livelihood of the family and the way community is created, while always hinting at the seasonal pattern and ritualistic character of the activities.

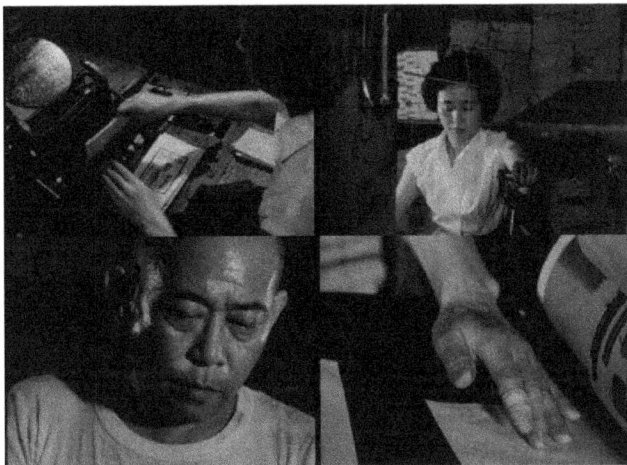

Figure 2. *Mother* (Shindō Kaneto, 1963).

Figure 3. *Tree Without Leaves* (Shindō Kaneto, 1986).

At the level of narration, this manner of presenting repeating gestures goes well beyond the length conventionally allowed for establishing shots in fiction films. In other words, what is anticipated to be an exposition instead ends up taking on something akin to the function of mise en scène. By drawing attention to the everyday activities, rather than using them for establishing characters and situations, these sequences seem to provide a statement on how the routine of labor creates meaning to the everyday lives and hardships of common people. In the last scenes of Shindō's final film, *A Postcard* (Ichimai no hagaki, 2011) (See Figure 4), another couple (Ōtake Shinobu and Toyokawa Etsushi), much like the one in *The Naked Island*, is shown carrying water on yokes to start anew and cultivate the land left behind by a disintegrated peasant family during the last months of the war. In this poignant allusion to what is perhaps his most enduring directorial work, Shindō reconfirms his most persistent metaphor on human existence in a characteristically self-referential manner.

Satō (2006, p. 147) has pointed out that, descended from an impoverished agricultural family, Shindō maintained the mindset he inherited from there for his entire career as a filmmaker. Indeed, many of his films are directly related to depicting the plight of agricultural workers. Interestingly, the very first record of Shindō's writing, an unproduced screenplay he entered in a competition by the journal *Eiga hyōron* (Film Criticism), *Farmers Who Lost Their Land* (Tsuchi o ushinatta hyakushō, 1937), tells the story of a village that is about to be flooded by land developers to make way for a new water supply for the rapidly growing city of Tokyo. It was based on the real-life case of Ogouchi Village that was gaining much attention in the press at the time. Ōya Sōichi, a prominent non-fiction writer, published a well-known reportage in *Chūō Kōron* in August 1937 and the Akutagawa prize-winning novelist Ishikawa Tatsuzō fictionalized it in *Hikage no mura* (Village Under a Shadow, 1937) (Takeda 2017, pp. 9–10). There was even a hit song, *Kotei no furusato* (Home Village at the Bottom of a Lake), performed by the popular singer Shōji Tarō. At any rate, this site caught the popular imagination, as well as that of various writers leaning towards documentary style.

Figure 4. *A Postcard* (Shindō Kaneto, 2011).

Shindō went to Ogouchi on what he calls 'scenario hunting' as early as summer 1936. He later wrote that despite taking extensive walks there, he had no interest in finding about the real life of the village—simply seeing it was enough for him to construct drama necessary for his screenplay (Shindō 1993, p. 73). This statement at once reveals Shindō's complex and paradoxical attitude towards documentary filmmaking. Shindō discloses his view on documentary more precisely in a short essay, 'The documenting nature of film' (Eiga no kirokusei, 1962), where he posits that the term 'non-fiction' is basically meaningless due to the involvement of the author (*sakka*), deeming any film fictional by default (Shindō 1981, p. 47). By claiming so, Shindō underlines how the viewpoint of the author interrupts and complicates the proposed actuality of any cinematic text. In the following sections, I will examine how Shindō has woven this understanding into the film texts themselves in various ways, both by enmeshing different cinematic modes of representation and inscribing his own presence as the filmmaker.

3. Quasi-Documentary

In his fiction films, Shindō pursued a semi-documentary style that enabled him to depict the everyday with heightened realism. Examining how Shindō approached the representation of intense and controversial historic events reveals yet another layer of his engagement with documentary film. (In)famously, a number of his works, such as *Children of Hiroshima* (Genbaku no ko, 1952) and *Sakuratai 8.6* (Sakuratai chiru, 1988), relate to the atomic bombings of his hometown, Hiroshima. Another film, *Lucky Dragon No. 5* (Daigo fukuryūmaru, 1959), is about the crew of the eponymous fishing vessel that was exposed to atomic fallout from nuclear testing. In these films, Shindo alternates documentary footage with reenacted sequences, which makes them semi-documentaries in the most literal sense, as well as enabling their retrospective labelling as docudrama or docufiction.

The passage from *Children of Hiroshima* (1952) that recreates the atomic explosion and its immediate aftermath with a Soviet montage influence, highly stylized shots of blood-mired and disfigured bodies, is certainly the most renowned and discussed one of Shindō's many versions of the disastrous event. A frame story about a teacher (Otowa) who visits the city in order to find her students and their families leads to a flashback when she is standing next to the A-Bomb Dome. Accompanied by the premonitory ticking of clocks, the city symphony-like calm and relaxed images of the everyday life of Hiroshima and its citizens suddenly transforms into a series of scenes which, in their pace and visceral horror, are reminiscent of the Odessa Steps sequence from *Battleship Potemkin* (Bronenosets Potyomkin, 1925, Sergei Eisenstein) (See Figure 5). The closeup of the hand of a clock that hits 8.15 acts as a trigger for the transition from one mode to the other.

Figure 5. *Children of Hiroshima* (Shindō Kaneto, 1952).

Shindō revisited the events of these August days decades later in *Sakuratai 8.6*, which focuses on the eponymous travelling theatre troupe unlucky to have been performing in Hiroshima on that fateful day. In this part-documentary film, a series of interviews with the victims' colleagues and friends (most of them notable Japanese actors) are effortlessly alternated and juxtaposed with reenacted footage of the attack and its consequences, including the painful deaths of the two prominent members of Sakuratai, Maruyama Sadao (1901–1945) and Sonoi Keiko (1913–1945), on 16 and 21 August 1945, respectively. Besides documentary footage of various radiation victims, there is also a scene from *The*

Rickshaw Man (Muhōmatsu no isshō, 1943, Inagaki Hiroshi) in which Sonoi had starred. In contrast to the interviews shot in color, the reenacted scenes are presented in a markedly grainy black and white cinematography, having the appearance of Japanese films from a few decades earlier.

The scene in *Sakuratai 8.6* where several people who have survived the explosion are making an effort to crawl clear from the rubble and help each other is presented in a much more realist style than the montage sequence in *Children of Hiroshima*, which has sometimes been criticized for its emotional detachment. Curiously, parts of the sequence, such as children playing in water, a baby crawling over the floor and a withering sunflower, are borrowed from the earlier film, in effect recycling one reenactment alongside the new one. Something similar happens in *A Postcard*, where the final stages of the war are represented by a brief passage with the same clock, treated as if already a form of documentary footage (See Figure 6). This is the point where semi-documentary at the same time becomes quasi-documentary that mixes ready-made 'documentary' footage with Shindō's new 'semi-documentary' passages. Ostensibly, this is also done out of convenience because the director can use whatever is readily available in his personal archive.

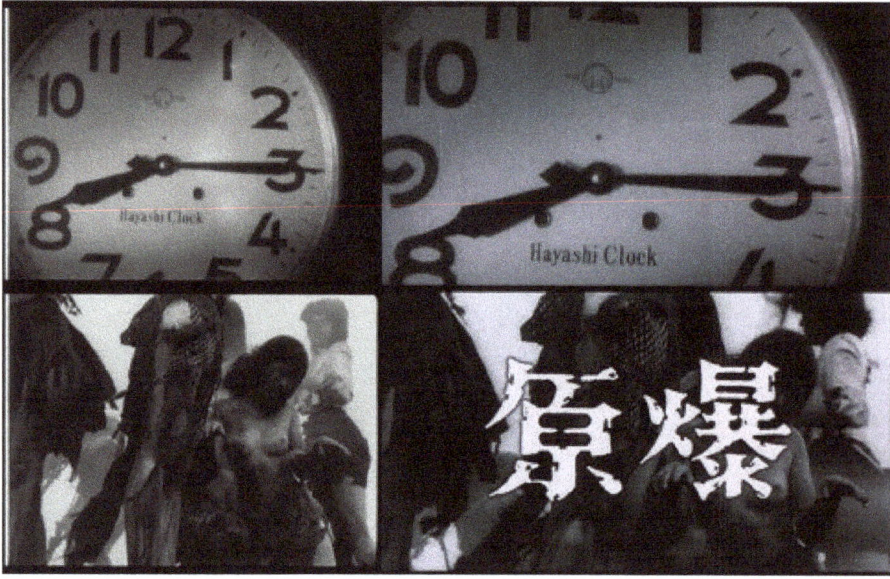

Figure 6. *Children of Hiroshima* (Shindō Kaneto, 1952); *A Postcard* (Shindō Kaneto, 2011).

Another example from *Sakuratai 8.6* that is even more telling of Shindō's self-conscious play with the cinematic medium shows a search party, two men in uniforms, entering a large building, one of the few still erect after the catastrophe. As they walk in, the camera pans to reveal film lighting equipment as well as a huge canvas with a life-size photo of the destroyed cityscape of Hiroshima standing against the wall (See Figure 7). The ensuing action then takes place in a stage play fashion, employing the photo as backcloth. By underlining artificiality and providing yet another mode of representation enmeshed with theatre that makes the film medium itself literally visible, Shindō points at the inevitability of staging in cinema and the impossibility of non-fiction.

Figure 7. *Sakuratai 8.6* (Shindō Kaneto, 1988).

Whereas human figures on the verge of disintegration surely allow for some striking cinematic images, the depiction of the consequences of the atomic bomb has never been the only device for Shindō when commenting on the main trauma of his generation, the Pacific War. There is also a much more intimate and subdued image that he has relied on (and recycled) in a number of films. In *The Story of a Beloved Wife* (1951), while the Shindō-like protagonist (Uno Jūkichi) is trying to finish his final draft of a script, people have gathered outside on the street to wave flags and sing songs to bid farewell to a young man from the neighborhood who has received his conscription orders. 'Banzai' is shouted but the general mood is somber. A few scenes later, heavy rain is falling on the same street while there is a silent funeral parade for the young soldier who has returned home in a small white wooden box carried by his mother.

A somewhat more light-hearted and humorous as well as explicitly political use of the same motif can be found in *The Strange Story of Oyuki* (Bokutō kidan, 1992). This time, the singing and hoorays are conducted by the prostitutes living in the Tamanoi red-light district, contrasted with documentary footage of the prime minister Tōjō Hideki on a military parade greeting schoolboys who have joined the army (See Figure 8). Shindō revisited this motif once more in *A Postcard*, again in an ironic vein, with a hint of black humor. The elder son of a peasant family receives his orders and is given a farewell ceremony in front of the family house. In the next scene, the same people walk into the same frame, this time in silence and carrying a small wooden box containing the soldier's bones. Not before long, the younger brother is also drafted, and all the rituals are repeated in an identical manner, frame by frame. Shindō is repeating a common trope of wartime cinema with a critical distance by establishing a stark contrast between the clamorous farewell paid to the soldier and the silent homecoming of his remains.

Figure 8. *The Strange Story of Oyuki* (Shindō Kaneto, 1992).

A Postcard takes as its premise Shindō's own real-life experience of spending the last days of the war in cleaning duty while the rest of his unit was killed in combat. However, this is not the only occasion when he has linked his own life with cinema and seminal events in modern Japanese history. Shindō's two-volume *History of Japanese Scenario* (*Nihon shinarioshi*, (Shindō 1989)) is organized along time frames that seem to overlap conspicuously with that of his own life and involvement in the film industry. The book starts with the infamous Zigomar incident in 1912, the year Shindō was born and the blurb on the cover of the book ambiguously characterizes it as 'the first autobiography of/in Japanese film' (Nihon eiga no hajimete no jijoden). Among comparable attempts at the historiography of Japanese cinema, it bears close affinity to Ōshima Nagisa's documentary, *100 Years of Japanese Cinema* (1995), with its often criticized gesture to include most of the director's own films within the survey up to the point when they seem to be structuring the entire history. In the final section, I will examine how Shindō, in those works more readily classifiable as documentaries, often actively infiltrates and interrupts the very text by inscribing himself as the author of the film.

4. Meta-Documentary

Arguably Shindō's most solid achievement as a documentary filmmaker is the feature he made about his one-time mentor, Mizoguchi Kenji (1898–1956). Shot over many years during various other projects, *Kenji Mizoguchi: The Life of a Film Director* (Aru kantoku no shōgai: Mizoguchi Kenji no kiroku, 1975) was very well received upon its release and placed first in the annual *Kinema junpō*'s critics' poll—the first such distinction for Shindō (he won again with *A Postcard* in 2011). Notably, the word *kiroku* is used in the film's original title as if to suggest that, this time, Shindō has finally managed to simply 'record' without relying on reenactments. Compared to the films previously discussed, the approach is indeed more straight-forward and mostly operates within the genre conventions of documentary film.

It is evident from *Kenji Mizoguchi: The Life of a Film Director* that Shindō reveres Mizoguchi but, at the same time, seems all too eager to expose the man behind the camera with all his human flaws. The film is structured around a string of interviews conducted with an impressive lineup of Mizoguchi's collaborators, often shot with the interviewer's shoulder visible, making Shindō's authorial presence ubiquitous (Figure 9). As an interviewer, Shindō emerges as a relentless interrogator, persistently forcing his witnesses to give away ground. For instance, he is teasing out testimonies from the actresses who had problematic relationships with Mizoguchi, such as Irie Takako (1911–1995) and, notably, Tanaka Kinuyo (1909–1977). Towards the end of the film, Shindō keeps pushing Tanaka towards a confession she probably would not even be able to make about the exact nature of her relationship with Mizoguchi. Shindō used material from this interview for writing *Tanaka Kinuyo: The Novel* (Shōsetsu Tanaka Kinuyo, 1983), subsequently made it into the film *An Actress* (Joyū, 1987) by Ichikawa Kon, where scenes from various films are reenacted with Yoshinaga Sayuri as Tanaka.

Figure 9. *Kenji Mizoguchi: The Life of a Film Director* (Shindō Kaneto, 1975).

Shindō appears again as an interviewer in *A Paean* (Sanka, 1972), shot around the same time as *Kenji Mizoguchi: The Life of a Film Director*. However, this film is an adaptation of Tanizaki Jun'ichirō's short story, *A Portrait of Shunkin* (Shunkinshō, 1933), and the director is made part of the multilayered fictional world of the original plot that comprises various conflicting sources telling the same story of the blind *koto* teacher, Shunkin, and her faithful servant, Sasuke. In a sequence where the author (Shindō) is interviewing Shunkin's maid Teru (Otowa), the shot/reverse shot technique suddenly reveals blood gushing from the edge of his mouth (See Figure 10). By way of a wry commentary on his own work as a filmmaker, Shindō seems to be alluding to the complexities of this role that never comes without strong authorial investment or violence inflicted upon its subject.

Figure 10. *A Paean* (Shindō Kaneto, 1972).

Elsewhere (Kitsnik 2018), I have argued that Shindō's voice and physical features that appear to belong to a rural laborer become the site of authenticity that supports the perception of his films as semi-documentaries. In the examples above, by bringing the documentarist to the screen, not unlike fellow filmmakers Werner Herzog, Nick Broomfield or Michael Moore, Shindō also takes a step from self-reference to self-reflexion and, by so doing, moves towards what could be called meta-documentary. In Japan, Shindō was not alone in positioning himself as an unreliable author: suffice to think of Imamura Shōhei's screen role in his *A Man Vanishes* (Ningen jōhatsu, 1967). Paradoxically, it seems that the more Shindō approaches documentary film proper, the more the focus shifts to the author and the agency of filmmaking.

Although very much invested in trying out various documentary styles, Shindō displays a (self-)critical stance towards the act of recording. In fact, one of Shindō's thematic preoccupations is the role he assigns to media reporting, both as part of film's context and narrative device. A characteristic example of this can be found in *Live Today, Die Tomorrow!* (Hadaka no jūkyūsai, 1970), a film based on the life and crimes of the spree killer (and later novelist) Nagayama Norio, named Yamada Michio in the film. After newspaper headlines report Yamada's capture, his mother, Take (Otowa), led by a police officer, is shown getting off a train. The platform is swarmed with news reporters and photographers who all try to get a hold of her for any comment about her son's past. In order to do so, they run in flocks over the tracks, climb over fences and follow her down the stairs to the waiting lobby. All this is captured by a violently shaking hand-held camera that adds both intensity and a documentary feel to the sequence. The mother, looking very tired, is eventually cornered by the members of the press and pushed against a wall. A montage of closeups from different angles shows the mother closing her eyes and fainting, while the camera lights keep flashing over her pale face (See Figure 11). The homicidal acts committed by Yamada at once become thematized alongside the violent behavior of the press craving to report them.

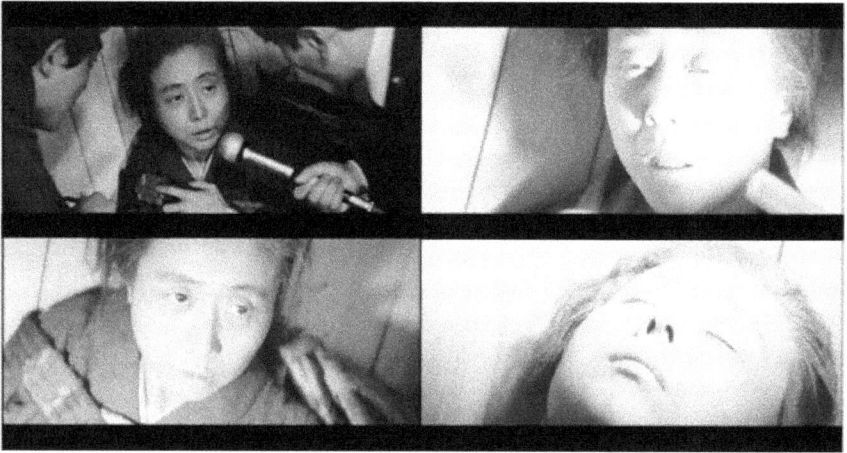

Figure 11. *Live Today, Die Tomorrow!* (Shindō Kaneto, 1970).

When making films on factual material such as *Live Today, Die Tomorrow!* or *Lucky Dragon No. 5*, Shindō includes the way these events were witnessed and reported at the time, turning media coverage into a crucial part of the film's narration. By so doing, Shindō reveals an affinity with the work of fellow filmmakers such as Matsumoto Toshio (1932–2017) and Ōshima Nagisa (1932–2013) who, in addition to working with both fiction and documentary, often employed topical issues and their media representation in their films. In *Lucky Dragon No. 5*, it is through the gradual uncovering of the evidence by the press that we first find out about the consequences of what occurred to the ship crew exposed to nuclear fallout near Bikini Atoll in 1954 and, upon reading a newspaper, so does the crew (See Figure 12). After the ship's captain (Uno) is taken to a hospital in Tokyo for treatment, we receive information about the changes in his medical condition by scenes that cross-cut between his hospital room and reports on the radio. When his health suddenly deteriorates, the bed is surrounded by doctors while the reporters wait at the staircase; when the patient's wife arrives at the hospital, she is followed by a crowd of reporters. When the captain regains consciousness, this information is once again transmitted by the image of a reporter running up the stairs and telling his colleagues about it; later, when he finally succumbs to the radiation disease, radio is the first to make the announcement.

Figure 12. *Lucky Dragon No. 5* (Shindō Kaneto, 1959).

By making the act of reporting such a visible presence on the screen, Shindō is in fact making an inquiry into media ethics. In the case of *Lucky Dragon No. 5*, it could be argued that the press was working within the confines of public interest. After all, it was the first to bring the devastating facts of nuclear fallout encountered by the fishing crew to the attention of the public. However, its treatment of the captain's struggle for his life, although clearly sympathetic to the victim and his family, contains clear hints of sensationalism. The latter tendency becomes much more evident in films such as *Live Today, Die Tomorrow!* and *The Strange Story of Oyuki*. In the latter, an adaptation of Nagai Kafū's (1879–1955) *A Strange Tale from the East of the River* (Bokutō Kidan, 1937), the timeline of this semi-autobiographical story is extended all the way to Kafū's (Tsugawa Masahiko) death. The famous last photograph taken by the yellow press, where the already deceased Kafū is discovered face down on the floor of his room, is reenacted in meticulous detail (See Figure 13). In contrast, *Kenji Mizoguchi: The Life of a Film Director* begins with Shindō entering the Kyoto hospital where Mizoguchi died, after which the picture of the walking director abruptly halts while the soundtrack goes on and provides a conversation with a hospital staff member who will not grant the crew admission to the premises. By way of compromise, Shindō agrees to simply shoot a scene of the empty corridor.

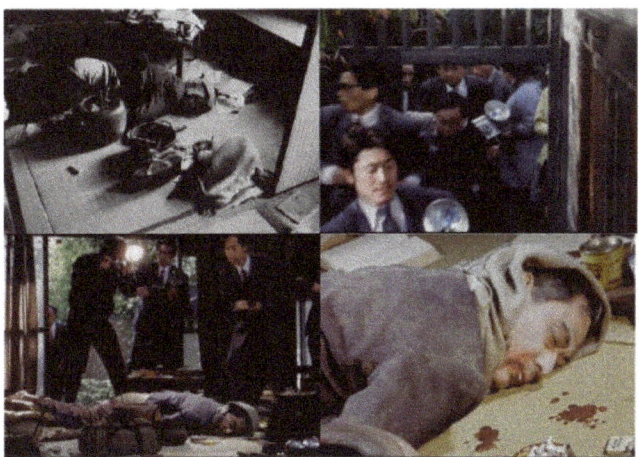

Figure 13. *The Strange Story of Oyuki* (Shindō Kaneto, 1992).

5. Conclusions

From early on in his long career, Shindō Kaneto displayed a strong interest in working with material based on real-life events and employing a variety of documentary film styles. This preoccupation can be traced from his first screenplay all the way to his final film, between which Shindō was invested in reproducing both the quiet drama of the everyday as well as controversial historical events. At the same time, Shindō expressed an awareness of the limitations of the cinematic medium, where the authorial position necessarily overrides any attempt of objective recording, rendering the notion of non-fiction all but meaningless. Equipped with this understanding, Shindō often mixed fiction and documentary styles in his films, whether reenacting events in a highly stylized manner or recycling the resulting footage in his own subsequent work. It could be argued that this propensity to challenge and blur the boundaries between different modes of representation was one of the causes for the inconsistency of his directorial career that, in various ways, sought to answer the dilemma of how to create drama by recording social reality.

Funding: This research was funded by the Japan Society for the Promotion of Science (JSPS KAKENHI Grant Number JP17F17738).

Conflicts of Interest: The author declares no conflict of interest.

References

Imamura, Taihei. 1940. *Kiroku eigaron*. On Documentary Film. Kyoto: Daiichi Bungeisha.
Kitsnik, Lauri. 2018. Real and slow: The poetics and politics of *The Naked Island*. *Asian Cinema* 29: 261–73. [CrossRef]
Satō, Tadao. 2006. *Nihon eigashi*. Japanese Film History. Zōhoban. Tokyo: Iwanami Shoten, vol. 3.
Shindō, Kaneto. 1981. *Shindō Kaneto eigaronshū*. A Collection of Shindō Kaneto's Film Theory. Vol. 2. *Shigotoba no deai*. Encounters at Workplace: What is Director, What is Scenario, What is Actress. Tokyo: Chōbunsha.
Shindō, Kaneto. 1989. *Nihon shinarioshi*. History of Japanese Scenario. 2 vols. Tokyo: Iwanami Shoten.
Shindō, Kaneto. 1993. *Shindō Kaneto no sokuseki*. Shindō Kaneto's Footprints. Vol. 1. *Seishun* [Youth]. Tokyo: Iwanami Shoten.
Takeda, Tōru. 2017. *Nihon nonfikushon-shi: Ruporutaaju kara akademikku jaanarizumu made*. A History of Japanese Non-Fiction: From Reportage to Academic Journalism. Tokyo: Chūō Kōron Shinsha.
Toba, Kōji. 2010. *1950 nendai: 'kiroku' no jidai*. The 1950s: The Age of 'Recording'. Tokyo: Kawade Bukkusu.

© 2019 by the author. Licensee MDPI, Basel, Switzerland. This article is an open access article distributed under the terms and conditions of the Creative Commons Attribution (CC BY) license (http://creativecommons.org/licenses/by/4.0/).

Article

Documenting a People yet to Be Named: History of a Bar Hostess

Bill Mihalopoulos

School of Language and Global Studies, University of Central Lancashire, Preston PR1 2HE, UK; BMihalopoulos@uclan.ac.uk

Received: 10 February 2019; Accepted: 24 March 2019; Published: 28 March 2019

Abstract: The paper focuses on Imamura Shōhei's *History of Post-War Japan as Told by a Bar Hostess* (*Nippon Sengoshi—Madamu Onboro no Seikatsu*), a documentary released for general viewing in 1970. The subject of the documentary was Azaka Emiko, the uninhibited middle-aged owner of the bar *Onboro* in the port city of Yokosuka, home to a U.S. naval base. Emiko embodied the phantasmagoric (*chimimōryō*) lowlifes who inhabited the nooks and crannies of Japanese cities and went about their lives without resentment or guilt, unburdened by familial responsibility and social norms that fascinated Imamura. While other intellectuals and film makers were obsessing about the status of Japanese democracy, Imamura chose to focus on people such as Emiko to identify the psychological and moral changes undergone by the Japanese people during three decades of post-war recovery and growth.

Keywords: Imamura Shōhei; *History of Post-War Japan as Told by a Bar Hostess*; fiction and documentary; history; memory; experience

1. Introduction

In the decade from 1960 to 1970, Imamura Shōhei (1926–2006) wrote and directed a body of work dealing with the carnality, squalor, greed and lurking violence that gave context to the lives of pimps, prostitutes, and peddlers of pornography. His focus fell on life in the streets and back alleys of urban Japan. Key to his aesthetic vision was the search for a cinematic practice with the capacity to extract stories directly from reality. If the camera had the ability to capture this thing called life, what was the role of cinema: to record or to interpret life? Imamura's response was to combine the world of the reality—the immediacy and authenticity associated with documentary film-making—with the world of the imaginary: the artifice of storytelling with its emphasis on character development and dramatic arc.

Imamura's turn to documentary film-making techniques was part of a wider quest to identify the sign under which post-war Japan was born. The people who were the subjects of his camera were without identity. They were an unassimilable heterogeneity, without representation and "outside" of history; the unchecked off-shoots of life that emerged as an overwhelming number of the rural poor migrated to cities looking for work and wealth. This heterogeneity living outside the pages of history is the subject of *Pigs and Battleships* (*Buta to Gunkan*, 1961), *The Insect Woman* (*Nippon Konchūki*, 1963), *The Pornographers* ("*Erogotoshitachi*" *yori Jinruigaku Nyūmon*, 1966), *A Man Vanishes* (*Ningen Jōhatsu*, 1967), and *History of Post-War Japan as Told by a Bar Hostess* (*Nippon Sengoshi—Madamu Onboro no Seikatsu*, 1970).

Imamura chose to focus his camera on the diversity of life and subjective experiences that grew shoots in the cities of high-economic growth Japan. The streets of urban Japan were the intersection of two contemporaneous historical forces. One force of history was post-war defeat, where the Japanese were forced to find a living in the bombed-out shells of once functioning cities. This historical duration was dominated by the question of food and survival. Food rationing and a lack of basic services forced people to sell their possessions one by one to afford the basic consumer goods available at exorbitant prices on the black market (Kramm 2017, p. 36).[1] For many city dwellers, especially women, survival meant selling the only object they possessed of value: their body.[2]

The other force of history crystallised around the U.S. Occupation, the dissemination of American democracy, and subsequent economic recovery. This historical trajectory involved the assimilation of Japan into the global market economy under U.S. hegemony and a fundamental transformation in the outer and inner life of the Japanese. The introduction of American-style democracy did not herald unprecedented freedom for the Japanese people, but rather initiated a radical change in personality. The economic miracle was founded on numbing homogeneity and cruel indifference, as post-war individualism reduced all forms of life to units of equivalence and exchange.

However, Imamura also discovered an important "truth" from his life as a black marketer in the years immediately after surrender. Defeat brought with it new possibilities. The war had scattered families far and wide. In the wake of defeat, people found themselves on their own, without any social constraints and familial obligations, "totally free" to survive as required (Nakata 1997, p. 111; Imamura 2001, p. 234). Those who survived the best played the game of "survival at all costs" with abandon, accepting the rules and rough and tumble of the street without reservation. In the everyday activities of prostitution, selling contraband cigarettes and hooch (*kasutori shōchū*), and smuggling gasoline off U.S. bases, Japan in the wake of defeat was a world full of new possibilities and expectations, far removed from the programs of austerity and sacrifice that defined the war years (Imamura 2004, p. 57). In the alleys of the black market, Imamura came to realise that food and sex gave value, direction and meaning to life in post-war Japan. Echoing the ironic detachment of essayist Angō Sakaguchi (1906–1955) who advocated "decadence" as the antidote for the counterfeit wartime morality that demanded sacrifice and righteous duty, Imamura too wryly noted that, after surrender, the staunch and steadfast soldiers of the Imperial army were "scattered as blossoms" across the wasteland of Japan where they survived as black marketers (Imamura 2004, p. 57).[3] From his experience of the black market, Imamura came to the conclusion that the biological materiality of the body was the foundation of all human activity (Imamura 2001, p. 234). The body did not follow any laws other than those of its physiology. The social and the biological were impossible to untangle. Cultural artefacts and social organisation were not signs of progress or the unfolding of the law of history, but a solution to the problem of sustaining the species.

2. Betwixt Fiction and Documentary

Imamura's body of work from 1960 to 1970 was defined by a curiosity for the changing nature of contemporary Japan in its own right. During this period, Imamura constantly returned to the same existential question: what are we Japanese becoming as people leave the village en masse to find new opportunities in the cities (Katori 2004, pp. 9–10)? He saw the everyday details of street life as a manifestation of contemporary culture. What amazed Imamura was how the phantasmagoric (*chimimōryō*) lowlifes who inhabited the nooks and crannies of Japanese cities went about their lives without resentment or guilt, free from the burden of familial responsibility and social norms (Imamura 2004, pp. 127–33). Racketeers, pimps, con artists, prostitutes and newly arrived migrants from the countryside to the city accepted the rules of the street as the ground of their historical reality.

---

[1] This practice was colloquially known as *takenoko seikatsu* (bamboo-shoot existence)—an analogy for living a life below subsistence, where securing access to a daily meal was reduced to stripping layers of bamboo shoots.

[2] It has been estimated that Allied servicemen contributed $150 million to the Japanese economy while they were on duty in Japan during the occupation. Around $75 million is alleged to have passed into the hands of sex workers. (Kramm 2017, p. 2).

[3] Here, Imamura is paraphrasing the opening paragraph of Angō Sakaguchi's well-known essay "Discourse on Decadence (*Darakuron*)" written in 1946.

To achieve his cinematic vision, Imamura turned to documentary film-making techniques in order to develop a cinematic style that was both effective and realistic.

Documentary film-making practice was also the process by which Imamura chose source material for his films. He firmly believed the raw moments of everyday life had the power to strip the actor of his or her artifice in front of the camera. Consequently, Imamura placed great value in researching and understanding time, place, cultural context, and beliefs. He saw background research as providing the authentic material from which to build narrative arc and character development.

However, Imamura came to the issue of authenticity and truth via cinematic practice. He was not content to leave his films as a record of the transformation of post-war Japan. He wanted to use the neglected, undervalued culture of Japanese street life to expose the oppressive ideologies that constituted post-war Japan (Tessier 1997, p. 64). Imamura was conscious that his project was double pronged. He was aware that he relied on the narrative grammar of film-making to create immediacy and drama in order to challenge prevailing ideas about Japanese identity and culture. However, at the same time, he was sensitive to the fact the effectiveness of his cinema lay in being able to appropriate a local cultural reality that was separated from mainstream knowledge and Japanese identity. Imamura was convinced that documentary film-making techniques had the power to break down the barriers between performance and action. For better or worse, Imamura firmly believed that documentary techniques had the potential to transform the quotient details of everyday life into an exposé of the psychological motives that grounded post-war social and historical experience (Imamura 2017, pp. 103–5; Imamura 2001, pp. 234–38).

In his quest for a new realism, Imamura was heavily influenced by the cinematic practice of directors such as Hani Susumu and Matsumoto Taisho who believed documentary techniques had the ability to extract stories directly from reality (Centeno Martín 2018a, p. 6). Akin to Hani, Imamura too thought that the boundaries between reality and artistic expression could be transcended by linking cinema to the current moment as it was unfolding (Centeno Martín 2019, pp. 55–56). He followed Hani and Matsumoto by experimenting with non-linear narratives, technical improvisation, filming close up through long takes, and favouring shooting on location rather than film sets as a way of capturing the complex beliefs and psychology of his characters (Imamura 2017, pp. 103–5; Imamura 2001, pp. 234–38; Centeno Martín 2018b, pp. 132–34). The novelty of Imamura's experimentation was that he privileged the body as the signpost of the present. The bodies that inhabited the back alleys of the city carved out a culture of freedom that came from the pursuit of pleasure, laughter and gratification. They were configured differently from the bodies dedicated to work, domesticity and self-sacrifice that had become the allegory for post-war development. For Imamura, the subjects of his films were a metonymy for the correlative transformations in Japanese character, sociability, and post-war economic recovery. The elements of personality that seemed private and accidental—greed, violence and cold indifference—were said to have a wider collective significance.

3. The History of Post-War Japan as Told by Imamura Shōhei

Imamura used the power of cinema to make visible the different temporalities which create the whole of the present. A brilliant display of Imamura's use of techniques to articulate multiple times is *History of Post-War Japan as Told by a Bar Hostess* (*Nippon Sengoshi—Madamu Onboro no Seikatsu*), released for general viewing in 1970. The subject of the documentary was Azaka Emiko, the uninhibited middle-aged owner of the bar *Onboro* (literally, shabby or ragged) in the port city of Yokosuka, home to a U.S. naval base.[4] As the title suggests, the film offered a subjective view of Japanese history as experienced and narrated by Emiko. Stripping away all cinematic artifice, a large portion of the film

---

[4] Yokosuka was also the setting of an earlier Imamura feature film, *Pigs and Battleship* (*Buta to Gunkan*). Since 1945, the Yokosuka naval base has been used to maintain and provide logistic, recreational, administrative support and service to the U.S. Seventh Fleet and other U.S. forces operating in the Western Pacific region.

consists of Emiko talking to the camera while ignoring the newsreel content and images projected on a screen behind her. Emiko, with beehive hair-do, heavy make-up and false eyelashes, ignores the visual cues on the projection screen and instead narrates her own highly personal history. As the film proceeds, a disjuncture develops between the visual image of the newsreels and the audio image of Emiko's narrative. A gap opens between the sanctioned history of post-war Japan—centred on U.S. occupation, reforms and subsequent economic recovery—and alternative histories of Japan lived by people on the margins of Japanese society due to the unevenness of post-war development. The brilliance of this film is the way Imamura presents the heterogeneity of Japanese culture—incompatible realms of Japanese life which coexist in the single space of the Japanese nation-state.

The documentary makes visible a Japan of multiple pasts, presents, and possible futures that are incompatible and outside the narratives of official history that form the conditions of shared memory. The lived experience of Emiko offers new spatial and perceptual situations that challenge the notion of a single Japanese identity as the fixed and immutable point of reference of all things Japanese. At the heart of film lies scepticism of the dominant post-war belief in the resurrection of democracy and freedom in Japan. The history of post-war recovery as experienced by Emiko is not about the advancements made by democratisation and the genesis of a new, mature Japanese species-being that has overcome all militaristic tendencies, but about how to make the best of given circumstances.

The historical question that drives the first two-thirds of *History of Post-War Japan as Told by a Bar Hostess* is: What have we Japanese become when we live in a world in which all principles have been shattered by defeat and the consequent "Americanisation" of Japan? Emiko's life-story stands in for the transformations in Japanese character and sociability during post-war recovery and growth where "success" in life was configured in terms of survival. Emiko was a proprietor of a bar that catered for American service men. Her life was based on calculations and trade-offs with exclusive reference to the means/ends of making money. Her success depended on her coldness to others. This trait in her personality and those around her was brilliantly revealed in the opening sequences of the documentary where Emiko and her mother, Etsuko, are shot speaking on the phone with Imamura's production team negotiating the monetary terms of her daughter's involvement in the film (Standish 2011, p. 127).

In terms of the collective experience, *History of Post-War Japan as Told by a Bar Hostess* tells of a post-war Japan doubly colonised by the adaptation of the pre-war emperor system to parliamentary ideology in the name of democracy and by the market forces unleashed and nurtured by the American occupation and subsequent patronage. These two strands of history are captured in the news footage that flickers on a screen behind Emiko and her personal narrative about how she came to money. The newsreels chronicle the marriage of the crown prince to a commoner (albeit a commoner whose father is a very rich industrialist), and the omnipresent, bone-shattering state violence that erupted in the open streets targeting mass democratic movements calling for an end to U.S. occupation. Emiko talks about her loves, losses, and her ability to survive based on her wits and ability to exploit others. On the personal level, the film offers a diagnosis of the transformation in the outer and inner life of the Japanese character due to the changes of orientation in life imposed by the U.S. guided post-war economic recovery. Emiko stands for a post-war individualism: a product of a market-driven economy and society that reduced all forms of life to units of equivalence and exchange. In her personal relations with men, Emiko offers money for personal qualities such as affection and sex. She supports her lovers by giving them money and work in return for sex.[5]

---

[5] *History of Post-War Japan as Told by a Bar Hostess* in many ways echoes the findings of an early diagnostician of urban life, Georg Simmel. Emiko's personal experience reveals a powerful internal contradiction that defines her everyday life, namely, how money robs things of their innate value and distinction by making everything interchangeable with money (Simmel 1990, p. 391).

4. A People Yet to Be Named

History of Post-War Japan as Told by a Bar Hostess seeks to show the force of the proliferating new cultural forms riding the wave of rapid economic growth. In official versions of history, people such as Emiko do not exist. In conception and praxis, Emiko occupies a space outside of history: she is neither a People nor a historical Subject. She has no identity. She and her like are insignificant. They are the flotsam and jetsam of society: a declassé mishmash of criminal marginals with a dubious origin and an unsavory means of subsistence. The events and details that make up her life are never subsumed into the official version of the history of Japan.

For Imamura, Emiko represents the eruption of heterogeneity and difference. Her marginal social space—as a *Burakumin*,[6] black marketer, prostitute, brothel madam, and bar hostess to American navy personnel based in Japan during the Vietnam War—represented an everyday organised around gratification, excess and expenditure that escaped the norms and cultural values espoused by the voices of post-war authority and rapid economic growth. The details of Emiko's life and her obscure localism from mainstream Japan allowed Imamura to deliberately use existing imagery to challenge the cherished beliefs that constitute post-war Japanese identity and present an alternative version of the type of individual post-war Japanese culture was cultivating. He did this by being both dependent and dismissive of mainstream post-war culture. Using a technique of doubling, through the manipulation of sound and image, Imamura placed the official history encapsulated in newsreel footage on top of the clandestine details of Emiko's life in such a way as to allow the lower layer to reveal itself through the imposed stratum. Imamura lets Emiko speak over the newsreel images that fill the screen. The disjuncture between the content and details of Emiko's spoken word and the newsreel visuals of "significant" events that define post-war Japan creates a jarring disjuncture. While the newsreel montage shows the major political disturbances that frame the evolution of post-war Japan—the Matsukawa incident (1949),[7] the May Day Incident (1952),[8] Sunagawa anti-base protests (1956)[9]—Emiko recollects her life as a child during the war, her co-habitation with a policeman during her late teen years, her forays in adultery, and selling contraband beef on the black market. The dissonance between the newsreel visual image and Emiko's oral narrative creates a moment of non-synchronicity: sequences of time fork or bifurcate into different pasts and presents. Emiko's "point-of-view" narration challenges and defies the "objective" view-point and facts of the newsreels projected on the screen behind her. The history revealed by the news footage, the chain of action and consequence that represents the political and cultural history of post-war Japan is doubled with the forces that shape and constitute the details of Emiko's life. This technique of doubling gives

---

[6] *Burakumin* are Japan's largest minority group. The so called *Brakumin* do not differ from the "mainstream" Japanese population ethnically or linguistically. The discrimination that they face is a deeply ingrained, based on ambiguous concepts of genealogy and pollution coupled with institutionalized practices of ostracization.

[7] On 17 August, 1949, three crewmen of a freight train were killed when a train derailed and overturned near the village of Matsukawa in Fukushima prefecture on the Tohoku Line. Twenty-one Japan National Railway [JNR] workers, including union leaders who had already been fired, were arrested and imprisoned on the suspicion of sabotage. Many of the arrested JNR workers were members of the fledgling Japanese Communist Party. In the narrative of the nation, the "Matsukawa Incident" was the first instance of violent opposition to the anti-communist measures of the U.S. Occupation, and the earliest flashpoint of an ongoing public struggle by leftist to democratize Japan.

[8] On the 1 May, 1952, two people were killed and over 1400 injured after 6000 demonstrators shouting "Yankee go Home!" and demanding a new government entered the Imperial Park and clashed with armed police. 1232 people were arrested. It took the Tokyo district court 17 years and nine months to pass verdict. Of the 219 people arraigned who did not plead guilty or partially guilty, 110 were acquitted, 93 were found guilty and either fined or imprisoned, and 16 died before a final verdict was reached.

[9] In 1955, protests erupted over the plans to extend the main runway of the American military airbase in Tachikawa through the heart of the nearby village of Sunagawa. The protests against the extension of the base were multilayered. At the time, Tachikawa was renowned as the city of black markets and drugs and, in the early 1950s, it was reportedly home to 5000 sex workers who worked in the bars and cabarets surrounding the base. Toxic runoff from the operations of the air base had also badly contaminated the local water supply. In October 1956, farmers, trade unionists and students staging a sit-in to prevent surveying of the land clashed with police, giving rise to an estimated 1000 casualties (Wright 2015).

Imamura the cinematic grammar to draw attention to heterogeneity of a present where time forks and diverges into incompatible worlds.

The schism between Emiko's narrative and the visual images of the newsreel turns the medium of the documentary itself into an aspect of the problem history, memory and point of view. Without a fixed and immutable point of common reference, history and memory are struck by uncertainty and begin to lose their moorings (Harootunian 2019, pp. 2–6).

History of Post-War Japan as Told by a Bar Hostess directly intervenes in the national narrative of post-war Japan. The documentary attacks two conceits: first, the tacit assumption that national history speaks for all and has the power to fit the multiplicity of experience into a single category, and second, that subjectivity is a fixed and secure property spread evenly and homogeneously across historical time. The documentary also issues a caution. Post-war consensus was produced by the telling of founding narratives about society, culture and modes of life via the determined fixed viewpoint of a homogenising nation-state (Igarashi 2000).

The documentary also offers a realization of the world Emiko inhabits. The montage at the beginning of the film comprises the following sequence of shots: Imamura on the phone talking money in order for Emiko to appear in the film; Emiko's mother in intense negotiation with Imamura's lawyer over Emiko's remuneration for appearing in the film; a speeding train; the killing of cattle at an abattoir; and a Vietnamese freedom fighter. The montage brilliantly reveals the forces that surround the actual occurrence of Emiko becoming the person she is today: her love of money, a love also shared by her mother, her birth in a *Burakumin* household, her migration to Yokohama to pursue her desire for fun and money, and her success as a bar owner catering to the wants of American navy personnel fighting a war in Vietnam. *History of Post-War Japan as Told by a Bar Hostess* reveals how Emiko is nothing more than the sum of her actions and the ensemble of relations that make up these undertakings.

5. The Never-Ending Pacific War

However, there was an element of Emiko's life that Imamura was very critical of: her direct involvement in the Vietnam War. The context for Imamura's scorn is his investment in the politics of *Beheiren*—the Citizens' League for Peace in Vietnam (*Betonamu Ni Heiwa O! Shimin Rengo*)—which also informed the series of documentaries he made in 1971 for Tokyo Channel 12 on Japanese soldiers who chose not to return home (Mihalopoulos 2018).[10] Imamura's challenge to national history and Japanese remembrance of the Pacific War, along with his spare, handheld camera and low production cost approach to documentary making, inspired other Japanese film makers to embark on similar projects most notably Hara Kazuo's *The Emperor's Naked Army Marches On* (*Yukiyukite Shingun*, 1987) and Matsubayashi Yoju's *Flowers and Troops* (*Hana to Heitai*, 2009).

Imamura situated the documentaries firmly within the politics of *Beheiren* for a Japanese television audience. The broad historical context that framed the documentaries was: (i) Japanese government involvement in the Vietnam War; and (ii) public concern that Japan's post-war affluence was founded on tacit collaboration by Japanese citizens with American Cold War conflicts in Asia. From February 1965, when the United States began Operation Rolling Thunder, the U.S. military was dependent on the unrestricted use of the 148 U.S. bases across the Japanese archipelago for their sustained bombing campaign against North Vietnam. Most of the 400,000 tons of monthly supplies needed to sustain the U.S. military in Vietnam also passed through the U.S. bases stationed at Yokosuka, Sasebo and Naha (Havens 1987, pp. 85–87). Fiscally, the Vietnam War was a windfall for the Japanese economy. Japanese manufacturers supplied commodity goods to the Allied forces and the equipment and materials for the U.S. war effort in Vietnam. Between the years of 1965 to 1968, Japanese exports to Southeast Asia increased 18% annually. An estimated one billion American dollars per year entered the Japanese

---

[10] *In Search of the Unreturned Soldiers in Malaysia* (*Mikikan-hei o otte: Marei-hen*, 1971) and *In Search of the Unreturned Soldiers in Thailand* (*Mikikan-hei o otte: Tai-hen*, 1971).

economy because of the Vietnam War from 1966 to 1971. By 1970, Japan had surpassed the United States as the leading trading power in Southeast Asia (Halliday and McCormack 1973, pp. 54–56).

Many Japanese citizens saw their government's willingness to allow Japan to be used as a base for U.S. war-making in Vietnam as unlawful. From mid-1967 to 1970, 18.7 million Japanese took to the streets to protest U.S. bombing raids originating in Japan. Such acts were seen as a direct contravention of Japan's 1947 post-war constitution and violating the sovereign will of the Japanese people who had renounced the right to war (Havens 1987, p. 133; de Bary et al. 2005, pp. 1029–36).

Beheiren activists drew attention to the fact that by allowing the U.S. to use its bases in Japan to bomb Vietnam, every Japanese going about their daily life was complicit in supporting the U.S. military. Oda Makoto and Tsurumi Yoshiyuki, the co-founders of *Beheiren*, claimed that under the Japan–U.S. Security Treaty, Japan was a client state of the United States. They pointed to the fact that the supply of special procurements for the Vietnam war by corporate Japan was a permanent and institutionalized feature of the Japanese economy and made possible the recent affluence enjoyed by most Japanese (Avenell 2010, p. 143). *Beheiren* spokespeople urged Japanese citizens to critically address their role in the historical circumstances that saw Japan once more perpetrating aggression against an Asian nation—this time by logistically supporting the U.S. military in Vietnam (Avenell 2010, p. 146).

The last section of *History of Post-War Japan as Told by a Bar Hostess* is uneven. A major reason is that the focus of the documentary moves from a diagnosis of what Japan is becoming to an exposé on the workings of power framed by the politics of the *Beheiren* movement. Following the cues of *Beheiren* activists, Imamura incorporated a victim–aggressor dynamic in his documentary based on the critique that for Japan to find peace with their Asian neighbors, individual Japanese needed to resist the state locked into supporting the U.S. war in Southeast Asia. Otherwise they would remain victims of the state while simultaneously the victimizers of fellow Asians (Avenell 2010, pp. 106–47). In *History of Post-War Japan as Told by a Bar Hostess*, Imamura attempts to illuminate how politics and culture were inseparable by showing how deeply the victim–aggressor dynamic was embedded in Japanese identity. Imamura's research discovered that one of Emiko's favorite American patrons was an officer on *USS Puelbo*, an unmarked U.S. Naval intelligence vessel captured at gunpoint by North Korean forces for spying on 23 January 1968. Imamura confront Emiko with this information along with photos of atrocities committed by U.S. forces in the Vietnam, while raising the possibility that the U.S. military personnel that frequented her bar were directly or indirectly responsible for the shattered bodies found in the photos. Aggressively pushing images from the conflict in front of her, Imamura badgers Emiko for her thoughts about her clientele being engaged in a war against other Asians. Emiko, however, refuses to see any linkage between her work, her clientele, and the wars in Asia. She adamantly refutes such a connection. Her belief lay in the confidence that her American military clients were gentlemen. They could not possibly be involved in such nasty business.

In the end, *History of Post-War Japan as Told by a Bar Hostess* proves to be a messy, uneven collision between history and memory, experience and the everyday. It would seem that when interrogated, any recollection—personal or collective, written or oral—reveals an investment in symbols, images and representations that constitute a specific subjectivity. The value Emiko attached to her self-image was greatly affected by the political and economic power that impinged on the relations she had with others. However, at the same time, the details of Emiko's everyday revealed the workings of power that effectively tied Japan's prosperity to the United States' global strategic policy aimed at containing communism via military involvement in East and Southeast Asia.

6. Conclusions

For *History of Post-War Japan as Told by a Bar Hostess*, Imamura directed the camera to focus on the new forms of subjectivity that were at work in the present, the variable creations that arose out of the processes of individuation which were brought to bear upon the people who left the countryside to fill the cities of post-war Japan. The camera recorded how the introduction of American-style democracy did not herald unprecedented freedom for the Japanese people, but rather initiated a radical change in personality. The camera also revealed that the elements of Emiko's personality that seemed private and accidental—greed, violence and emotional suffering—had a wider collective significance. They pointed to the double-colonization of Japan by the adaptation of the pre-war emperor system to parliamentary ideology in the name of democracy, and by the new market forces unleashed and nurtured by American occupation.

The camera's recognition of the lived experience of people such as Emiko challenged the notion of a single Japanese identity as the fixed and immutable point of reference of all things Japanese. For Emiko, post-war Japan was a world full of new possibilities and expectations far removed from governmental programs aimed at cultivating bodies singularly dedicated to work and self-sacrifice. Emiko stood for a spontaneous post-war individualism: a product of a market-driven economy and society that reduced all forms of life to units of equivalence and exchange.

The power of Imamura's documentary lay in the way the camera captured the positive and inventive process of life that occurred from the affirmation and embrace, rather than the rejection and avoidance of, chance events. He was drawn by the vitality, energy, spontaneity, and resourcefulness in which the game of chance was played, and the exhilarating feeling of freedom that accompanied it. In *History of Post-War Japan as Told by a Bar Hostess*, Imamura's cinematic practice was the ethics of *amor fati*—the love of what is. He did not hone his camera in search for higher standards of truth or morality from which to order and judge post-war Japanese culture, but to locate the unexamined forces that frame action and belief in the 'now' of present.

Funding: This research received no external funding.

Acknowledgments: I am indebted to the generous feedback and guidance of Mark R. Plaice and Marcos Centeno Martín on earlier drafts of this article. I would also like to thank the astute and considerate feedback of the two anonymous referees, which helped to improve this article considerably.

Conflicts of Interest: The author declares no conflict of interest.

Filmography

Pigs and Battleships (*Buta to Gunkan*). 1961. Dir. Imamura Shōhei.
The Insect Woman (*Nippon Konchūki*). 1963. Dir. Imamura Shōhei.
The Pornographers (*"Erogotoshitachi" yori Jinruigaku Nyūmon*). 1966. Dir. Imamura Shōhei.
A Man Vanishes (*Ningen Jōhatsu*). 1967. Dir. Imamura Shōhei.
History of Post-War Japan as Told by a Bar Hostess (*Nippon Sengoshi—Madamu Onboro no Seikatsu*). 1970. Dir. Imamura Shōhei.
In Search of the Unreturned Soldiers in Malaysia (*Mikikan-hei o otte: Marei-hen*). 1971. Dir. Imamura Shōhei.
In Search of the Unreturned Soldiers in Thailand (*Mikikan-hei o otte: Tai-hen*). 1971. Dir. Imamura Shōhei.
The Emperor's Naked Army Marches On (*Yukiyukite Shingun*). 1987. Dir. Hara Kazuo.
Flowers and Troops (*Hana to Heitai*). 2009. Dir. Matsubayashi Yoju.

References

Avenell, Simon. 2010. *Minding Japanese Citizens: Civil Society and the Mythology of the Shimin in Postwar Japan*. Berkeley: University of California Press.
Centeno Martín, Marcos. 2018a. The limits of fiction: politics and absent scenes in Susumu Hani's Bad Boys (*Furyō Shōnen*, 1960). A film re-reading through its script. *Journal of Japanese and Korean Cinema* 10: 1–15. [CrossRef]
Centeno Martín, Marcos. 2018b. Method Directors. Susumu Hani and Yasujirō Ozu: A Comparative Approach across Paradigms. In *Yasujirō Ozu und Die Ästhetik Seiner Zeit*. Edited by Andreas Becker. Marburg: Büchner-Verlag, pp. 125–52.
Centeno Martín, Marcos. 2019. Postwar Narratives and the Avant-garde Documentary: *Tokyo 1958* and *Furyō Shōnen*. In *Persistently Postwar: Media and the Politics of Memory in Japan*. Edited by Blai Guarné, Artur Lozano-Méndez and Dolores P. Martinez. New York: Berghahn Books, pp. 41–62.

de Bary, Wm. Theodore, Carol Gluck, and Arthur L. Tiedemann. 2005. *Sources of Japanese Tradition-Volume 2*, 2nd ed. New York: Columbia University Press, pp. 1029–36.

Halliday, Jon, and Gavan McCormack. 1973. *Japanese Imperialism Today: Co-Prosperity in Greater East Asia*. New York and London: Monthly Review Press.

Harootunian, Harry. 2019. *Uneven Moments: Reflections on Japan's Modern History*. New York: Columbia University Press.

Havens, Thomas R. H. 1987. *Fire Across the Sea: The Vietnam War and Japan, 1965–1975*. Princeton: Princeton University Press.

Igarashi, Yoshikuni. 2000. *Bodies of Memory Narratives of War in Postwar Japanese Culture, 1945–1970*. Princeton: Princeton University Press.

Imamura, Shōhei. 2001. *Toru: Kannu kara Yamiichi e*. Tokyo: Kōsakusha.

Imamura, Shōhei. 2004. *Eigawa Kyoki no Tabi de Aru: Watakushi no Rirekisho*. Tokyo: Nihon Keizai Shinbunsha.

Katori, Shunsuke. 2004. *Imamura Shōhei Densetsu*. Tokyo: Kawade Shobō Shinsa.

Kramm, Robert. 2017. *Sanitized Sex: Regulating Prostitution, Venereal Disease, and Intimacy in Occupied Japan, 1945–1952*. Oakland: University of California Press.

Nakata, Toichi. 1997. Shohei Imamura Interview. In *Shohei Imamura*. Edited by James Quandt. Toronto: Toronto International Film Festival Group, pp. 107–24.

Simmel, Georg. 1990. *The Philosophy of Money*. London: Routledge. First published 1900.

Standish, Isolde. 2011. *Politics, Porn and Protest: Japanese Avant-Garde Cinema in the 1960s and 1970s*. New York: Continuum International Publishing Group.

Tessier, Max. 1997. Shohei Imamura Interview. In *Shohei Imamura*. Edited by James Quandt. Toronto: Toronto International Film Festival Group, pp. 57–67.

Wright, Dustin. 2015. 'Sunagawa Struggle' ignited anti-U.S. base resistance across Japan. *Japan Times*. May 3. Available online: https://www.japantimes.co.jp/community/2015/05/03/issues/sunagawa-struggle-ignited-anti-u-s-base-resistance-across-japan/ (accessed on 18 March 2019).

Imamura, Shōhei. 2017. Betwixt fiction and documentary. Translated by Bill Mihalopoulos. *Asian Cinema* 28: 101–5.

Mihalopoulos, Bill. 2018. The never-ending Pacific War: Imamura Shōhei and the ruse of memory. *Japan Forum*, 1–19. [CrossRef]

© 2019 by the author. Licensee MDPI, Basel, Switzerland. This article is an open access article distributed under the terms and conditions of the Creative Commons Attribution (CC BY) license (http://creativecommons.org/licenses/by/4.0/).

Article

Blurred Boundaries: Ethnofiction and Its Impact on Postwar Japanese Cinema

Jennifer Coates

Sainsbury Institute for the Study of Japanese Arts and Cultures, University of East Anglia,
Norwich NR14DH, UK; j.coates@sainsbury-institute.org

Received: 24 December 2018; Accepted: 31 January 2019; Published: 2 February 2019

Abstract: This article explores the use of ethnofiction, a technique emerging from the field of visual anthropology, which blends documentary and fiction filmmaking for ethnographic purposes. From Imamura Shōhei's *A Man Vanishes* (*Ningen jōhatsu*, 1967) to Hou Hsiao Hsien's *Cafe Lumieré* (*Kōhi jikō*, 2003), Japanese cinema, including Japan-set and Japan-associated cinema, has employed ethnofiction filmmaking techniques to alternately exploit and circumvent the structural barriers to filmmaking found in everyday life. Yet the dominant understanding in Japanese visual ethnography positions ethnofiction as an imported genre, reaching Japan through Jean Rouch and French cinema-verité. Blending visual analysis of Imamura and Hou's ethnofiction films with an auto-ethnographic account of my own experience of four years of visual anthropology in Kansai, I interrogate the organizational barriers constructed around geographical perception and genre definition to argue for ethnofiction as a filmmaking technique that simultaneously emerged in French cinema-verité and Japanese feature filmmaking of the 1960s. Blurring the boundaries between Japanese, French, and East Asian co-production films, and between documentary and fiction genres, allows us to understand ethnofiction as a truly global innovation, with certain regional specificities.

Keywords: ethnofiction; Japan; documentary; non-fiction; dramatization

1. Introduction

Scholarship on global cinemas is scarred by a number of organizational barriers. One of the most detrimental to a holistic understanding of the field may be the division of film texts along national lines, and by genre. In practice, such divisions are often meaningless. A significant number of filmmakers innovate across national boundaries in relation to setting, funding, casting, and exhibition, while genre-defying film texts have tested scholarly definition since the beginning of Film Studies. Certain key trends in Japanese feature filmmaking clearly illustrate the value of taking a more inclusive approach to understanding genre development, thematic trends, and technical innovation. This article explores Japanese cinema's use of ethnofiction, a technique associated with visual anthropology that blends documentary and fiction filmmaking for ethnographic purposes. From Imamura Shōhei's *A Man Vanishes* (*Ningen jōhatsu*, 1967) to Hou Hsiao Hsien's *Cafe Lumieré* (*Kōhi jikō*, 2003), postwar Japanese feature films, including Japan-set and Japan-associated films, have employed ethnofiction filmmaking techniques to explore the human condition, alternately exploiting and circumventing the structural barriers to filmmaking that are presented by the physical constraints of bringing a camera into everyday lives and spaces. Feature films such as Imamura and Hou's discussed below draw from spontaneously occurring events in the lives of everyday people, and from the environments in which these people live, to create semi-documentary or partly fictionalized stories. The close relation that these stories bear to a lived reality or perceived truth then allows the filmmaker to make claims about their depiction of an imagined human condition.

As the first part of this article demonstrates, fictionalized elements including staging, re-enactment, the use of props, and scripted scenes and dialogue, have been a part of the broader genre of documentary film in Japan since the beginnings of film itself. Yet in the field of anthropology, the dominant understanding in Japanese visual ethnography positions ethnofiction as an imported genre, arriving in Japan in the late 1950s through the work of Jean Rouch and French *cinema verité*. Blending analysis of Imamura and Hou's ethnofiction films with an auto-ethnographic account of my own experience of four years of visual anthropology work in Kansai, I interrogate the organizational barriers constructed around geographical and genre definitions to argue for ethnofiction as a filmmaking technique that simultaneously developed in French *cinema verité* and Japanese feature filmmaking of the 1950s, 1960s, and 1970s, continuing to influence contemporary filmmaking in East Asia today. While it is not possible within the limits of this essay to deal with the development of ethnofiction techniques in commercial filmmaking through the 1980s and 1990s, I hope these two examples from either end of the postwar ethnofiction trend demonstrate how the technique became more mainstream, both across genres and across East Asia more broadly. Blurring the boundaries between Japanese, French, and East Asian filmmaking, and between documentary and fiction genres, allows us to understand ethnofiction as a truly global innovation, with certain regional specificities.

There are numerous definitions of ethnofiction (also written ethno-fiction), but for the purposes of this article I will use the definition adopted by the ethnofiction study group I joined at The National Museum of Ethnography in Osaka, Japan. As the last section of this article describes, the study group was largely comprised of Japanese practice-based researchers in the field of anthropology, working in fieldsites other than Japan. During the making of my own documentary film on memories of postwar cinema in Japan (Coates 2018), I screened several of Imamura's films for the group, initiating an on-going discussion about the history of ethnofiction filmmaking in Japan outside the specific scholarly field of anthropology.

Group members worked from Johannes Sjöberg's outline of ethnofiction as a genre in which "the camera simply follows the subjects' improvisations of their own, and others', lived experiences" (Sjöberg 2008, p. 229). Sjöberg identifies ethnofiction as emerging in 1950s France in the work of director Jean Rouch, and the term as a coinage of the film critics of the era (Sjöberg 2008, p. 229). Paul Stoller describes Rouch's method as follows:

> It is not a documentary that attempts to capture an observed reality. By the same token it is not a melodrama the filmmakers dreamed up to titillate our emotions ... These films are stories based on laboriously researched and carefully analysed ethnography. In this way Rouch uses creative licence to "capture" the texture of an event, the ethos of lived experience (Stoller 1992, p. 143).

While I am arguing here for the development of ethnofiction filmmaking as multi-local and simultaneous, as well as for more scholarly blurring of the boundaries between documentary and feature film, the "varying degrees of commitment to ethnographic research that was represented through fiction" in Rouch's work (Sjöberg 2008, p. 230) provides a working definition of the term ethnofiction for the discussion that follows. However, I do not wish to imply that any director, auteur, or even anthropologist may be credited with independently developing something like a 'true' ethnofiction. Given the formal and informal media flows of the 1950s and 1960s, including amateur film club screenings and study group screenings conducted in the Japanese film studio workplaces which are difficult to trace, it is not possible to argue with any certainty that the filmmakers discussed below were not influenced by one another's films and methods. Instead, I wish to demonstrate how ethnofiction is presented in filmmakers' own discourse as a commonsense technique for developing and communicating stories about everyday life. The final paragraphs contrast this approach to ethnofiction-like techniques with the more canonical account of ethnofiction in visual anthropology in Japan today.

2. Results

2.1. Early Ethnofictions and the Problem of Terminology

The question of language is crucial to understanding the emergence and development of techniques such as ethnofiction in two broad aspects—definition and translation. When we speak across disciplinary boundaries and language barriers, we are often using different words to talk about the same phenomenon, or conversely, using shared terms to discuss very different concepts. Tracing the emergence and development of ethnofiction through Japanese cinema history makes clear the confusions, misunderstandings, and miscommunications that can occur when we try to discuss visual techniques in multiple languages, and from different academic fields or perspectives.

Focusing first on the question of definition, it is clear that this problem is not unique to ethnofiction filmmaking. In fact, the multiple origin stories of filmmaking and cinema exhibition in Japan revolve around the question of our definition of "cinema". Closely following the arrival of Thomas Edison's Kinetoscope in Kobe in November 1896, and the Vitascope in 1897, the Lumière brothers' Cinematograph was brought to Japan by businessman Inabata Katsutarō. While Edison's technology was exhibited in the style of an interactive museum object, with viewers approaching the Kinetoscope one by one to look through the lens, Inabata hosted the first open commercial film screening at the Nanchi Enbujo Theatre in Osaka from 15 February 1897 after a two-week trial screening in Kyoto from 20 January 1987. The commercial Kyoto screening later opened to the public in March 1897. Kobe, Kyoto, and Osaka city governments have all erected plaques claiming their respective sites as the birthplace of cinema in Japan. Was Kobe's technological exhibition, Kyoto's public theatre-style screening, or Osaka's commercial fee-paying event the first instance of cinema in Japan? It all depends on your definition of "cinema".

In addition to bringing the Lumières' apparatus to Japan, Inabata was also influential in bringing the first images of Japanese everyday life to global film audiences, though the version he was involved in creating was perhaps closer to ethnofiction than classical documentary. Francois-Constant Girel, a Lumière cameraman who travelled to Japan with Inabata, was encouraged by his host to film the elite life of the Inabata family, showing members at dinner and engaging in domestic and social activities (Toki and Mizoguchi 1993). These images showed a marked contrast to the orientalist exotica that the Lumière cameramen recorded in Japan, such as *The Ainu of Ezo* (*Les Ainu a yeso*, 1897), *Japanese Fencing* (*Escrime au sabre japonaise*, 1897), *Japanese Actors* (*Auteurs japonais*, 1898), and *Geisha Riding in Rickshaws* (*Geishas en jinrikisha*, 1898). Inabata appeared determined to ensure that the cameramen returned to Europe with recordings of Japanese life that challenged any idea of Japan as quaint, backwards, or uncivilized.

The influence of Inabata's engineered representations of everyday life in Japan is clear in these first cinematic recordings, blurring documentary and scripted re-presentation. These early films can be understood as ethnographic in their intention, attempting to show how everyday people were living in Japan to audiences on the other side of the world. At the same time, they already contained fictionalized elements of a propagandistic nature. Non-Japanese cameramen emphasized difference, exoticizing the representation of Japan in order to increase the attractiveness of their footage for viewers in Europe. Wealthy and worldly participants such as Inabata instead insisted on an equally fictionalized representation of Japanese people as models of civilization and Westernized deportment, demonstrating the use of Anglo-European customs, furnishings, fashions, and utensils in early twentieth century Japan.

This early engineering of the nation's public image was quick to catch on in Japanese filmmaking. News films visualized the exciting developments of the early twentieth century for domestic audiences, focusing on glorified stories such as Japan's success in the Russo-Japanese war of 1904. Hiroshi Komatsu identifies a degree of fictionalization at this early stage of news reporting, distinguishing constructed news films (*kōseisareta nyūsu eiga*) from fake news films (*nisei nyūsu eiga*) (Komatsu 1994). Re-enactments, stage sets, and props including miniature models were used in constructed news films based on real events, often mixed with reportage from scenes of battle. Fake news films showed re-enactments of events filmed outdoors, including imagined dramatic death scenes. While these "fake documentaries" (Komatsu 1994) can be attributed to the lack of available documentary footage of the war, the practice of fictionalizing and re-staging events continued even after the 1905 ratification of the Treaty of Portsmouth that ended the war.

It is important to note that these early war films, like those to follow in the 1930s and 1940s, no longer followed the ethnographic imperatives of the earliest film recordings. Propagandistic goals supported increasing fictionalization, as censors and filmmakers strove to represent the Japanese military effort favorably. Before the strict censorship of the 1930s however, the end of the Russo-Japanese war saw a decline in the production of war films, documentary or otherwise. As cinema theatre content moved on from war films to "slapstick, comedy, tragedy, fairy tale, and historical dramas" (Anonymous 1910, p. 21, trans. Gerow 1994), little distinction was made between observational recordings of spontaneous occurrences, and scripted, enacted, or created content. Overall, Komatsu argues, writers on film culture of the early 1900s appeared "not [to] possess a cinematic point of view presupposing the concept of fiction; accordingly, the idea of nonfiction does not exist for him [sic] either" (Komatsu 1994). As such, we can understand the prewar and interwar news and documentary films featuring fictionalized elements as a kind of early ethnofiction, with a strong connection to the more fully developed ethnofiction films of the postwar period.

The translation of key terms and genre nomenclature further disrupted the possibility of clearly defining fiction from documentary film. As Hikari Hori notes, the role of translator and scenario writer Atsugi Taka was crucial here. Atsugi translated Paul Rotha's 1935 *Documentary Film*, which was published in Japan in 1938 under the title *Bunka eiga ron*. Hori translates the title as "Treatise on Culture Film" in order to emphasize the difference between "documentary" and "culture film" as the genres are understood today (Hori 2018, p. 117). The Kyoto-based publisher Daiichi geibun sha recommended that the title should include the term *bunka eiga*, on the grounds that it was "one of the better-known terms for nonfiction films in Japan" (Hori 2018, p. 117). Yet Atsugi also used the word *dokyumentari* (a phonetic transcription of "documentary") throughout the translated text, and her translation spread the term *dokyumentari* widely across Japan (Hori 2018, p. 117).

Rotha himself was not against "creative dramatization of actuality" in documentary film (Hori 2018, p. 131), intentionally conflating the genres of documentary and dramatic films and promoting the use of fictionalized and re-staged episodes in documentary filmmaking (Higson 1995, p. 204). The use of amateur actors "was practiced as part of Rotha's reception" (Hori 2018, p. 142), though the method has previously been understood in Japan as promoted by Soviet directors such as Vsevolod Pudovkin and Sergei Eisenstein. Yet the degree to which fictionalization was considered acceptable was much debated. Critic Iwasaki Akira denounced Kamei Fumio's *Fighting Soldiers* (*Tatakau heitai*, 1939) as exemplifying the trend for abusing "dramatization" by using acting too freely (Hori 2018, p. 131). Iwasaki argued that the term "dramatization" had become almost a "slogan" in "the new school of culture film" (Hori 2018, p. 131). Yet he did not advocate abandoning the practice entirely. Instead, he argued that the purpose of dramatization should be to "introduce the voices of people and social issues" (Hori 2018, p. 132). Iwasaki's focus on the use of dramatization to foreground the voices of everyday people and their concerns suggest the ethnographic imperative. Yet the political mood of the moment saw this goal superseded by the use value of cinema as a tool of political persuasion. Iwasaki recommended that culture film become more "argumentative" (*shuchōsei*), moving on from simply recording a subject to persuading the audience of a political objective as a kind "argument film" (*giron eiga*) or "thought film" (*shisō eiga*) (Hori 2018, p. 132).

While recognizing the practice of dramatization and the use of actors as widespread in the documentary and culture films of the 1930s, Iwasaki located a second stage of fictionalization in the editing of drama and documentary genres alike. "Living actuality fast becomes artistic reality when it is selected, edited, and formed, and since this is when truth appears, documentary cinema is also no different from the fiction of theatrical film" (Iwasaki quoted in Sugiyama 1990, p. 179, trans.

Nornes 2003, p. 101). The wartime Japanese government came to similar conclusions in 1939 on the passing of the Film Law, which privileged the screening of documentary film over fiction film, and at the same time drew a wide marker around the definition of documentary. In 1939, the Education Ministry recognized 985 documentary films, while registered documentary films totaled 4460 by 1940 (Naimushō keihōkyoku 1941, p. 103; quoted in Kasza 1993, p. 240). Markus Nornes argues that, "by the end of the 1930s it would be more appropriate to conceptualize fiction and nonfiction as two overlapping spheres with constant flux between them" (Nornes 2003, p. 95). We can see a similar attitude in the more fully developed ethnofiction films of the postwar.

While this history lays the ground for the development of ethnofiction filmmaking in the postwar era, it is important to note that fictionalization in the service of propaganda is of a different order to the research-based and participant-led fictionalizations of filmmakers such as Rouch and Imamura in the 1950s and 1960s. The 1930s "blurring of the boundary between fiction and documentary film" (Nornes 2003, p. 97) developed into a second era of wartime filmmaking that blended documentary recordings of actual events into fictional narrative structures. Narrative fiction films such as *Dawn of Freedom* (*Ano hata o ute*, Abe Yutaka and Geraldo de Leon, 1944) included recordings of real events taken at the time of their occurrence, as well as footage of people re-enacting recent events from their own experience, for example, American prisoners of war re-enacting their own defeat and surrender. Such techniques fell out of favor after the war, perhaps tainted for audiences by memories of wartime propaganda. Occupation era (1945–1952) censorship scrutinized films for references to the war and the Occupation itself, restricting the exhibition of spontaneously recorded footage of real-life events, as the representation of Occupation personnel, English language signage, black market dealing, and other everyday occurrences were banned.

While the early postwar film industry re-focused largely on narrative film, with the exception of Kamei Fumio's ill-fated *Tragedy of Japan* (*Nippon no higeki*, 1947), a return to documentary style filmmaking in the early 1950s included from its beginning an element of ethnofiction or scripted reality. Nornes argues that "the first questioning of postwar realism" began in 1957, when the nature documentary *The White Mountains* (*Shiroi sanmyaku*, 1957) was found to include species from other environments, and even a stuffed bear (Nornes 2002, p. 43). In the late 1950s and early 1960s, documentary filmmaking began to move back towards the *cinema verité* or ethnofiction style of the wartime and pre-war. While Hani Susumu's well-regarded *Children of the Classroom* (*Kyōshitsu no kodomotachi*, 1954) and *Children Who Draw* (*E o kaku kodomotachi*, 1955) observed the largely non-interventionist methods of direct cinema, by *Bad Boys* (*Furyō shōnen*, 1961) the director was employing the residents of a home for delinquent youths to play characters based on themselves, re-enacting experiences told to the filmmaker.

Ethnofiction, or the use of fictionalized or dramatized elements in the representation of a factual or historical event or situation, significantly predated the 1960s global boom in practice and discussion of the technique. Drawing from Japanese cinema's long blurring of the boundaries between fiction and non-fiction, the next section of this article investigates the work of experimental director Imamura Shōhei, a near contemporary of Jean Rouch. Examining Imamura's first uses of ethnofiction filmmaking techniques, I argue for the development of ethnofiction in Japan as near-simultaneous with its French counterpart, rather than a later import from France, as it is commonly understood in the field of Japanese anthropology. Like Kamei Fumio, who borrowed Erik Barnouw's notion of "parallel developments" to argue that "the genre of documentary film was simultaneously emerging globally" (Hori 2018, p. 130), I am suggesting that ethnofiction developed in parallel in Japan and Europe in the 1950s and 1960s, contextualized by the historical blurring of the boundaries between documentary and fiction film in the first half of the twentieth century in Japan.

2.2. "Between Fiction and Documentary" in Japan: The Ethnofictions of Imamura Shōhei

While Jean Rouch was establishing ethnofiction in France, a new generation of filmmakers were emerging in Japan. Shōchiku studio personnel were keen to connect these young innovators to developments in France, despite the filmmakers' resistance. At Nikkatsu studios, Imamura's first three films were released in quick succession throughout 1958, all classic studio era narrative fiction features. Throughout his career, Imamura became progressively more committed to exploring and representing human nature. The director famously referred to himself as an "anthropologist" asking, "What is a human being? I look for the answer by continuing to make films" (Laprévotte 1997, p. 101). From the 1960s on, Imamura began to weave some of the documentary filmmaking techniques associated with anthropology into his studio films.

For example, *The Insect Woman* (*Nippon konchūki*, 1963) follows the protagonist (Hidari Sachiko) from youth to middle age, depicting a woman who, like an insect, simply exists while life goes on around her. The scenario was influenced by the life story of a living woman, and re-written so that it could be filmed in a "fly on the wall" documentary style (Mihalopoulos 2008, p. 282). Though the protagonist is played by a professional actress, the film style reflects the mood of an ethnofiction film in which "the camera simply follows the subjects' improvisations of their own, and others', lived experiences" (Sjöberg 2008, p. 229). We can think of Hidari's performance under Imamura's direction as a kind of joint improvisation of "others' lived experiences". Stoller defines ethnofiction films as "stories based on laboriously researched and carefully analysed ethnography" (1992, p. 143). While Imamura's use of a living woman's memories doesn't quite constitute laborious research, the mood of *The Insect Woman* certainly echoes the "way Rouch uses creative licence to "capture" the texture of an event, the ethos of lived experience" (Stoller 1992, p. 143), with the "varying degrees of commitment to ethnographic research" found in Rouch's work (Sjöberg 2008, p. 230). When questioned about his research process by interviewer Nakata Toichi, Imamura reflected that, "It may be that some of my fiction films look a bit like documentaries because I base my characters on research into real people" (Imamura trans. Nakata 1997, p. 116). While Imamura was by no means the first or only proponent of ethnofiction filmmaking techniques in postwar Japan, his account of practicing "research into real people" as the basis of narrative development highlights the shift from ethnofiction-like practices in the prewar and wartime eras that focused on recreating historical events, to the postwar use of ethnofiction to explore the human condition in an anthropological manner.

In 1965, Imamura left Nikkatsu to establish Imamura Productions, and his first independent film, *The Pornographers*, made explicit his deepening interest in anthropology and its methods. The title is literally translated as "An Introduction to Anthropology by Pornographers" (*Erogotoshitachi yori jinruigaku nyūmon*, 1966). The plot was adapted from a novel by Nosaka Akiyuki. Yet on recalling this period, Imamura returns to his emphasis on the idea of generating film content directly from human experience.

> For me, the idea for the film lies in its attitude to human beings. In my case, this attitude is one of obsession . . . . In my work, people take centre stage. I am much more interested in mankind than I am in other filmmakers (Imamura 1997, p. 125).

Imamura addresses the gap between fiction and documentary in his films of this era in a chapter titled "Between Fiction and Documentary" (*Fikushon to dokyumentari no awai de*) (Imamura 2001). Recalling the early years of Imamura Productions, he remembers working simultaneously on plans for *A Man Vanishes* while writing the scenario for *The Pornographers*, and drafting *The Profound Desire of the Gods* (*Kamigami no fukaki yokubō*, 1968) (Imamura 2001, p. 234). While *A Man Vanishes* was completed a year before *The Profound Desire of the Gods*, working like this, Imamura recalled feeling that the two films "blur into one" (Imamura 2017, translated by Mihalopoulos 2017, p. 103). While *The Profound Desire of the Gods* is perhaps Imamura's most explicitly ethnographic film, *A Man Vanishes* was similarly developed through a process of researching a particular event, finding and enlisting participants to play versions of themselves, and following their movements with a film crew. Author of *The Pornographers* Nosaka Akiyuki was also invited to co-write *A Man Vanishes*, which wears its provocations openly.

Originally intending to investigate twenty-six cases of disappearances in postwar Japan, in the end, Imamura focused on the remnants of one specific family (Nakata 1997, p. 117). Protagonist Hayakawa Yoshie searches for her husband, who has disappeared, as Imamura's camera follows her less than surreptitiously. Imamura's "research" included lodging himself and his crew in the room next door to Hayakawa for one year, observing her "every bad quality imaginable" (Imamura quoted in Nakata 1997, p. 118). Actor Tsuyuguchi Shigeru played the role of interviewer, and Imamura instructed him to romance Hayakawa to draw out the grasping side of her nature. When Tsuyuguchi expressed dismay at Hayakawa's romantic interest in him, Imamura allowed himself to be captured on camera urging him on, "That's exactly what I want". "So much for cinema verité" critic Donald Richie wrote archly of this scene (Richie 2005, p. 189). In fact, Imamura's open depiction of how he manipulated the real people playing versions of themselves in his film recalls Jean Rouch's own presence in *Chronicle of a Summer* (*Chronique d'un été*, 1961), specifically the scene in which he persuades a reluctant Marcelline Rozenberg to speak about her time in Auchwitz-Birkenau, before encouraging the other participants to turn on her critically.

As in much of his previous work, Imamura remains attracted to the space between documentary and fiction, or truth and fiction, in content as well as form. As *A Man Vanishes* builds to a climax, this becomes the film's central theme. Sitting in a small private dining room of an inn or restaurant, Hayakawa Yoshie confronts her sister Sayo in the presence of Imamura and Tsuyuguchi. "What is truth?" asks Hayakawa, and on cue, the walls of the room fall away, the lights become brighter, and the camera moves out to reveal that the room sits in the centre of a film studio. Imamura answers, "This is fiction". Richie claims that only Imamura knew what was about to happen (Richie 2005, p. 190), but the viewer questions how the protagonists could have been brought to the room without realizing that the structure was not part of a regular restaurant building. Imamura would only say, "I collapsed the set in the end with the intention of revealing the betwixt of drama and documentary" (Imamura 2017, translated by Mihalopoulos 2017, p. 103). Here, we can see an element of fictionalization in the discourse surrounding the film, as well as the film itself, in that certain details are omitted or manipulated to preserve the auteur's persona. Imamura's accounts of both the practical elements of creating such scenes, and the use of documentary and ethnofiction-style techniques more broadly, should be understood in relation to his budding auteur persona, arguably better served by a focus on his innovations than by references to other filmmakers such as Rouch.

In his interview with Nakata, Imamura expressed regret at the deception of Hayakawa during filmmaking. While he stressed that she had "given her explicit consent" to being filmed, she was not aware of the hidden cameras used to film some of the footage (Nakata 1997, p. 118). Hayakawa had taken time off work for the project, and was paid a salary. Imamura asserted that "she approached the project as a job, and she soon took on the role of an actress in front of the camera" (Nakata 1997, p. 118). While he argued that, "She used the cameras as much as we used her as a subject", he acknowledged the "serious ethical questions involved" in the treatment of Hayakawa during filmmaking (Nakata 1997, p. 118). Yet he invoked the ethnographic aspect of the project as an excuse for the risk to which Hayakawa was exposed, arguing that while she did not know what the outcome of the project would be, "we behind the camera didn't know where reality was going to lead us either" (Imamura quoted in Nakata 1997, p. 118).

In the end, Imamura recalled the experience of making *A Man Vanishes* as leading to his realization that "fiction—no matter how close to reality—could never be as truthful as unmediated documentary" (Imamura quoted in Nakata 1997, p. 118). In the early 1970s, he began a series of documentaries for Tokyo Channel 12 television channel dealing with the lives of former Japanese soldiers of the Japanese Imperial Army living in Southeast Asia: *In Search of the Unreturned Soldiers in Malaysia* (*Mikikanhei o otte—Marei-hen*, 1971), *In Search of the Unreturned Soldiers in Thailand* (*Mikikanhei o otte-Tai-hen*, 1971), and *Outlaw Matsu Returns* (*Muhomatsu kokyō ni kaeru*, 1973). The last playfully blends the titles of 1950s fiction film hits *The Rickshaw Man* (*Muhomatsu no issho*, Inagaki Hiroshi, 1958) and *Carmen Comes Home* (*Karumen kyokō ni kaeru*, Kinoshita Keisuke, 1951), suggesting that even these straight documentaries have some connection to the fictionalized worlds of narrative cinema.

Imamura stepped away from narrative fiction filmmaking in the 1970s and 1980s to focus on documentary, and it is in that genre that we can most easily chart the continuing use of ethnofiction-style techniques. For example, the work of Hara Kazuo, particularly *Extreme Private Eros: Love Song 1974* (*Gokushiteki erosu: renka 1974*, 1974) and *The Emperor's Naked Army Marches On* (*Yuki yukite shingun*, 1987) continued the provocative use of the camera modeled by Rouch and Imamura. Markus Nornes has argued for the early to mid-1970s as a break in documentary filmmaking, "with new filmmakers rejecting the dominant conception of documentary practice" and turning to more individualist models rather than collective filmmaking practice (2002, p. 64). At the same time, fiction filmmaking practices were also changing as the studio system contracted due to a decline in audience attendance, which plummeted sharply from a peak in 1958. Critics, scholars, and filmmakers themselves note the decline of the documentary genre in the 1980s, characterizing the period as one of "groping in the darkness", to quote the title of the 1998 Yamagata International Documentary Film Festival (Nornes 2002). As the students of Hara and Suzuki Shiroyasu, another prominent documentary filmmaker of the 1970s, began to produce their own documentary films, Nornes argues that a focus on the individual self continued into the 1990s in such films as Kawase Naomi's *Embracing* (*Nusumarete*, 1992) and he "self-nudes" of Kamioka Fumie, Wada Junko, and Utagawa Keiko (Nornes 2002, pp. 64–65). A number of these early 1990s films are "fake documentaries" (Nornes 2002, p. 65), involving an element of fictionalization reminiscent of ethnofiction. Rather than focusing on ethnofiction in Japanese documentary cinema however, I am interested in how ethnofiction techniques became the commonsense approach to representing everyday life in commercial narrative film, and the divergence between this trend and current discourses on ethnofiction in visual anthropology today. The next sections will return to the commercial fiction film and the field of visual anthropology to consider how ethnofiction is practiced and discussed in the 2000s. As a secondary point, the discussion of Hou Hsiao Hsien's *Café Lumière* below demonstrates the flow of ethnofiction-style techniques not only across the boundary of fiction and documentary genre films, but also geographically, as the Taiwanese director adapted ethnofiction approaches to plan and film a story set in Japan.

2.3. Contemporary Ethnofictions: Café Lumière

Imamura eventually returned to fiction filmmaking, while the ethnofiction-style approach demonstrated in *A Man Vanishes* remains apparent in contemporary films made in Japan today. For example, Hou Hsiao Hsien's *Café Lumière* draws from a number of the ethnofiction techniques discussed above, including ethnographic research as the basis for narrative development, and the use of hidden or surreptitious cameras to film events as they unfold in public spaces. *Café Lumière* was commissioned by Shōchiku studios to commemorate the centenary of Ozu's birth. Hou's film was originally planned as one of three short films to celebrate Ozu's centenary, though the others were never made and Hou's expanded to feature length. The quiet naturalistic narrative follows protagonist Yōko, played by singer Hitoto Yō, as she travels by train through the centre of Tokyo, visiting a bookshop run by her anthropologist friend Hajime to research a book about a Taiwanese composer. Later, we learn that Yōko is pregnant by a Taiwanese partner now living in Thailand, and considering her options for the future.

Hou based Hitoto's character on a Taiwanese friend living in Tokyo and working as a freelance writer. In interviews, Hou has emphasized basing his film characters on real people, and mimicking the mechanics of their everyday lives. The narrative development proceeded alongside character development, based on real events and experiences told to the director.

> ... the main outline of the story came out of conversations with friends and what I knew of their backgrounds. It usually works like this. I'd start with a concept, and develop a structure, and then I'd start exploring some concrete instances (Hou and Liu 2008, p. 181).

Research included scoping the landscape of Tokyo, "trying to figure out which part of Tokyo, and on which railway line, people like my characters usually lived" (Hou and Liu 2008, p. 181). As Yōko tries to imagine a future life with the Taiwanese father of her child, the shifting distinctions between Japan and Taiwan are mirrored in the star persona of Hitoto, born to a Taiwanese father and Japanese mother, and in her character's research on Taiwanese composer Jiang Wen-Ye (1910–1983), who left his Japanese wife to teach in occupied China (1938). Jiang's real life mirrors Yōko's fictional situation in that the Taiwanese father of her child has moved to Thailand and she must decide whether to join him. In this way, Hou creates characters and narratives by weaving together information based on ethnographic research conducted among Taiwanese friends living in Japan, the family background of his leading actress, and the historical figure of a Taiwanese composer.

> I have a friend called Kosaka who married a Taiwanese. Part of the storyline was copied from her life. She was a 'cafe girl.' What I mean is that she did all her work at the coffee shop, including having meetings with people, writing, and organizing her work. The funniest was the day when she took an entire suitcase to the coffee shop when she met with us. She put some of her stuff into her suitcase and took some more out while she was explaining herself to us. Before we came, she was waiting for her parents at the coffee shop to pick up her kid. The coffee shop was her office. This part of the story came from her (Hou and Liu 2008, p. 181).

The settings, including Yōko's family home, were similarly borrowed from friends and a whole sub-plot concerning visiting family graves was inspired by the director learning about the August O-Bon festival and its customs by observing friends' activities in this month (Hou and Liu 2008, p. 181). The film layers these elements over a naturalistic representation of Tokyo, privileging the environmental sounds of the city and the surrounding countryside over dialogue and emphasizing the capture of the everyday sounds of real life. Anthropologist Hajime is even shown recording the sounds of the Tokyo railway system for an ethnographic art project, in a self-referential scene that mirrors the process of the ethnographer-director.

In part due to the constrictions of filming these scenes, the style of Hou's film suggests similarities with the quasi-documentaries and ethnofiction films of the late 1960s and 1970s. Hou was unable to secure permission from Japan Railways to film on the Yamanote line (Hou and Liu 2008, p. 181). As a result, the camera crew were forced to go undercover, packing minimal equipment into backpacks and assembling camera rigs on the train (Hou and Liu 2008, p. 182). Cameramen were asked, "to keep a low profile and do it casually" (Hou and Liu 2008, p. 182), operating according to similar principles to the ethnofiction filmmaker. Like Rouch and Imamura before them however, the camera sometimes gave the filmmakers away. "We said 'shoot it secretly' but all of our staff laughed about it because we were pretty obvious" (Hou and Liu 2008, p. 182). Hou did exercise directorial agency over particular shots; for example, the scene in which Yōko and Hajime pass one another in separate trains had to be shot eighteen times. Nonetheless, the filming style and dialogue emphasize a sense of reality, as Hajime muses that his recordings of train sounds might assist a criminal investigation, "Someone might need to hear a tape as evidence of something".

Café Lumière demonstrates the on-going use of ethnofiction-style filmmaking techniques and narrative development in feature films made in Japan today. At the same time, the increasing availability of filmmaking equipment for non-professional filmmakers, including researchers, has encouraged an increase in the use of filmmaking for research purposes. While filmmaking has had a central place in visual ethnography since the 1950s, the cheaper equipment and editing software currently available has increased the number of graduate students and ethnographic researchers using filmmaking for research purposes in Japan. As a scholar of classical narrative Japanese cinema turned documentary filmmaker, I was interested in how these researchers understood the history of ethnographic filmmaking in Japan, including the development of ethnofiction. In the concluding paragraphs, I present some observations on contemporary understandings of the development of ethnofiction techniques in Japanese visual anthropology.

3. Discussion: Ethnofiction as Research Practice at The National Museum of Ethnography

With my background in Japanese film studies, the texts discussed above were at the forefront of my mind as I set out to make my own documentary film about the memories of early postwar audiences in the cinema theatres of the Kansai region. I joined a filmmaking study group at The National Museum of Ethnography, home to leading practitioner-researchers making anthropologically-influenced ethnographic films, including Professor Omori Yasuhiro, one of Jean Rouch's last students. Rouch's approach has been the subject of much discussion at the museum, known colloquially as Minpaku. In part, this is due to Professor Omori's connections, but conversations with and around Rouch and his methods are also sustained by Minpaku's relationship with the University of Manchester in the United Kingdom, the Granada Center at the university, and the Filmmaking for Fieldwork collective working there. Kawase Itsushi, Associate Professor at Minpaku, facilitates connections between the Osaka-based institute and counterparts in Manchester, and many researchers and graduate students from Minpaku enroll on the summer filmmaking courses offered by the Granada Center for Visual Anthropology, and the associated Filmmaking for Fieldwork collective. Manchester visual anthropology situates the work of Jean Rouch as an example of the origins of ethnofiction in documentary cinema. Rouch's *cinema verité*, using the camera to instigate events rather than documenting events that spontaneously occurred in the vicinity of the camera, is a common approach to ethnofiction at Minpaku.

In 2016, I was included in a small research group dedicated to studying ethnofiction filmmaking, and screened Imamura's *A Man Vanishes* and *A History of Postwar Japan as Told by a Bar Hostess* at consecutive meetings. The attending graduate students and researchers had not viewed Imamura's films before, and their response to the screenings was immediate interest in this home-grown example of ethnofiction filmmaking developing around the time of its French counterpart. One graduate student later wrote that he was "stunned by how innovative his films were/are". The student particularly praised "the reflexive viewing method Imamura utilized in *A History of Postwar Japan*, where Madam Onboro talks out her opinions and memories while viewing the footage of war", noting that this "is one of the trends in contemporary anthropological filmmaking". The question "What is truth?" raised by Hayakawa Yoshie in *A Man Vanishes* was also identified as particularly relevant to the group members' own fieldwork and filming.

Minpaku anthropologists were open to the inclusion of Imamura in the historiography of the development of ethnofiction filmmaking techniques, and like Kamei Fumio before us, we agreed on the possibility of ethnofiction as a simultaneous development, occurring in France and Japan at around the same time. I offer this short auto-ethnographic vignette in closing not to justify the argument above with the agreement of a small group of visual anthropologists, but to suggest that researchers and filmmakers in various fields may be more open to the blurring of boundaries between visual anthropology and film studies, and between narrative fiction film and feature film, than the current organization of disciplines and genres suggests. The Minpaku discussions suggested to me the importance of overcoming the organizational barriers that have been constructed around geographical and genre definitions to understand ethnofiction as a truly global innovation, with certain regional specificities. Scholars of studio-era narrative cinema collaborating with visual ethnographers and practice-based filmmaker researchers can blur the constructed boundaries between the fields, revealing alternative historiographies of innovation and development that give a more holistic picture of the productive intersections of fiction and non-fiction film.

What might this ultimately mean? The humanities and social sciences, within which film studies and anthropology are generally housed, are positioned as fields of enquiry into the human condition, broadly defined. Likewise, documentary cinema purports to reveal the conditions and environment in which we exist. Tracing ethnofiction and associated techniques through early actuality film, news production, war propaganda, classical narrative fiction film, and documentary cinema both for research and entertainment purposes emphasizes the limitations of the camera in telling the whole story, and reveals our reliance on discourse about the filmmaking process to better understand what we are watching. The persuasive influence of discourse suggests the importance of getting our stories straight, and that includes the story of how ethnofiction developed in Japanese and East Asian cinema. Understanding ethnofiction as a global innovation with regional specificities gives us a clearer picture of its emergence, development, uses, and abuses, revealing the blurry line between truth and fiction to be geographically and temporally shared.

Funding: This research received no external funding.

Acknowledgments: I am grateful for the kind support of researchers at The National Museum of Ethnography in Osaka, Japan, including Kawase Itsushi, Yanohara Yushi, and Muratsu Ran. Jamie Coates gave much appreciated feedback on early drafts of this paper, and Michael Raine and Marcos Centeno's guidance on the abstract greatly shaped the final version. I also appreciate the feedback and suggestions of my two autonomous reviewers.

Conflicts of Interest: The author declares no conflict of interest.

Filmography

A History of Postwar Film as Told by a Bar Hostess/Nippon sengoshi: Madamu Onboro no seiketsu, dir. Imamura Shōhei, Imamura Productions, 1970.
A Man Vanishes/Ningen Jōhatsu, dir. Imamura Shōhei, Imamura Productions, 1967.
A.K.A Serial Killer/Ryākusho: renzoku shasatsuma, dir. Adachi Masao et al., 1969 (screened 1975)
Café Lumière/Kōhi jikō, dir. Hou Hsiao-Hsien, Shōchiku, 2003.
Carmen Comes Home/Karumen kokyo ni kaeru, dir. Kinoshita Keisuke, Shōchiku, 1951.
Chronicle of a Summer/Chronique d'un été, dir. Jean Rouch, Argos Films, 1961.
Dawn of Freedom/Ano hata o ute, dir. Abe Yutaka and Geraldo de Leon, Toho, 1942.
Fighting Soldier/Tatakau heitai, dir. Kamei Fumio, Toho, 1939.
Geisha Riding in Rickshaws/Geishas en jinrikisha, dir. Francois-Constant Girel, Lumière catalogue, 1898.
In Search of the Unreturned Soldiers in Malaysia/Mikikanhei o otte—Marei-hen, dir. Imamura Shōhei, Tokyo Channel 12, 1971.
In Search of the Unreturned Soldiers in Thailand/Mikikanhei o otte-Tai-hen, dir. Imamura Shōhei, Tokyo Channel 12, 1971.
Japanese Actors/Auteurs japonais, dir. Francois-Constant Girel, Lumière catalogue, 1898.
Japanese Fencing/Escrime au sabre japonaise, dir. Francois-Constant Girel, Lumière catalogue, 1897.
Kamigami no Fukaki Yokubō/The Profound Desire of the Gods, dir. Imamura Shōhei, Imamura Productions, 1968.
Outlaw Matsu Returns/Muhomatsu kokyo ni kaeru, dir. Imamura Shōhei, Tokyo Channel 12, 1973.
The Ainu in Yeso/Les Aïnous à Yéso, dir. Francois-Constant Girel, Lumière catalogue, 1897.
The Insect Woman/Nippon konchūki, dir. Imamura Shōhei, Nikkatsu, 1963.
The Rickshaw Man/Muhomatsu no issho, dir. Inagaki Hiroshi, Toho, 1958.

References

Anonymous. 1910. *Katsudo Shashinkai [Moving Picture World]*, July 21.
Higson, Andrew. 1995. *Waving the Flag: Constructing a National Cinema in Britain*. Oxford: Clarendon.
Hori, Hikari. 2018. *Promiscuous Media: Film and Visual Culture in Imperial Japan, 1926–1945*. Ithaca and London: Cornell University Press.
Hou, Hsiao-Hsien, and Petrus Liu. 2008. Cinema and History: Critical Reflections. *Inter-Asia Cultural Studies* 9: 173–83.
Imamura, Shōhei. 1997. My Approach to Filmmaking. In *Shohei Imamura*. Edited by James Quant. Toronto: Toronto International Film Festival Group, pp. 125–28.
Imamura, Shōhei. 2001. *Toru: Kannu kara Yamiichi e*. Tokyo: Kōsakusha.
Imamura, Shōhei. 2017. "Betwixt fiction and documentary" [Fikushon to Dokyumentari no Awai de]. Translated by Bill Mihalopoulos. *Asian Cinema* 28: 101–5.
Kasza, Gregory. 1993. *The State and the Mass Media in Japan 1918–1945*. Berkeley: University of California Press.
Komatsu, Hiroshi. 1994. Transformations in Film as Reality (Part One): Questions Regarding the Genesis of Nonfiction Film. Trans. Aaron Gerow. Documentary Box 5: 1–5. Available online: https://www.yidff.jp/docbox/5/box5-1-e.html (accessed on 19 December 2018).

Laprévotte, Gilles. 1997. Shōhei Imamura: Human, All Too Human. In *Shohei Imamura*. Edited by James Quant. Toronto: Toronto International Film Festival Group, pp. 101–7.

Mihalopoulos, Bill. 2008. Becoming Insects: Imamura Shōhei and the Entomology of Modernity. In *The Power of Memory in Modern Japan*. Edited by Sven Saaler and Wolfgang Schwentker. Folkestone: Global Oriental, pp. 277–90.

Naimushō keihōkyoku 1941. Eiga kensetsu nenpō.

Nakata, Toichi. 1997. Shohei Imamura Interview. In *Shohei Imamura*. Edited by James Quant. Toronto: Toronto International Film Festival Group, pp. 107–24.

Nornes, Abé Markus. 2002. The Postwar Documentary Trace: Groping in the Dark. *Positions* 10: 39–78. [CrossRef]

Nornes, Abé Markus. 2003. *Japanese Documentary Film: The Meiji Era through Hiroshima*. Minneapolis: University of Minnesota Press.

Richie, Donald. 2005. *A Hundred Years of Japanese Film: A Concise History, with a Selective Guide to DVDs and Videos*. Tokyo and New York: Kodansha International.

Sjöberg, Johannes. 2008. Ethnofiction: Drama as a creative research practice in ethnographic film. *Journal of Media Practice* 9: 229–42. [CrossRef]

Stoller, Paul. 1992. *The Cinematic Griot: The Ethnography of Jean Rouch*. Chicago: Chicago University Press.

Sugiyama, Heiichi. 1990. *Imamura Taihei*. Tokyo: Libroport.

Toki, Akihiro, and Kaoru Mizoguchi. 1993. A History of Early Cinema in Kyoto, Japan (1896–1912). Cinemagazinet! No. 1. Available online: http://www.cmn.hs.h.kyoto-u.ac.jp/NO1/SUBJECT1/INAEN.HTM (accessed on 31 January 2017).

© 2019 by the author. Licensee MDPI, Basel, Switzerland. This article is an open access article distributed under the terms and conditions of the Creative Commons Attribution (CC BY) license (http://creativecommons.org/licenses/by/4.0/).

MDPI
St. Alban-Anlage 66
4052 Basel
Switzerland
Tel. +41 61 683 77 34
Fax +41 61 302 89 18
www.mdpi.com

Arts Editorial Office
E-mail: arts@mdpi.com
www.mdpi.com/journal/arts

www.ingramcontent.com/pod-product-compliance
Lightning Source LLC
LaVergne TN
LVHW070600100526
838202LV00012B/522